W9-BUB-851

TORSO

TORSO

The Story of Eliot Ness and the Search for a Psychopathic Killer

Steven Nickel

John F. Blair, Publisher
Winston-Salem, North Carolina

Library of Congress Cataloging-in-Publication Data

Nickel, Steven.
    Torso : the story of Eliot Ness and the search for a
psychopathic killer / Steven Nickel.
        p.   cm.
    Bibliography: p.
    Includes index.
    ISBN 0-89587-246-3 (pbk.)
    1. Serial murders—Ohio—Cleveland—Case studies.
2. Homocide investigation—Ohio—Cleveland—Case studies.
3. Ness, Eliot. 4. Detectives—United States—Biography.
5. Police—United States—Biography.   I. Title.
HV6534.C55N53   1989
364.1'523'9077132—dc19   89-792
                                                CIP

Acknowledgments

I am indebted to the following for their assistance and cooperation: the staffs of the Cleveland and Chicago public libraries; Claire Fenrich at the *Cleveland Plain Dealer*; Ann Sindelar and Michael McCormick at the Western Reserve Historical Society; Dr. Elizabeth K. Balraj at the Cuyahoga County Morgue; David Yawn; Bryon Sellers; and especially my wife, Karen, for her help, encouragement, and patience while I was preparing the manuscript.

TORSO

Introduction

This is a story about crime in Cleveland, Ohio, from the fall of 1935 to the spring of 1942.

During this period—a time marked by rampant lawlessness at its beginning and a dramatic decrease in crime by its end—headlines in the city were dominated by two widely divergent individuals. One was an energetic young lawman whose colorful exploits propelled him into the public limelight and restored a sense of hope and pride to a beleaguered community. His name was Eliot Ness. The other was a mysterious, phantomlike killer, never caught, never identified, whose horrible crimes plunged the city into a state of terror. Newspapers called him the Mad Butcher, the Headhunter, and the Torso Murderer.

Like most big cities, Cleveland is marked by strong contrasts. The natural beauty of the region is muted by rampant industrialization; majestic skyscrapers overlook festering slums; and the affluent walk the same streets as the needy. Even opinions about the city vary dramatically, some hailing Cleveland as "the best location in the nation" while others mock it as "the mistake by the lake." It is appropriate, then, that at a crucial time in the city's history, one of the two central figures in this story came to represent what was good and decent in Cleveland, while the other came to symbolize what was reprehensible and wicked.

The Torso case might be regarded as the missing chapter in the saga of Eliot Ness. Thanks to *The Untouchables*—book, television series, and motion picture—Ness has become one of the most celebrated figures among twentieth-century American lawmen. In the process, fact has been largely eclipsed by fiction. Readers will find a demythicized Eliot Ness in the following pages, a man who helped create his own larger-than-life image and then struggled to live up to it.

By contrast, the Torso Murderer remains curiously unrecognized in the annals of crime. In many ways, the case qualifies as an American version of London's infamous Ripper murders. In each instance, a knife-wielding maniac operated alone and unseen in the heart of a huge city, preying upon the lowest stratum of society, the series of grisly killings suddenly ending and the unknown slayer vanishing into oblivion.

London authorities were absolutely baffled by the Ripper murders and endured tremendous criticism as a result. Sir Charles Warren, head of the metropolitan police, became the prime target of the public's furor and eventually resigned. In Cleveland, when the embarrassed and exasperated police force continually failed to catch the Torso Murderer, the city looked in desperation to Eliot Ness. When he, too, failed, the critics descended like wolves on Ness and his exalted image.

The failure of police to capture either Jack the Ripper or the Torso Murderer was no doubt due, in large part, to the fact that they were dealing with what was then a rare phenomenon. The Ripper was history's first pattern killer and sexual psychopath. Victorian law enforcement officials quite honestly didn't know what to make of him. In like manner, though he appeared on the scene a full fifty years later, the Torso Murderer was, with a few arguable exceptions, America's first serial killer. He was also one of the most prolific if certain evidence is considered. The official body count in Cleveland reached twelve, but at least one of the detectives closest to the case maintained that a number of similar killings outside the city were the work of the same man.

As with the Ripper murders, the mystery surrounding the Torso case has only deepened with the passage of time. Despite the abundant evidence and the parade of suspects (including one Eliot Ness did not speak of until twenty years later), the identity of the Torso Murderer and his method of eluding capture in what was one of the most massive homicide investigations in history remain impenetrable after half a century.

Clevelanders got their first look at Eliot Ness in August of 1934. For some, especially those who had followed the accounts of the government's battle against organized crime, his reputation preceded him. In Chicago, as a young agent of the Justice Department, Ness had led a special squad of gangbusters known as the Untouchables that helped to smash the bootlegging empire of Al Capone. In the course of his two-and-a-half-year crusade against the underworld figures of the Windy City, Ness had won fame as a resourceful, courageous, and incorruptible crime fighter.

Cleveland had a desperate need for a lawman with the talent and integrity of Eliot Ness. America's seventh largest city (with a population of just under a million), Cleveland was infested with so much crime and corruption that it had earned a reputation as an untamed town. The public had long ago lost faith in its police and city officials and was starved for a hero.

Ness, however, was not coming to town to combat the gargantuan problem of metropolitan crime. He was still the property of the federal government, and his arrival was rather routine as he settled into his new post as investigator in charge of the Treasury Department's Alcoholic Tax Unit in the northern district of Ohio.

There were still a curious few, most of them reporters, who turned out to get a look at the already legendary G-man as he arrived at his new office in the Standard Building in downtown Cleveland. The majority, no doubt expecting to see a rugged-looking lawman, were genuinely surprised to find a well-dressed, handsome young man with a pleasant smile and a soft voice. Eliot Ness was just thirty-one, and he looked even younger. Standing six feet and weighing 180 pounds, he possessed what some would term a baby face, round and cherubic with a ruddy complexion in the cheeks, a weak, dimpled chin, wavy brown hair parted in the middle, sleepy blue-gray eyes, and a sharp nose crossed by a faint band of freckles. His slender build and slim waist were offset by broad, powerful shoulders.

He looked like a youthful business executive and possessed a confident yet modest manner, blushing slightly as he answered questions. Ness downplayed his role in the Capone case. Although he and his Untouchables had performed some spectacular feats in busting up mob distilleries and breweries, he credited revenue agents for collecting the actual evidence that had put the scar-faced ganglord behind bars. He appeared more enthusiastic about his present assignment, announcing that his goal was to "clean out" bootleggers from the region. When the newsmen pressed for more details, Ness replied, "I'm just finding my way around Cleveland. I'd rather talk about what we can do after we do it."

Ness wasted no time fitting into his new role and making an impact on the city. With thirty-four agents under his command, he methodically tracked down, raided, and destroyed a string of illicit alcohol operations throughout Cuyahoga and Lake counties. Ness's new squad earned a reputation for hitting a still a day. They arrested hundreds. In one of their most sensational raids, they captured what was believed to be the largest distillery in northeastern Ohio, operating behind a legitimate business on East Thirtieth Street. Ness and his agents seized and demolished over a hundred thousand dollars' worth of equipment capable of producing a thousand gallons of bootleg liquor a day, cheating the government out of close to thirty thousand dollars a week in taxes.

Clevelanders read the newspaper accounts of Ness's exploits with only casual interest. With the repeal of Prohibition the previous year, bootlegging had ceased to be a major crime. As part of the overall Cleveland crime picture, efforts to halt the flow of illegal liquor seemed a trivial and outdated attempt at law enforcement.

On the morning of September 5, 1934, Cleveland skies were gray and overcast. At the foot of East 156th Street on the far eastern outskirts of the city, Frank La Gossie, a twenty-one-year-old carpenter, found Euclid Beach nearly deserted. As he strolled along the shoreline watching the clouds roll in over Lake Erie and seeing what the waters had cast up, he spied a curious object protruding from the sand. Brushing aside some driftwood, La Gossie suddenly realized, to his horror, that he had stumbled upon the partial remains of a human body.

An hour later, the grisly find arrived at the Cuyahoga County Morgue, where Coroner Arthur J. Pearse and his pathologists conducted an examination. The object proved to be the lower half of a female torso, neatly severed at the waist between the second and third lumbar vertebrae. The thighs were still attached, but the lower legs had been cut off at the knees. Pearse announced that the woman had been dead close to six months, and in the water three to four months. He immediately ruled out the possibility that the torso was a discarded specimen from a medical lab.

The following day, Cleveland police were contacted by Joseph Hejduk, a handyman from North Perry, Ohio, some thirty miles east of Euclid Beach. Two weeks earlier, Hejduk had found what he believed was part of a human body on the shore close to his home. He had informed a local deputy, who theorized that the remains were those of an animal and suggested that Hejduk bury them. After doing as the deputy recommended, the handyman had thought nothing more of the matter until reading about the torso discovery at Euclid Beach.

Inspector Cornelius W. Cody, Homicide Detective Emil Musil, and several others from Central Station accompanied Hejduk to North Perry. With night falling and a storm approaching, Hejduk led the officers to the site of the makeshift grave, but he had difficulty in pinpointing the exact spot. A fierce rain began to beat on the search team. Determined to finish, the lawmen pulled down their hats, turned up their collars, and continued digging. Their efforts paid off, as the object was finally unearthed. It proved to be the upper half of a woman's torso, minus the head and arms.

The upper torso matched the previous section perfectly. Assembling the pieces, Coroner Pearse was able to determine that the woman had been about five foot six, 120 pounds, and in her mid- to late thirties. Her uterus had been surgically removed at least a year before her death. The dismemberment, according to Pearse, was notably skillful, performed with a razor-sharp, butcher-type knife. Only in one instance did the cutting appear sloppy; in removing the right arm, the killer had missed the joint and spent considerable time and effort hacking through the shoulder blade to complete the separation. Otherwise, the work was flawless.

Most curious of all was the odd discoloration of the victim's skin. The police had initially surmised that it had been charred in a bungled attempt to burn the body. The medical examiners, however, concluded that a chemical preservative—possibly calcium hypochloride or chloride of lime—had been applied, accounting for both the unusual tinge of the flesh and the fact that the pieces were not more decomposed. The presence of the chemical also explained why a gull that had apparently feasted on part of the remains was found dead beside the site of the North Perry section.

On September 8, police began to drag the shallow lake waters in the hope of retrieving the missing body parts. They concentrated their efforts around Euclid Beach, North Perry, and the thirty miles of shoreline between them. Police also searched a stretch of beach closer to the city where, six weeks earlier, a little girl had scrambled frantically to shore screaming that she had stepped on a human leg. A portion of an upper arm eventually turned up near Euclid Beach; Pearse felt certain that it belonged to the body. But the rest of the arms, the lower legs, and the head were never found.

Inspector Cody examined the missing persons records of women who had disappeared from the Cleveland area in the previous twelve months. Beginning with more than sixty files of women aged sixteen to seventy-four, he managed to eliminate all but two using the meager details supplied by the coroner. Another week of extensive investigation convinced him that neither was "the Lady of the Lake," as detectives had come to call her. The victim, whoever she was, had apparently left no mourners in the vicinity. The investigators concluded that her remains could have come from almost anywhere, even Canada.

A reporter for the *Cleveland Plain Dealer* asked Cody if this was the perfect crime. "No," the inspector responded, "but so close to perfect that we don't know what to do next."

With no solution in sight and none expected, the case was officially classified as unsolved and filed away with the coroner's conclusion, "Causes unknown; probable homicide." Cleveland police had no idea that the most bizarre and baffling case of multiple murder in the history of American crime was just beginning.

ONE

On September 22, 1935, the Seventh National Eucharist Congress opened in Cleveland.

Never before had the Ohio metropolis witnessed such an ostentatious display of religious exuberance and pageantry. Cleveland was one of the great American strongholds of Roman Catholicism, a fact due largely to the enormous immigrant labor force that had poured into the city for close to a century to radically alter its New England Protestant foundation. Even non-Catholics, however, seemed to share in the excitement of the prestigious event. Thousands attended the services at St. John's Cathedral, which were overseen by New York's Patrick Cardinal Hayes, the presiding papal legate. Tens of thousands more gathered as spectators along Euclid Avenue to observe the procession down Cleveland's main thoroughfare. For the final ceremonies, a crowd in excess of 150,000 jammed into Municipal Stadium, the city's grand canyon sports arena on the lakefront, for a midnight mass.

One spectator, obviously caught up in the ecclesiastical fervor, exclaimed that it was as if "the Kingdom of Heaven has come to Cleveland."

Only a few blocks west of where the ecstatic worshippers thronged, in what is generally considered the heart of the city, the landscape was more like a vision of hell.

Sixty feet below street level along the sprawling basin of the Cuyahoga River are the Flats, Cleveland's great industrial valley. It is an awesome sight. The immense factories appear innumerable and endless; iron and steel mills, oil refineries, mammoth warehouses, and plants of all kinds produce and store machinery, tools, electrical equipment, chemicals, paint, and much more, helping Cleveland earn the reputation of manufacturing anything and everything.

After sundown, many factories were dark and deserted; others ran continuously through the night. Inside the mills, the open-hearth and blast furnaces operated at close to three thousand degrees. Black smoke gushed from the towering stacks atop the factories, producing a fallout of soot that filtered down over the area and the surrounding city. From a few of the giant columns, flames rose into the black sky, casting a hellish, eerie aura over the entire valley. The pungent stench of gas fumes, burning oil, diesel engines, and smelting ore was overpowering.

When night descended on the Flats, a legion of lost souls appeared—drunks, derelicts, degenerates, vagabonds, scavengers, the outcasts of society, the dregs of humanity. Some were simply the destitute, the unemployed, the homeless. Many wandered aimlessly all night among the factories, along the twisting banks of the river, or across the maze of train rails running up and down the valley. A few prowled through the rubbish heaps that were everywhere. Others crawled into a darkened niche and tried to sleep on a bed of excelsior, newspapers, or bare concrete. Some gathered around campfires sharing a bottle and their philosophies of life, speaking of their troubles, a better past, unreal expectations for the future.

Where they came from and where they were going were enigmas. What could be done for them was a more significant but equally unanswerable question. It was the time of the Great

Depression, and Cleveland was a city grown all out of proportion and hit hard by economic crisis. There were nearly seventy thousand on work relief, and more than a quarter of the total population was dependent on some form of government aid. The city was powerless to either help its needy or rid itself of its misfits.

Many of the ragged figures roaming the nocturnal world of the Flats were hobos who drifted into town in a steady stream aboard trains. There were many in the depression days who had taken to riding the rails. It was a romantic notion, as well as a means of escaping the harsh realities of the times, to stow away aboard a freight and see the country from Oregon to Maine. A number of the major routes through the Midwest passed through Cleveland and the Flats. Most of the hobos were gruffly ejected by the railroad detectives, or "bulls," as they were called. Many hobos found themselves stranded, at least temporarily, in the city.

A few were content for the moment. The majority, however, realized that it was late September and that Cleveland winters come quickly and are notably cruel. Many began to search for a southbound freight to take them to a more moderate climate. Boxcars were plentiful and usually easily accessible along the Flats. But the bulls checked them frequently and thoroughly; only a few vagabonds were wily or fortunate enough to remain aboard when the trains departed.

The tracks of the Erie, Nickel Plate, and other railroads exited the valley through a side gully called Kingsbury Run. A prehistoric creek of some size branching off the mighty Cuyahoga had once flowed through the Run, forming a natural ravine sweeping eastward along the underbelly of the city. Over two dozen sets of train rails snaked through the rocky, dried bed toward the East Fifty-fifth Street train yards. Between the Flats and the brightly lit railroad yards, Kingsbury Run stretched in an arc for more than a mile, shrouded in almost total blackness except for the red and green signal lights along the rails.

The younger, bolder, more agile vagabonds often ventured into the dark, forbidding gully. There, they could hop a freight unobserved as it rambled along the tracks, concealing themselves on board before reaching the yards. It was a dangerous method, but, for some, it was preferable to falling into the hands of the bulls, who were notorious for their mistreatment of tramps. Yet there were others who refused to enter the Run at night. In the hobo camps and shantytowns, wherever men sat around flickering fires, there was talk that the Kingsbury ravine was haunted, that the night swallowed up people there without leaving a trace. During the next few years, the ghost stories about the Run would increase dramatically.

Monday, September 23, the first day of fall, was a sunny, pleasant seventy-one degrees in the city.

Kingsbury Run seemed only slightly less desolate in the daylight. The floor of the wide gully was largely barren and strewn with trash. Sunflowers, clumps of sumac bushes, an occasional willow tree, and weeds of all kinds grew there. "Waste land," was the way one city councilman described it to a reporter. Housing could not be erected close to its steep banks. Streets were interrupted and continued confusedly on the opposite bank. Expensive bridges spanning the ravine at East Thirty-seventh Street, East Fifty-fifth Street, and Kinsman Road had to be maintained.

There had been a few, nevertheless, who looked upon the Run as a valuable and useful resource. Among these were the Van Sweringen brothers, a pair of reclusive but enterprising tycoons who left their mark upon Cleveland as few others have. The brothers had paid more than $8 million to purchase the Nickel Plate Railroad so they could acquire the rights to Kingsbury Run. It had seemed a curious move, since the Van Sweringens were real estate barons, not train magnates. Their aim was soon revealed to be the construction of a commuter service linking their most ambitious project, suburban Shaker Heights, with downtown Cleveland. Oris, the elder brother, had viewed the eastward-sweeping Kingsbury ravine as the ideal route for a rapid-transit line. Construction had begun in 1916, setting the commuter tracks along the northern edge of the Run, separate from the intercity rails. Residents of the Heights and other eastern suburbs were provided with a fast, inexpensive means of traveling to and from the city. The Van Sweringens' properties had, as a result, flourished remarkably.

Twice a day, commuters found themselves staring out upon the bleak, craggy sides of the gully. Railroad crews could often be spotted at work in the Run, men in grimy, sweat-soaked T-shirts repairing sections of rusty rails. An unusual but not uncommon sight was that of children, most of them neighborhood boys attracted by the rugged terrain and, of course, the trains. Occasionally, on a dare, youngsters attempted to hop slow-moving freights as they had seen the hobos do. It was a perilous but time-honored means of proving adolescent courage. Sometimes, the railroad bulls charged after the young culprits with nightsticks in hand. The clubs, however, were only used on the tramps. For the boys, it was all part of the game; seldom was one caught.

Shortly before five o'clock that bright afternoon, a pair of youths fresh from school—sixteen-year-old James Wagner and twelve-year-old Peter Kostura—were scampering along the southern cliffs of the Run. Close to where a short stretch of East Forty-ninth Street dead-ends against the ravine, the pair came to a weed-covered slope known as Jackass Hill. They decided to race each other to the gully sixty feet below.

Reaching the bottom first, the older boy turned triumphantly to look back at his companion. As he did, a curious, white patch in the knee-high brush a few feet away caught his eye. Young Wagner took a couple of steps closer, then froze. A moment later he was scrambling back up the slope, shouting to his friend that there was "a dead man with no head down there." The two boys ran until they spotted an adult and breathlessly informed him of their gruesome discovery. The man phoned the police.

Sergeant Arthur Marsh and Patrolman Arthur Stitt of the Erie Railroad Police were the first to arrive at the foot of Jackass Hill to find what had sent Jimmy Wagner fleeing in terror. It was the remains of a young white male, naked except for a pair of black socks. The body was not only headless but emasculated as well. The two officers began to search for the missing parts. In some thick brush thirty feet away, Stitt halted and called out to his partner.

"You find the head?" March reportedly asked.

"No," Stitt answered. "It's another body."

By five-thirty, city police started arriving on the scene. The first were Detectives Emil Musil and Orly May, only blocks away when they heard the report on their car radio. It was immediately apparent to May—a tall, no-nonsense lawman with a mustache—that the victims had been killed elsewhere and at different times. He noted how the bodies were neatly laid out, arranged with arms tucked at the sides and legs and heels together. Both detectives were also struck by the fact that there was no blood on the ground or the corpses. They could only surmise that the murderer had washed the bodies before discarding them in the Run, a peculiarity that May admitted gave him "the creeps."

The second body—that of a shorter, older man who had also been decapitated and emasculated—was completely nude and more decomposed. The skin had an unusual reddish tinge and was tough like leather. Next to an embankment, about twenty feet from the first body, the lawmen discovered the genitalia of both victims, as if indifferently cast there by the killer. Nearby, Patrolman Stitt noticed some dark hairs sticking out of the dirt. He carefully dug around the spot, uncovering a human head. Seventy-five feet from the other corpse, a second head was located in a similar shallow grave.

The area was soon being combed and clogged by dozens of lawmen—more detectives from Central Station (including Assistant Police Chief Emmet J. Potts), others from the nearby East Fifty-fifth Street Station, and officers of the Erie and Nickel Plate railroad police. Spectators gazed down from atop Jackass Hill, and more were lined along the cliffs on both sides of the Run. Not far away, the rapid-transit trains rushed by regularly, their cars jammed with rush-hour passengers returning home to the comfortable suburbs. A few may have caught a fleeting glimpse of the policemen at work and wondered what was happening.

Searching the terrain around the bodies, police discovered some clothing—a blue suit coat with the label of B. R. Baker and Company (a local department store), a white shirt, a dark gray cap, and underwear, all bloodstained. The articles appeared to fit the older victim. Police also found some rope and a rusty bucket containing oil drained from an automobile engine. Lab chemists would later detect blood and hair in the oil. Some detectives theorized that the killer had brought the bucket to the site intending to burn the bodies but had either been interrupted or simply changed his mind.

After the corpses were removed and the crowds had broken up, some of the lawmen remained in the fading sunlight of the Run to discuss the case. A few pointed to the railroad signal tower not far away, wondering how the murderer placed the bodies where he had without being seen. Others talked about possible motives for the killings. Detective May, who had spent the last four of his eighteen years on the force working Homicide, declared to his partner that he had never seen anything like it before, adding in an ominous tone that he had "a bad feeling about this one."

Shortly after supper, Dr. Arthur Pearse, Cleveland's potbellied, good-natured coroner, began the autopsies on the Kingsbury Run corpses. The examination of the older man proved puzzling and frustrating. The strange discoloration of the skin was credited to an unknown chemical employed as a preservative. The body, nevertheless, was badly decomposed. Although Pearse had viewed this bizarre feature before, he never imagined any connection to the female remains he had encountered the previous year. The condition of the body made fingerprinting useless. It also meant that Pearse could not be precise in assigning a time of death; he estimated that the victim had been dead one or two weeks. The man had been about forty-five years of age, with a short, stocky build. He had stood five foot six and weighed 165 pounds, with brown eyes, dark brown hair, and perfect teeth.

The fresher corpse belonged to a young man with a handsome face who had been dead only two or three days. He was a lanky five foot eleven, 150 pounds, with a light complexion and brown hair. His head had been cleanly and skillfully removed between the third and fourth cervical vertebrae with a large, heavy, very sharp knife. The absence of blood in the heart and the retracted muscles in the neck led the coroner and his assistants to a startling conclusion—the act of decapitation itself had been the cause of death. Pearse believed that the older victim had died the same way, but he could not be as certain. The examiners also noted that there were rope burns on the younger man's wrists, indicating that he had struggled violently while bound. Fingerprints identified the victim as Edward A. Andrassy of 1744 Fulton Road.

Twenty-eight-year-old Edward Andrassy had been a resident of the near west side, where he had lived with his parents and his younger brother, John. He had a modest police record. In 1931, he had been arrested for carrying concealed weapons and sentenced to thirty days in the Warrensville Workhouse. His favorite hangout had been the notorious Third Precinct, a triangular area covering the ten square miles of decaying neighborhoods south of Prospect Avenue, bordering on the Flats, East Fifty-fifth Street, and Kingsbury Run. Police called it the Roaring Third. Andrassy had been a familiar face to the cops working there. He had been tagged by some as a troublemaker and a "snotty punk." He had often been picked up for being drunk and disorderly, for barroom brawling, or for suspected involvement in small-time gambling or swindling operations.

His parents, Joseph and Helen Andrassy, arrived at the morgue to confirm the identification and claim the body. They agreed to speak with Inspector Cornelius Cody about their son. It was a sad tale Cody had heard many times. Eddie had been a good kid, always decent at home, but he had taken up with a rough crowd. The senior Andrassy stated that he had last seen his son leaving their house around eight o'clock Thursday night, September 19. The young man had not said where he was going or when he would return.

Photographs of Edward Andrassy gave an indication of the double life he had led. In some, he appeared as a well-dressed young man with thoughtful eyes and a look of boyish innocence. Police shots showed the same Andrassy glaring into the camera with a smirking grin and a defiant, cocky look. It was the latter, darker side that almost everyone outside his family seemed to have encountered.

Detectives diligently traced their way through Andrassy's seedy past hoping to uncover some clue to his murder or, at the very least, to learn the identity of the man found beside him. For nearly four years, Andrassy had worked as an orderly in the mental ward of the west side's Cleveland City Hospital. There, he had met and married a nurse in 1928. The couple had divorced after less than a month. The woman had later borne Andrassy's child, whom he had never made an attempt to see. Andrassy had quit his hospital job and, as far as is known, stayed unemployed for the remainder of his life.

Living quietly at the home of his parents, Andrassy had often crossed the river at night and entered the world of the Roaring Third, a sleazy landscape of flophouses, brothels, saloons, pawnshops, pool halls, and crowded tenements. Andrassy had seemed to fit in well with the hustlers inhabiting the region. He had shot craps in alleys and cheap rooms and made the rounds of local bars with his cronies. He had often been seen in the company of young women, some of whom he pimped for, it was said. From the record of his frequent scrapes with the law, his favorite pastime appeared to have been getting intoxicated and picking fights, usually getting the worst of it. About two months before Andrassy's death, a cabdriver had found him lying along a curb on East Ninth Street, his head bleeding. There was also an unconfirmed report that he had stabbed an Italian in a fight and that the victim and his friends were looking to get even. The story struck a chord with a pair of detectives who learned that a neighbor claimed to have seen a pair of Italians in Kingsbury Run near the site of the bodies on the Friday before the discovery. Railroad police also reported that they had on several occasions observed an Italian in a green coupe parked atop Jackass Hill. Detectives later found the man but swiftly cleared him of the murders and any association with Andrassy. Still, the theory that Andrassy had fallen victim to a gang of Italians remained one of the prime possibilities in the eyes of the police.

As the detectives dug deeper into Andrassy's nocturnal activities in the Third Precinct, evidence came to light portraying the young man as a sexual deviate. Although Andrassy had been regarded as something of a ladies' man, more than a few acquaintances were discovered who alleged he had taken male lovers, while there were others who claimed he had attempted to entice them into homosexual acts. One young man told of having accompanied Andrassy to a house where he watched him have sex with a black man. When police searched Andrassy's room, they discovered a collection of muscle magazines. Also found was a list of names and addresses he had written in the margin of a newspaper. Many, it was learned, were known perverts. There was also evidence that Andrassy had acquired young males for an older homosexual and had been paid for his services.

More sordid details eventually surfaced. Andrassy had dealt in pornographic literature; he had smoked marijuana; he had gone to Detroit earlier in the summer and had been forced to leave suddenly after angering an Oriental gangster; he had been romantically involved with a married woman whose husband had vowed to kill him. Few people would have made a more likely candidate for murder than Edward Andrassy. And yet with all the investigators learned, there were no solid clues to the identity of his killer. According to the coroner, Andrassy had been murdered late Friday or early Saturday, a little over twenty-four hours after leaving his home. Police could not find a single person who admitted seeing him during that time.

Possible motives were plentiful, and each man working on the case seemed to have his favorite. Detective Sergeant Bernard Wolf, head of the Homicide Unit, believed the double murder was the result of a perverted love triangle. A number of his men agreed, since the emasculation of the bodies suggested sexual slayings. Other detectives were convinced that the butchery performed on the victims indicated a foreign ritual of revenge, such as an Italian, Greek, or Slavic vendetta. A few pointed out that it was not uncommon when the body left behind in a Mafia killing had its genitals mutilated.

In early October, Inspector Cody resigned after twenty-eight years of distinguished service with the Cleveland police. At a testimonial dinner, he expressed regret at not solving his final case. Gradually, all of the detectives working on the double murder were reassigned, leaving the case unsolved and a multitude of questions unanswered. Why had the killer washed and drained the bodies before bringing them to Kingsbury Run? Why had he taken the time and effort to bury the heads while leaving the torsos in plain sight? Who was the older victim? He was not one of Andrassy's known acquaintances, and none of Andrassy's friends remembered having seen him. A check of missing persons drew a blank, and no one came forward to identify him.

Most perplexing of all was how the killer had managed to deposit the corpses where they were found. Police were sure that the difficult task had been performed in the predawn gloom on on Monday. Any later and the murderer would certainly have been observed. Attempting to reconstruct how he had done it, detectives theorized that he must have brought the bodies by car to the top of Jackass Hill. The slope is so steep, however, that it is dangerous for vehicles to come closer than a hundred feet from the site where the bodies were laid out. It is doubtful that he would have hazarded any nearer at night. From that point, the killer must have operated on foot. Why he hadn't simply tossed the bodies down the hill was a mystery. The physical evidence was conclusive; neither corpse had rolled down the slope, nor had they been dragged. Incredibly, the killer must have carried his victims down the steep, sixty-foot slope, neatly placing them in the brush at the bottom. It must have been an exhaustive and time-consuming process—bringing down one body, climbing back up the hill, descending again with the second, and then burying the heads. All this, furthermore, had been performed in almost total darkness.

These facts suggested to the police that a gang was involved, or at least two individuals working together. It was only much later, when it was apparent they were hunting a single murderer operating alone, that investigators thought back to the bodies below Jackass Hill and attempted to find another explanation of how the killer had placed them there. Unfortunately, there wasn't one.

What the *Plain Dealer* labeled "the most bizarre double murder" in the city's history seemed, at least initially, only a minor part of the overall Cleveland crime picture.

At the core of Cleveland's lawlessness was a tremendous rise in organized crime. Many mobsters who had acquired enormous wealth and power during Prohibition flaunted their fortunes with a haughty, above-the-law arrogance. Citizens could not help believing that the mobs controlled the city, or at least a good share of the police and the politicians.

Cleveland's first recognized ganglord was Joseph "Big Joe" Lonardo, an ambitious but illiterate three-hundred-pound Italian who, with his brothers, John and Frank, had foreseen the fantastic potential for bootlegging wealth before the Eighteenth Amendment even became law. Lonardo had commissioned thousands of Italians and Sicilians dwelling in the city's Woodland district, which bordered the eastern edge of the Roaring Third, to brew cheap booze. Almost overnight, Big Joe had found himself presiding over a vast empire with tremendous profits he was unwilling to share with anyone. Rival bootleggers were promptly and savagely dealt with. But there had been a few in Lonardo's own organization who looked upon his prodigious income—represented best by his palatial $120,000 house—and decided that it was too much for one man. The disgruntled faction was led by the seven Porello brothers. On October 13, 1927, Big Joe was lured into a trap and shot to death. His two brothers had quickly followed him to the grave.

About a year later, a diminutive figure with a prominent nose and an affable smile had arrived in Cleveland. His name was Moe Dalitz. Dalitz had held executive status in Detroit's notorious, predominantly Jewish Purple Gang but had fled when conflicts with opposing gangs grew too bloody. In Akron, he had formed an alliance with bootlegger Sam Tucker, who managed a modest but steady income with associates Morris Kleinman and Louis Rothkopf. Once Dalitz applied his genius to the business, profits had soared, and the quartet had moved its operations to downtown Cleveland. Dalitz's numerous contacts in Canada gave them almost total mastery over the lucrative rum-running across Lake Erie, which supplied the public with a high-quality alternative to the rotgut of the Woodland stills.

A clash with local Italian mobsters had seemed inevitable. As it turned out, the Italians were too busy warring with each other. The Porellos, having successfully overthrown the Lonardo empire, were being challenged by the Mayfield Road Mob, a collection of rising young mafiosi operating around Cleveland's Little Italy on the extreme east side of town. The Mayfield leaders were Frank Milano and Alfred Pollizi. Members of the gang included Milano's brothers, Peter and Tony; Pollizi's adopted brother, Charles; Big Angelo Lonardo, eldest son of the slain Big Joe; Lonardo's cousin, Little Angelo Scirrca; and the three Angersola brothers.

Instead of remaining neutral, Dalitz had carefully surveyed the opposing sides and thrown his support behind the Mayfield Road Mob. The Porellos were swiftly wiped out; four were gunned down and the remaining three fled. Their demise had marked the birth of the powerful Cleveland syndicate. Thanks largely to the efforts and wisdom of Dalitz, who tirelessly propagated his belief that there was enough for everyone, mob bosses dwelt in harmony, enjoyed tremendous prosperity, and cultivated profitable ties with gangsters in Buffalo, Detroit, Kansas City, and many other mid-western towns.

Bootlegging was only the foundation upon which the mobsters had built their empires. Foreseeing the end of Prohibition, they had begun to branch into new fields of illegal income. Prostitution, narcotics, loansharking, labor racketeering, and various forms of extortion all proved to be prosperous avenues. But the most lucrative, by far, was gambling. Bookie joints and betting parlors were as common as restaurants in the city, if not quite as visible, while in the suburbs and nearby Lake County plush, fashionable casinos like the Harvard Club, the Thomas Club, the Mounds Club (the personal enterprise of Dalitz), and the Pettibone Club operated openly and unmolested by local law officers, who reportedly shared in the profits. Patrons were assured of a safe, comfortable atmosphere in which to gamble and drink the night away.

It was no secret why crime had thrived in the city. Rarely had the fine art of purchasing police and political protection been handled so smoothly and on such a vast scale as in the Cleveland area during the early and mid-thirties. Once again, credit must be given Dalitz. His personal policy, as well as his exhortation to fellow gangsters, was to use bribes in place of bullets.

"The fix was really in in Cleveland," Alvin "Old Creepy" Karpis later recalled in his autobiographical account of his outlaw days. Along with St. Paul, Minnesota, and Hot Springs, Arkansas, Cleveland had been one of the three locations that criminals regarded as "safe" cities, where they could always be assured of a secure place to lay low.

Karpis had come to Cleveland upon hearing that it was a good town for criminals. Local gangsters had not only set up Karpis and his girlfriend with a comfortable place to stay but also paid the bank robber and kidnapper, one of the most wanted men in the nation at the time, to work at the Harvard Club. When, after many months, federal agents caught wind of his presence and moved in, Karpis was alerted and long gone by the time they reached his hideout. Karpis later claimed that the tip had come from the district attorney's office.

Corruption had spread everywhere, from the highest echelon of the city police to the average cop walking a beat, from the county sheriff's department to the city council and, some said, even the mayor's office. Many of those in the police department not on the take were indifferent or incompetent. Some simply felt powerless to have any positive effect. In the meantime, mobsters flourished. A deluge of crooks attracted by the breakdown in law and order had poured into Cleveland, some (like Karpis and his associates in the Ma Barker gang, Pretty Boy Floyd, and assorted others) seeking a haven, others looking to practice their criminal talents in an atmosphere that threatened little peril.

All this, in turn, had contributed to the general crime scene. Neighborhood crime—muggings, robberies, burglaries, and juvenile delinquency—greatly increased, as did murder. And nowhere in the city was the state of lawlessness more evident than on the mean streets of the Roaring Third.

The Third Precinct had long been an eyesore and a trouble spot, especially for cops in uniform. It was, moreover, the city's great melting pot, a region marked by a spectrum of cultural, racial, and linguistic differences. One survey reported that nearly half of the school-age children could not speak English. Virtually all its inhabitants were foreign born or the offspring of immigrants. The groups congregated according to their ethnic heritages. In the Roaring Third, thirty-nine different languages were spoken by some forty-eight different nationalities, among them Lithuanians, Yugoslavians, Italians, Irish, Hungarians, Poles, Jews, Russians, Swiss, Greeks, Welsh, Germans, Romanians, Bohemians, and recent arrivals like Hispanics, Orientals, and blacks, all jammed together in conditions that were often squalid. The cultural clashes among the groups were frequent and bloody.

The general public—including many honest, hardworking residents of the Third Precinct—was deeply distressed by the lack of effective law enforcement in the city. All agreed that the greatest part of the blame rested with Mayor Harry L. Davis, a hopelessly inept politician who had managed in the course of his two-year term to plunge city hall into new depths of corruption, indifference, and incompetence. One of his most towering blunders had been his appointment of Martin J. Lavelle, a former police captain, as the director of public safety, the official invested with supreme authority over municipal law enforcement and fire fighting. Lavelle had not only made a mockery of the position but also outraged citizens with his personal conduct. Once, he had attended a wild drinking party aboard a yacht which ended with a young woman's falling overboard and drowning. Lavelle had failed to report her death, igniting a tremendous sensation in the city when the truth was revealed. The incident was only one of many scandals during the Davis administration.

With the fall election approaching and Davis's term coming to a merciful end, Clevelanders began to scrutinize the candidates in the mayoral contest in search of one who could restore law and order to the city. The choice soon became clear. Harold Hitz Burton, a former state representative, was an independent Republican running without his party's endorsement on the promise of bringing civic duty and pride back to city hall. Burton was originally from Massachusetts, the only son of Swiss immigrants. During World War I, he had served in Belgium and France and been decorated for heroism twice. He was best known in Cleveland as law director for the city manager and county commander of the American Legion.

Burton mounted a vigorous campaign, devoting sixteen hours a day to public appearances. Proud of his immigrant ancestry, he spent considerable time among the city's great mass of minorities. His speeches were strictly antipolitical. He charged that corrupt officials and political favoritism were the major causes of Cleveland's enormous problems. Eliminate the corruption, Burton claimed, and the way would be open to wage war on crime and make the streets safe again. It was the message people wanted to hear. Burton possessed a convincing, straightforward manner that satisfied many that he was a sincere and capable statesman intent on keeping his word. On November 5, 1935, the voters chose him as their new mayor by the largest margin in the city's history.

In selecting the staff for his new administration, Burton gave careful consideration to filling the position of safety director. Instead of making a political appointment, he wanted to find and install a man of unquestionable integrity with a distinguished background in law enforcement and the special skills needed to command the entire municipal system of crime prevention, fire fighting, and traffic control. He narrowed his list of candidates to four. The name at the bottom was Eliot Ness.

Burton had never heard of Ness until two weeks earlier. Wes Lawrence, a city hall reporter for the *Plain Dealer*, had been the first to recommend Ness as the best man for the job. Soon, a parade of local businessmen and city officials had mentioned the young G-man's name to Burton. Still, the newly elected mayor had his doubts. Ness simply seemed too young and too unfamiliar with the city and its politics to take on the responsibilities of public safety director.

Burton's other choices—a former United States assistant district attorney, the agent in charge of Cleveland's FBI office, and a special investigator for the United States attorney general—appeared much more qualified. Burton finally settled upon the latter candidate, Joseph Keenan, but Keenan declined, suggesting that Ness would be a better man for the post. After closely examining Ness's impressive record, the mayor put in a call to Chicago to Assistant United States Attorney Dwight W. Green, one of the federal prosecutors in the Capone case. Green could not say enough good things about Ness. Burton was slowly won over. The clincher came, perhaps, when he learned that Ness was a faithful Republican.

On the morning of December 11, Burton called Ness to his office for an interview. Ness arrived at city hall shortly before noon. Their meeting was brief. Burton carefully outlined the duties of safety director and promised that there would be no political interference; Ness would have complete freedom as long as he got results. At twelve-thirty, Ness was sworn in as director of public safety, at age thirty-two the youngest in Cleveland history.

Word of the mayor's unexpected choice spread quickly. Reporters flocked to city hall to catch Ness. A few tagged along as Ness returned to his Treasury Department office in the Standard Building—where he shook hands with his fellow agents, cleaned out his desk, and gathered his files—and then followed him back to the mayor's office. Ness talked freely the whole time. It was no secret that he liked newsmen and the attention of the press. Several of the reporters, including Wes Lawrence and Ralph Kelly of the *Plain Dealer*, were already good friends.

"I'm not going to be a remote director," Ness announced, promising he would be "right in the front lines combating crime." He had no specific plans to share, but he stated that he wanted to remain "as conservative as possible" until he became more familiar with the police force and the local crime scene. After some prodding by the newsmen, he admitted that his first order of business would be a "shake-up" and reorganization of the police department, a task he thought would be "lots of fun." Ness said, "After that, I don't know what I'll do, but I hope to act first and talk about it later."

A few reporters were still lingering at city hall several hours later when Ness departed, cradling a heavy load of books and pamphlets. "It's my homework," he explained. He intended to spend the evening studying the city charter and Cleveland crime reports at the modest home in the western suburb of Bay Village that he and his wife, Edna, shared with their six cats.

All Cleveland was buzzing over the news of Ness's appointment. The reactions of the public and the press were largely favorable. Ness was hailed as the answer to the city's staggering problem of lawlessness, while Mayor Burton was praised for choosing the flamboyant young crime fighter who had taken on the Capone mob, demonstrating that his campaign promises were not hollow political rhetoric. At the same time, a tremor was felt through the police department and various political circles when it was realized that Burton had handed the safety director's job to a man without political ties or aspirations who had a spotless record of battling corruption.

There was good reason for the corrupt to be concerned and for the honest to be optimistic. Ness was one of the new breed of lawmen catching the public's eye—young, well-dressed, college-educated agents from the Justice and Treasury departments and from a formerly obscure government agency called the Division of Investigation, officially renamed the Federal Bureau of Investigation that year. "G-men," George "Machine Gun" Kelly reportedly called them when they cornered him in a Tennessee bungalow, though Kelly later denied he had ever used the term. Wherever the nickname came from, it became part of the evolving mystique. Not only had the likes of Kelly and Al Capone and associates been placed behind bars by the government lawmen; in the previous year, such celebrated desperados as John Dillinger, Pretty Boy Floyd, Baby Face Nelson, Ma Barker, and many more had fallen before the guns of the federal agents.

Great numbers of local law officers around the country openly resented the young "feds" and their sophisticated, collegiate approach to crime fighting. It was much the same in Cleveland. A few notable voices in the department termed the new safety director a "Boy Scout" and a "college cop." Worse yet, there were some who considered Ness an outsider or a crusader who was only looking to make a name for himself at the expense of the force. There were others, too, who were not outwardly hostile but who voiced serious doubts about Ness after observing his boyish good looks and his open, friendly manner with the press. They claimed that his accomplishments in Chicago had been grossly exaggerated and that he was little more than a paper pusher who lacked the street toughness to tackle Cleveland's crime.

The cynicism of Cleveland cops was best expressed in a saying credited to a policeman that was already circulating through the city: "Safety directors come and go, but crooked cops remain forever."

Very few at the time might have predicted that Ness would serve in the office of safety director for six and a half years. Fewer still could have foreseen that he would launch one of the most zealous and successful campaigns against crime and corruption ever witnessed in an American city. But no one, not even Ness himself, could have imagined that along with battling the racketeers, the vice lords, the corrupt officials, and the rogue cops, the former Untouchable was destined to encounter a totally different kind of criminal—a shadowy, faceless psychopath stalking his victims among the hobo jungles of the Third Precinct and Kingsbury Run, leaving behind a gruesome trail of a dozen dismembered bodies. The two beheaded bodies discovered beneath Jackass Hill, almost forgotten by the time Ness took office, were only the beginning of the horror. Before long, Cleveland's new safety director and numerous others would be drawn into an exhaustive, massive manhunt unparalleled in the city's history.

TWO

In the opening pages of *The Untouchables*, Eliot Ness and coauthor Oscar Fraley describe an occasion in the summer of 1929 when Ness was introduced to a Chicago attorney actively involved in the fight against local mobsters. Upon learning that Ness was an agent of the Justice Department's Prohibition Bureau, the man grew suddenly cold and tight-lipped. It was obvious that he immediately assumed, as did many, that Prohibition agents were on the take.

The truth was that many government operatives in Chicago during the dry years were taking bribes; some were even on mob payrolls. But Eliot Ness was not, and he found it personally hateful to be lumped with what he termed "the bad apples" in his department. It is evident that this unfair association played a major part in the intolerant attitude Ness developed toward corruption. In his eyes, the dishonest public servant hiding behind a badge or a political office was more detestable than the criminal who openly broke the law.

Yet there was more to Ness's crusade against crime than a personal quest to prove his integrity. Above all else, he possessed a fierce, unshakable belief in the sanctity of the law. Some said it was as much his passion as his duty to rid society of its illegal elements.

His steadfast honesty and his zeal in enforcing the law were virtues Ness credited to his immigrant parents and his strict, moral upbringing. Peter Ness, a Norwegian baker, came to America in 1881. His bride was Emma King, daughter of a British engineer and a Norwegian mother. The couple settled on Chicago's south side. Peter founded a wholesale bakery that blossomed over the years into a thriving business with four shops and a small fleet of delivery trucks. Three daughters were born to the couple, then two sons. The younger, Eliot, was born on April 19, 1903.

According to his parents, Eliot was an exceptional child. "He was so terribly good he never got a spanking," his mother proudly declared later to reporters. "I never saw a boy like him." As the baby of the family, Eliot was adored and pampered but notably out of place. His father was fifty when he was born; his brother, Charles, was thirteen years his senior; and each of his sisters had married and moved away by the time he was three. One of them, Clara, wed Alexander Jamie, an agent with the Chicago division of the Justice Department. Young Eliot was a frequent visitor at their home. Their son, Wallace, became his favorite playmate. But most of all, Eliot enjoyed listening to his brother-in-law tell of his exploits as a lawman. With the permission of Eliot's parents, Jamie instructed him in marksmanship, with frequent visits to a local Coast Guard firing range.

In most ways, Eliot was a typical, freckle-faced, apple-cheeked youngster who spent much of his time with neighborhood buddies at nearby Palmer Park playground. For most of his adolescent years, Eliot faithfully worked a paper route and managed to help in his father's bakeries almost every day, delighting especially in riding aboard the delivery trucks. At Pullman Elementary School, he was a bright, attentive student. Although a notably active boy, he displayed a great fondness for reading. During evenings at home, he could often be found absorbed in a Sherlock Holmes novel, fancying himself a protégé of the fictional master sleuth.

After graduating from Fenger High School in the top third of his class, he worked briefly in a munitions plant, then in a real estate office. Finally giving in to the desires of his parents, Eliot enrolled in the University of Chicago, where he studied commerce, law, and political science. Quiet and studious in the classroom, he kept his athletic skills sharpened by becoming an exceptional tennis player on campus and by training in jujitsu three nights a week.

Ness graduated in 1925. Instead of going into the business world, he chose a poorly paying job as an investigator with the Retail Credit Company. For over a year, he checked credit ratings and insurance claims, experiencing for the first time the strenuous legwork and tedious paperwork that would mark his entire career in public service. At nights, he did a year's graduate study under famed criminologist August Volmar. In 1927, Ness passed civil service tests qualifying him to enter the Treasury Department as a special agent.

After a few months, he was transferred to the Justice Department and assigned to the Prohibition Bureau, becoming one of nearly three hundred Chicago-area agents saddled with the herculean task of drying up the Windy City. Supplying a thirsty public with bootleg liquor had become a multimillion-dollar business for mobsters who raked in the profits from an estimated twenty thousand speakeasies in the city. Through the violent, colorful decade of the Roaring Twenties, Chicagoans witnessed the rise of one ganglord to preeminence—a stocky, cigar-chomping young Italian-American named Alphonse Capone.

Born in Brooklyn (not in Italy, as his early biographers reported) in 1899, Capone migrated to Chicago at the age of twenty and was introduced into local gangdom by boyhood friend Johnny Torrio. Capone's arrival was well timed. That same year, Congress passed the Eighteenth Amendment, making Prohibition the law of the land. Although proclaimed "the noble experiment," Prohibition proved to be tremendously unpopular and virtually unenforceable. All across America, gangs of criminals pooled their resources and organized behind an enterprise that thrived on public approval. In Chicago, as elsewhere, bootlegging swiftly developed into a booming business. Capone was simply more ruthless, shrewd, and greedy than his competitors.

By 1925, when Torrio abruptly retired from the Chicago scene after narrowly escaping an attempt on his life, Capone was firmly established as the undisputed master of a vast criminal empire with an annual income of close to $120 million. He rode through the streets of the Windy City in a seven-ton, armor-plated, chauffeur-driven limousine specially built for him by General Motors at a price of $30,000. His custom-fitted suits were all in bright, gaudy colors, and they cost $135 apiece. Diamonds sparkled on his tie clasp, his stickpin, his watch and chain, and his belt buckle; on his index finger was a $50,000, eleven-carat ring. Almost every personal item he owned, from silk shirts to bed sheets and from handkerchiefs to underwear, bore the monogram AC. Capone filled his house on Prairie Avenue in Chicago and his plush estate on Florida's Palm Island with costly furnishings and decorations—Oriental rugs, antique furniture, exquisite jade pieces, and priceless sculptures and paintings.

Capone entertained lavishly and showered acquaintances with expensive gifts. Local politicians and national celebrities attended his parties. At restaurants and nightclubs, he often handed out tips of a hundred dollars, and never less than twenty dollars. On Chicago's streets, people waved and cheered at the sight of Capone. When he appeared at a racetrack or at Wrigley Field, hundreds rose and applauded him.

Although Capone was the recognized criminal czar of the city, his reign was not uncontested. His bloodiest and most prolonged gang war was with the predominantly Irish North Side Gang. Nearly five hundred mob-related killings, many perpetrated in broad daylight, occurred in Chicago during the twenties. Most gangland figures hid themselves while police investigated the slayings; Capone held press conferences. In denying the allegations against him, he could be charming, and although he had never progressed beyond the sixth grade, he made a sincere effort to sound educated. He portrayed himself as a victim of false accusations and unfavorable publicity. It was a credit to his charisma that in spite of the bloodshed he created, his popularity with the general public remained for the most part intact. After all, he was, in his own words, "a businessman supplying a public demand." Besides, the popular saying among Chicagoans claimed that "the gangsters only kill each other."

But the gang killings increased dramatically as the decade neared its end. In 1928, Ness's first full year as a Prohibition agent, there were seventy-two mob murders in the city, an all-time high. The carnage reached its peak on February 14, 1929, when seven members of the North Side Gang were savagely slain in a Clark Street garage by assassins dressed as policemen. There was little doubt about who had engineered the slaughter. North Side chieftain George "Bugs" Moran told reporters, "Only Capone kills like that."

The St. Valentine's Day Massacre proved to be a monumental mistake for Capone, generating the first real public outcry against him. Angered by their city's international infamy, two prominent Chicago publishers—Frank Knox of the *Daily News* and Robert McCormick of the *Tribune*—journeyed to Washington and voiced their concern about the millionaire ganglord who lived above the law to President Herbert Hoover. Hoover immediately instructed Secretary of the Treasury Andrew Mellon to work on putting Capone behind bars.

The government forces approached the Capone case from two different angles. A Treasury Department task force was formed under the command of Special Agent Frank J. Wilson; its assignment was to collect enough evidence to build a case of income tax evasion against the scar-faced mobster. At the same time, agents of the Justice Department would concentrate on connecting Capone to his bootlegging operations and bringing him to federal court on charges of Prohibition violations.

Selecting a team of agents from the ranks of the Prohibition Bureau to work exclusively on the Capone case was a difficult assignment in itself. The reason, simply, was that the bureau was riddled with bad apples. The backbone of the Capone organization was its bankroll, which enabled the ganglord and his associates to purchase the protection of perhaps as many as a thousand Chicago-area law officers. Capone's statement, "I own the police," was no idle boast. A number of local politicians, including Chicago Mayor William Hale "Big Bill" Thompson, were also in Capone's hip pocket. In the suburb of Cicero, where Capone's control was almost total, the mobster once kicked the mayor down the steps of city hall in front of several policemen who did nothing.

The widespread corruption among Prohibition agents was well known. Nationally, between 1921 and 1928, over 700 agents were fired and 257 were prosecuted for taking bribes. In Chicago, the inability of the government men to stop the flow of alcohol by either locating mob-owned distilleries and breweries or closing down speakeasies was sufficient proof that there were more than a few leaks in the department. One conservative estimate calculated that as many as a third of the 300 Chicago-area agents were tainted by Capone's payoffs.

Realizing this, United States District Attorney George Emmerson Q. Johnson and his assistant, William J. Froelich, struggled to create a special Capone squad—a small band of trusted, incorruptible Justice Department agents acting independently of the bureau. The pair consulted with Alexander Jamie, who had risen to one of the most respected positions in the Chicago division. Drawing up a list of candidates for leader of the special squad, Jamie offered an enthusiastic recommendation for his young brother-in-law.

At the time, Eliot Ness was twenty-six years old and still living with his parents. He was engaged to longtime sweetheart Edna Staley, and he earned twenty-eight hundred dollars a year as a federal agent. Studying Ness's record with the Prohibition Bureau, Johnson found that Ness had exhibited the qualities of honesty and resourcefulness he was searching for. The file stated that Ness displayed "coolness, aggressiveness and fearlessness in raids," that he had "far more than the average number of arrests," and that he didn't "shirk assignments or complain about extra hours." Most of all, Johnson was impressed by the young man's outspoken jabs at the bureau for holding back in its fight against the mob and for not "cleaning house."

On September 28, 1929, Johnson summoned Ness to his office and, after a brief interview, informed him that he was the selection for leading the Justice Department's special task force. Ness was stunned and elated, but he managed to retain his composure as he listened to District Attorney Johnson describe the duties of the squad. Ness was to select his own men, no more than a dozen. They were to be accountable only to Johnson and Froelich, and they were to act independently of bureau supervision. Their assignment, simply put, was to track down and destroy the mob's bootlegging operations in Chicago and to collect evidence connecting Capone and his cronies to violations of federal Prohibition laws. Johnson stressed that by closing down Capone's distilleries and breweries, they could dry up or at least severely impair the mobster's main source of income, which brought him an estimated $75 million annually. If Ness and his small band could cripple Capone financially, Capone would lose his powerful web of police and political protection and become vulnerable to the law.

Ness eagerly went to work choosing his men. He searched the personnel records of the Justice Department for men with impressive arrest records and no apparent Achilles' heels. From a list of fifty possibilities, he narrowed the field to fifteen men and finally settled upon nine.

Five—Martin Lahart, Samuel Seager, Lyle Chapman, Barney Cloonan, and Thomas Friel—were Chicago agents Ness had worked with or who came highly recommended by Jamie. The four others were outsiders recruited for their special talents. They were Paul Robsky, a wiretap expert from the New Jersey division; Michael King, a Virginia agent renowned for his ability to tail suspects; William Gardner, an expert at undercover work from the Los Angeles office; and Joseph Leeson, an exceptional driver from Detroit who, at age thirty, was the oldest member of the team. Like their leader, all nine were single men with at least two years of experience in the Justice Department. Each was an excellent marksman and possessed a spotless, noteworthy record and a distinctive background. Seager had been a guard at Sing Sing. Friel was a former Pennsylvania state trooper. Robsky had been an army officer at the age of nineteen, flying planes in the 199th Aero Squadron. Gardner and Chapman had been highly acclaimed football players in college.

By mid-October of 1929, the special unit was ready to begin its war on Capone's bootlegging empire. The timing was fortuitous. The previous May, Capone had been arrested at a Philadelphia train station for carrying a concealed weapon. The embarrassing incident had landed him in Holmesburg Prison for a ten-month stretch. In his absence, the mob's operations were overseen by

Frank "the Enforcer" Nitti, chief lieutenants Jake Guzik and Charley Fischetti, and Capone's elder brother, Ralph. But while these men were capable and fearful figures, they lacked Capone's criminal genius, and the rackets, as a result, did not run smoothly. Furthermore, like every other business in America, the Chicago mob was about to feel the devastating effects of the stock market crash that October.

With gangland activities already suffering financially and Capone temporarily absent, Ness and his men went to work locating the mob's alcohol-producing plants and shutting them down. The majority of their leads came from anonymous phone calls, many of which they suspected were from rival gangsters. Some plants were discovered only after weeks or months of exhaustive legwork and surveillance. Lahart and Gardner, posing as out-of-town criminals, actually managed to infiltrate the ranks of the Capone organization and to pick up leads as they rubbed elbows with top henchmen. The agents also used paid informants.

Phone taps were another source of information, the most valuable ones placed on Jake Guzik, who was the mob's business manager, and on the Montmartre Cafe, a plush Cicero speakeasy that served as the headquarters of Ralph Capone. Ness later described the planting of the Montmartre bug as one of the most harrowing experiences of his career. Four of his agents—Leeson, Seager, Cloonan, and Gardner—distracted a small army of gangsters long enough for Ness and Robsky to creep silently into an alley behind the cafe. Robsky scaled a telephone pole and applied his expertise to the terminal while Ness, his Colt .38 in hand, stood guard in the dark alley below. Usually cool in the most intense situations, Ness found himself nervously twitching at every sound and straining his eyes in the darkness to detect any movement. When Robsky finally bridged the lines and descended, the pair left the alley unnoticed. Over the next two years, the tap on Ralph Capone's private line proved invaluable, not only supplying useful information to the squad but also revealing the identities of three local Prohibition agents who were snitching to the mob.

On March 17, 1930, Al Capone was released from Holmesburg Prison and immediately resumed command of his gangland empire. He emerged to find America suffering under the first year of the Great Depression and his bootlegging organization slowly crumbling at the edges. Ness and his agents were a small but nagging factor in the mob's financial misfortunes. At first, Capone appeared to take his losses in stride. Playing the role of public benefactor, he sponsored a soup kitchen on the south side that fed thousands. Once, an elderly Italian woman, overwhelmed with gratitude, knelt before Capone and kissed his hand.

Ness was disgusted by the public image enjoyed by the gangster he was fighting to put behind bars. He was also dismayed at the lack of progress by his special squad. During their first six months, they had captured a total of nineteen distilleries and six breweries, costing Capone an estimated $1 million. It was a nice total on paper, but mere chicken feed to the Capone organization. Worse yet, Ness's raids had failed to produce a single arrest.

The reason was that locating Capone's operations proved much easier than entering them. Hacking through doorways with axes or battering them down with sledgehammers was often a slow, exhaustive endeavor that allowed those inside to destroy evidence and escape through secret exits. In one raid on a huge warehouse at 2271 Lumber Street that housed an operation worth seventy-five thousand dollars, the occupants silently slipped away through a special escape route via the roof while Ness and his men clumsily bashed their way in thinking they had all possible exits covered.

Ness realized that his special unit had to develop a faster, more efficient means of entering marked buildings. Leeson and Chapman, after many months of work, came up with a solution—a ten-ton flatbed truck equipped with ladders and a giant steel ram specially constructed for smashing through brewery or distillery doors.

On June 13, 1930, the agents tested their new weapon. With Leeson at the wheel, Ness riding shotgun, and the others riding in back or covering exits, the truck crashed through the doors of a Capone operation at 2108 South Wabash Avenue. Five mob employees found on the premises were taken prisoner.

The raid forced Capone to regard the squad as a serious threat to business. As Ness later told the story, a young underworld figure known as "the Kid" appeared at his office in the Transportation Building a few days later. Claiming that he spoke for "the Big Guy," the Kid offered Ness a bribe of two thousand dollars to "lay off," and assured him that another two thousand would follow each week he behaved. In an uncharacteristic rage, Ness jammed the bulky envelope back into the Kid's jacket pocket and growled, "Listen, and don't let me ever have to repeat it: I may only be a poor baker's son, but I don't need this kind of money. Now you go back and tell those rats what I said—and be damn sure you give them back every penny or so help me I'll break you in half."

The next morning, Lahart and Seager rushed into the office announcing that they, too, had received a bribe offer. While they had been tailing a truckload of booze, a vehicle containing a pair of thugs had suddenly pulled alongside them. One of the thugs had tossed an object through their open window. For an instant, the two agents had believed they were the recipients of a live grenade and thought they "were goners." But the object had proven to be "a wad of bills big enough to choke an ox." Seager had stepped on the gas and managed to catch the gangsters' car. When they were parallel again, Lahart had hurled the roll of cash back at them.

Ness told the pair he was "damned proud" of them.

"What the hell, Eliot," Seager said. "We want to beat 'em, not join 'em."

It was time, Ness declared, to share their story with the public. After discussing his idea with the other agents, he contacted the press and informed them that he had some interesting material to relate. That afternoon, a horde of newsmen descended upon the agents' office and listened as Ness told of the attempts to buy off the squad. Bribes and bullets, he proclaimed, would not deter them from their crusade against Capone. It was a writer for the *Tribune*, in an article printed the next day, who first called the tiny band of gangbusters "the Untouchables."

For the first time, Eliot Ness experienced the public spotlight, and he was obviously enthralled by the attention of the media. From that point on, whenever the agents raided a building, Ness made sure that there were plenty of reporters and photographers on the scene moments after the doors had been battered down.

Public officials and fellow lawmen were openly critical of the squad's publicity, charging that its effectiveness would be impaired by press coverage and that Ness was only seeking to make a name for himself. Ness sincerely defended his actions. He stressed that it was important that both Capone and the public learn of their determination and honesty. Ness also maintained that a tough reputation and a positive public image would help rather than hinder the squad. Ironically, and in a way Ness did not realize at the time, the publicity did help the government's case. Thanks in part to the attention that the Untouchables received, the team of Treasury Department agents working undercover to gather evidence of Capone's tax evasion was able to operate without detection.

At first, it appeared that Ness's critics were correct in blasting the unit for its overexposure in the press. For the next few months, the Untouchables were miserably ineffective. Capone had tightened security around his bootlegging plants, training his lookouts to recognize each of the ten agents. If an Untouchable was spotted near a plant, the operation was moved immediately. Other mobsters kept a vigilant watch on the squad, tailing them wherever they went. Ness even discovered that their office phones had been tapped.

After a considerable dry spell, the agents managed to resume their operations by expertly evading their tails and feeding the mob false information. Leeson and Seager located an old factory at the corner of Thirty-eighth and Shields where the mob cleaned the barrels used to hold its booze. By following the trucks leaving the factory, Ness and his men began to discover the sites of several major operations.

At five o'clock on the morning of March 25, 1931, the Untouchables crashed their truck through the doors of a Capone brewery at 1642 South Cicero Avenue. Ness leaped out of the cab, fired a single shot into the ceiling, and held his gun on five paralyzed, wide-eyed mobsters as the rest of the squad rushed in. The prisoners were Frank Conta, a known Capone aide; Steve Svoboda, reportedly the mob's ace brewer; and three truck drivers. Only Conta was armed. The agents destroyed thirty thousand gallons of beer.

On April 4, the squad successfully raided another operation only a block away from their previous capture. One week later, on April 11, the agents stormed the Old Reliable Trucking Company at 3136 South Wabash Avenue. Inside, they found a bootlegging operation worth a hundred thousand dollars and over forty thousand gallons of unbarreled beer. Among the five prisoners captured in the raid was, once again, brewmaster Svoboda, who had been released on a bail of five thousand dollars. "You won't get out so quickly this time," Ness told him.

Late one night during this period as Ness and a fellow Untouchable sat in an automobile staking out a suspected brewery, half a dozen gunmen suddenly appeared aiming shotguns and submachine guns at the pair. Bert Delaney, a Capone associate, walked up and ordered the others to put away their weapons. Then, turning to Ness, he asked, "How much you guys want?" Delaney started at six hundred dollars and gradually increased his offer as Ness continued to stare silently at him. Finally, Delaney barked, "All right, you guys set your own price."

Ness started the car. "You haven't got enough money," he remarked as he pulled away.

A few days later, Robsky was at a headset listening to a conversation between Ralph Capone and a gangster named Fusco on the Montmartre wiretap. Fusco was told to "go ahead with the South Wabash deal." When Ness read the transcript, he realized that the "South Wabash deal" might be a reference to a brewery the Untouchables had just closed down. He ordered Chapman and King to watch the building. Three days later, they reported that during the early morning hours "gangster-types" had been moving all kinds of equipment back inside.

The agents waited until the brewery was in full operation, then smashed through the reconstructed doors with their truck. Six men including Bert Delaney were taken into custody along with two trucks and equipment worth a hundred thousand dollars.

Not long after this sensational series of raids, Ness learned from one of his informants that a Capone "torpedo" (mob slang for a gunman) had been assigned to tail and kill him. Another contact informed Ness that the hit man's name was Michael Picchi. Ness obtained a mug shot of Picchi and carried it with him everywhere. A few days later, Ness was riding with Lahart through the city's south side when they noticed a car following them. The agents made a screeching turn and pursued the vehicle. After a wild chase, they managed to force the car to the curb, then leaped out with guns drawn. The driver was Picchi. Ness disarmed him and examined his weapon. It was a killer's gun—the serial numbers had been filed off, and it was loaded with dumdum bullets. Showing the slugs to Lahart, Ness remarked, "I bet these were meant for me."

Picchi was taken to the nearest police station, and he was eventually charged with attempted assualt on federal officers.

It was obvious that Capone was becoming desperate. The wiretap on the phone of Jake Guzik revealed how bad the mob's business was. In one conversation, Ness and his men overheard a speakeasy owner pleading for liquor, with Guzik replying that he was unable to furnish any. Another time, Guzik was contacted by a mob employee asking how much he should pay some local policemen. "Nothin'," Guzik answered.

"Whatta ya mean, nothin'?"

"Listen, Hymie," Guzik explained, "you'll have to tell the boys they'll have to take a pass this month."

"They ain't gonna like it."

"Too bad, but we just ain't makin' any dough. And if we ain't got it, we can't pay for it."

Ness and his men congratulated themselves on their apparent success in crippling the mob's booze operations. With their primary goal accomplished, the agents began to concentrate on their secondary objective of building a legal case against Capone and his associates. From the start, the job of assembling evidence gathered in the raids had belonged to Chapman, the tall football star who was a wizard at paperwork. Once, Chapman had even managed to trace the purchase of a beer truck confiscated in a raid to Capone himself.

On June 12, 1931, Ness, armed with Chapman's voluminous mass of data, appeared before a federal grand jury and secured indictments against Capone and sixty-eight members of his mob for conspiracy to violate the Volstead Act. Five thousand separate offenses against Prohibition laws were cited.

Ironically, Capone would never be brought to trial on any of the Prohibition charges. The Treasury Department agents working under Special Agent Wilson—the unsung heroes of the Capone case—had beaten their Justice Department counterparts by one week, having supplied evidence on June 5 to indict Capone for income tax evasion. United States District Attorney Johnson chose to prosecute the ganglord on the tax charges, holding Ness's Prohibition indictments in reserve should Capone evade conviction. A trial date was set for that fall.

In the meantime, adding insult to injury, the Untouchables continued to wreak havoc on Capone's bootlegging operations, making six arrests at a $125,000 brewery in a garage at 1712 North Kilbourn Avenue and raiding a $100,000 plant at 222 East Twenty-fifth Street.

This time, Capone responded with violence. An ex-convict who was a good friend of Ness's and who occasionally worked as the eleventh member of the Untouchables suddenly disappeared. His body turned up in a ditch near Chicago Heights a few days later. The apparent victim of a "one-way ride," he had been horribly tortured before being shot to death.

Ness was greatly shaken by the brutal murder of his friend, but his defiance of Capone was also reinforced. After some careful planning, the Untouchables staged a bizarre parade past Capone's headquarters at the Lexington Hotel. Early in the day, Ness phoned the Lexington and, after great persistence, managed to get Capone himself on the line. "What's up?" Capone had asked.

"I just wanted to tell you that if you look out your front window at eleven o'clock today you'll see something that will interest you," Ness had said.

At the appointed time, Capone and his chief henchmen appeared at the windows. Moving along Michigan Avenue at a pace of fifteen miles an hour was a caravan of forty-five trucks that the Untouchables had seized in their raids. The vehicles were on their way to a public auction. The next morning, Ness learned from one of his underworld contacts that the sight of the convoy had thrown Capone into a violent rage. Capone had smashed two chairs over a table and screamed, "I'll kill 'im, I'll kill 'im with my own bare hands!"

There followed, in quick succession, three attempts on Ness's life. In the first, he narrowly escaped a hail of bullets fired from a passing car. Next, he was almost run down by a speeding automobile that veered straight at him as he crossed an intersection outside his office. Days later, Ness was about to climb into his car when he noticed that the hood latches were unfastened; examining the motor, he discovered a dynamite charge wired to the starter.

Around that time, the Untouchables heard rumors of a super-plant that supplied the Capone empire with the greater part of its alcohol. Their efforts to locate the operation failed repeatedly until an anonymous phone call—this one from a woman—furnished a possible location. Ness and Lahart checked out the site, a six-story building on Diversey Avenue. They discovered that the first four floors housed a legitimate business. The top floors, however, were occupied by a mysterious paint company that, according to their information, had no record of any business dealings whatsoever.

After dark, Ness and Lahart crept up a fire escape to a window. They were greatly surprised by the brightly lit interior bustling with activity. The center of attention was a colossal, forty-foot still rising through a hole in the fifth-floor ceiling to almost touch the sixth-floor ceiling.

Ness and his raiders returned the next night. Unable to use his favorite method of smashing down the doors with their truck, Ness again climbed the fire escape with Lahart. At the prearranged moment—exactly midnight—the pair crashed through the windows and aimed their sawed-off shotguns at the startled workers. Moments later, the other Untouchables rushed in from a service entrance. The largest Capone booze operation ever uncovered fell without a single shot. The giant still was capable of producing an awesome twenty thousand gallons of alcohol per day. The entire setup was valued at close to a million dollars.

Capone was hurting. One estimate reported that his liquor production in the city had dwindled to a mere 20 percent of what it had been just ten months earlier. By the end of the summer, the mob had to resort to buying alcohol outside the city and smuggling it in, a more lengthy and costly procedure. Still on the offensive, Ness and his men began intercepting the shipments. They also entered rural areas beyond Cook County to track down Capone's suppliers, on one occasion arresting a small-town police force of a sheriff and two deputies who were operating a still.

Capone finally went to trial for income tax evasion on October 6, 1931. Ness was present in the courtroom each day, a mere spectator instead of the government's star witness. Capone was found guilty and sentenced to eleven years in a federal penitentiary.

On May 3, 1932, the Untouchables escorted Capone from the Cook County Jail to Dearborn Station. Their five-car caravan arrived uneventfully at the train depot, where thousands had gathered to catch a final glimpse of Chicago's most infamous and colorful criminal. Ness and his squad encircled Capone as policemen cleared a path through the mass of people. After turning over the prisoner to the two United States marshalls assigned to deliver him to the federal penitentiary in Atlanta, the agents stood guard on the platform until the train departed. It was the last mission of the Untouchables. The squad was disbanded and the agents reassigned.

In recognition of his outstanding service as the unit's leader, Ness was appointed chief investigator of the Chicago Prohibition Bureau. But Prohibition was coming to an end. Late in 1933, Ness was transferred to Cincinnati to supervise an entirely different kind of alcohol enforcement—the tracking down and destroying of thousands of hillbilly stills scattered throughout the "Moonshine Mountains." Directing operations over a vast territory that included southwestern Ohio, most of Kentucky, and parts of Tennessee, Ness encountered a hostile environment with its own laws and code of silence not unlike those of the Chicago underworld. Numerous times, his still-hunting expeditions ended in gunfire, usually with Ness and his fellow agents running for their lives.

As his new position offered all of the danger and none of the glamour of his days in Chicago, Ness was considerably displeased. He was, moreover, a city boy who yearned to be battling crime in the center of a metropolis. After less than a year as a revenuer, he requested reassignment. Ness's nephew and boyhood friend Wallace Jamie contacted him shortly thereafter. He offered Eliot a municipal law enforcement job in St. Paul, where Jamie had been appointed the city's assistant safety director. Ness seriously considered the proposal but finally decided that he was not ready to resign as a federal agent. In late July of 1934, the Treasury Department's post in northern Ohio was offered to Ness. He accepted and moved to Cleveland, where, sixteen months later, he became the city's director of public safety.

His first full day on the job, December 12, 1935, Ness attended a succession of routine meetings at city hall with the mayor and various officials including Police Chief George J. Matowitz and Fire Chief James E. Granger.

It wasn't until after nightfall that the city got a clearer indication of what could be expected from its new safety director. Ness was finishing dinner with his wife and some friends at a downtown restaurant when sirens were heard outside. After kissing Edna and arranging for her return home, Ness raced to a site a block away where police were investigating a burglary. He joined the investigating officers in a rooftop search, but the perpetrator escaped.

The evening still young, Ness asked a pair of patrolmen if he could ride with them. The officers could hardly refuse the man invested with almost absolute authority over Cleveland's twenty-four hundred policemen and fire fighters. For the next few hours, Ness was treated to a tour of the crime-infested Third Precinct. He accompanied the officers on routine calls and to the scene of a five-alarm fire. The night ended on a less than satisfying note when Ness and his companions attempted to raid a brothel on Orange Avenue. As the lawmen stormed the front, the occupants escaped out the rear. "That was a quick getaway," Ness commented with a grin to a reporter inquiring about the unsuccessful raid. Some of the subsequent news stories poked mild fun at the new safety director, implying that he was rapidly adjusting to the level of police incompetence in Cleveland.

There was no laughter, however, on December 17, when Director Ness discharged two patrolmen, Joseph Dunne and Michael Corrigan, from the force for drinking on duty. Intoxication was considered a negligible offense among Cleveland police, even though Dunne had been on school traffic duty at the time of his dismissal. The officers, moreover, were veterans of fourteen and twelve years, respectively. Their superiors in the department, along with some citizens and scattered comments in the press, claimed that the new safety director had overstepped his authority, and they demanded that the pair be reinstated. But Ness stood his ground, and the *Plain Dealer* backed him in an editorial.

In an interview, Ness stated emphatically, "I will not stand for this sort of thing in my department. It is this simple. Either we have a decent, law-abiding community, or we don't. Either we have decent, law-abiding policemen to show us the way, or we don't. These men have a past record of prior offenses. They don't fit."

He was just beginning to mold the police force in his image. Two days before Christmas, Ness sprang what was termed "the biggest departmental shake-up in years" when he announced the transfer of 122 policemen, including a captain and twenty-seven lieutenants. He also replaced the head of the Detective Bureau with a man more to his liking, and he warned all precinct captains that they would be held accountable for any misconduct among the men under their command.

Shortly after New Year's, Director Ness delivered his assessment of the city's crime scene in a speech before the Cleveland Advertising Club. The ineffectiveness of Cleveland police, he declared, was the result of widespread corruption and complacency. "In any city where corruption continues," he told his audience, "it follows that some officials are playing ball with the underworld. If town officials are committed to a program of 'protection,' police work becomes exceedingly difficult, and the officer on the beat, being discouraged from his duty, decides it is best to see as little crime as possible."

Ness informed his listeners that there was evidence that Cleveland officers were not only accepting bribes but acting as informants and even enforcers for the mobs. Those officers, however, were only a small percentage. The greatest offenses of Cleveland cops were apathy and carelessness. The average patrolman was sloppy in his appearance. Some were known to drop in at bars along their beat for a couple of quick ones. It was no surprise that the public had lost confidence in the police.

With the rise in corruption and the poor discipline and morale among the police, organized crime flourished in the city. Ness startled his audience when he quoted figures reporting that gambling raked in over two hundred thousand dollars a week in Cleveland, and he vigorously refuted the belief that gambling was a harmless vice. Ness admitted that he had no moral objection to the practice and that he was not averse to the movement by some city councilmen to legalize certain forms of gambling (a daring statement since his boss, Mayor Burton, *was* opposed). But that was not the issue, Ness said. As long as gambling was illegal and provided a prodigious source of income for the mob, it was the duty of every citizen to oppose its spread through the community. The fantastic success of illegal gambling had cleared the way for other criminal activities, among them prostitution and drug dealing as well as union racketeering, a new vice that was finding an extremely profitable atmosphere in blue-collar Cleveland. The unhindered expansion of the underworld had, furthermore, opened the door for criminals of all kinds to operate freely in the city.

It was obvious that Cleveland needed someone who could reverse the breakdown in law and order. The critical question that people were asking was whether Eliot Ness was the man for the job. A few days later, the question was answered.

At five o'clock on the afternoon of Friday, January 10, 1936, County Prosecutor Frank T. Cullitan attempted to spring a raid on the Harvard Club, the notorious gambling joint flagrantly operating on the outskirts of Newburgh Heights. Brandishing a warrant issued by Judge Frank J. Lausche and accompanied by twenty constables he had specially recruited, Cullitan was met at the front entrance by James "Shimmy" Patton, one of the three disreputable owners of the club, who defiantly refused to admit the raiding party. When the prosecutor tried to push his way in, a pair of thugs appeared behind Patton cradling submachine guns. With a smug grin, Patton informed Cullitan that his men would mow down anyone attempting to get past him. The lawmen beat a hasty retreat down the road to a gas station, where Cullitan phoned local officers for reinforcements. Incredibly, the village and county authorities he contacted refused to intervene. In desperation, the prosecutor put in a call to Eliot Ness at city hall.

The safety director was attending a meeting of the city council when an aide summoned him to his office to answer an urgent call. Ness listened as Cullitan gave a detailed account of the abortive raid and Patton's arrogant threat. "We need help," Cullitan said.

"Hold everything," Ness reportedly answered. "I'll be there."

He quickly placed a call to the office of the sheriff of Cuyahoga County, John L. "Honest John" Sulzman. Deputy William Murphy answered and informed Ness that the sheriff had gone home.

Ness explained, "Prosecutor Cullitan is at the Harvard Club with several of his staff and their lives are endangered. As a citizen, I am calling on you and the sheriff to send some men out there to protect them."

Murphy responded that the sheriff advocated a policy of noninterference. "We can't send men out there without a call from the mayor of Newburgh."

Ness refused to be put off. "Will you go out or won't you?"

"I'll have to call the sheriff and I'll call you back."

"To hell with calling back," Ness barked. "I'll wait on the phone."

After several minutes, Murphy returned to the line and stated, "No. We won't go out there."

Ness hung up in disgust. Before leaving city hall, he met briefly with the mayor and informed him of his decision to join the officers at the Harvard Club. Burton advised Ness against it. Newburgh Heights was not part of the safety director's jurisdiction. Burton also pointed out that Cullitan, a prominent Democrat, had been a vocal opponent of the new Republican administration. But Ness remained adamant, saying that he would go to the scene as a private citizen to lend support to lawmen in the performance of their duty. If their campaign for law and order was to succeed, Ness added, it was vital that they establish credibility by taking a stand and backing lawmen throughout the Cleveland area without regard to politics. Burton reluctantly gave his consent.

Minutes later, the safety director marched into nearby Central Station and announced that he was looking for recruits to assist him in a raid. "I want only volunteers," Ness said. "Preferably men going off duty."

Meanwhile, Cullitan and his men had resumed their position outside the Harvard Club, anxiously standing in clusters in the bitter cold discussing their next move. Many had started to talk of abandoning their efforts when, at ten-thirty, a caravan of police vehicles roared into view. As they screeched to a halt, the passenger's door of the lead car flew open. Cullitan instantly recognized Eliot Ness. The spur-of-the-moment posse Ness had assembled at Central Station numbered twenty-seven patrolmen, ten motorcycle cops, and four plainclothesmen. Most carried either a sawed-off shotgun or a high-powered rifle. Two had tear gas guns. More headlights were approaching in the distance. Reporters had already caught wind of the story, one source later claiming that Ness himself had tipped them off.

Cullitan was frankly startled at the sight of the reinforcements and their arsenal. As he shook hands with Ness, the prosecutor stated almost sheepishly that he wanted no bloodshed. Ness nodded, then walked boldly to the doorway and rapped vigorously until a pair of eyes peered from the peephole. "I'm Eliot Ness," he reportedly announced. "I'm coming in with some warrants."

There are conflicting accounts as to what occurred next.

In his personal version told many years later to Oscar Fraley, Ness claimed that he had been refused access and that he had kicked in the door—something of a superhuman feat, since reliable souces made note of the fact that the front entrance to the Harvard Club was constructed of steel. Ness said that once inside, he had been forced to wrestle a gunman to the floor using jujitsu, clearing the way for Cullitan and his men.

The official account was far less dramatic. After identifying himself, Ness reportedly waited with the other officers five minutes in the cold before the door was finally opened. As lawmen and reporters jammed inside, a tough-looking character in a tuxedo appeared from the back of the club and walked straight to Ness, growling that the intruders had no business entering. "Who the hell you guys think you are?" he asked. Ness flashed his identification, a special badge engraved with Eliot Ness, Public Safety Director, City of Cleveland. Surprised, the man took a couple of steps back. Ness smiled, put away his identification, and walked past him without a word. The only reported incident of violence occurred when a photographer for the *Cleveland Press* attempted to snap a picture of one of the club's employees and was roughly shoved away. A fellow reporter quickly intervened and decked the thug with a blow to the jaw.

The raid was hardly a spectacular success. Ness, Cullitan, and the others walked into the club's gambling parlor—a huge room with a high ceiling that had once been used for dance marathons and that could accommodate close to two thousand guests—and discovered that the interior was void of patrons and stripped of its crap tables and roulette wheels. Sometime during the five-and-a-half-hour stretch between Cullitan's first attempt at entry and Ness's appearance, Patton and some of his employees (including Alvin Karpis) had slipped away into the night with all the furnishings and gambling equipment. Cullitan vowed to keep the building empty.

Despite the rather anticlimactic ending, the raid was a glorious triumph for the new safety director. Newspaper accounts described his arrival on the scene as if it had been the cavalry coming to the rescue. For an overcrowded city riddled with crime and corruption and struggling through the Great Depression, Eliot Ness suddenly emerged as a valiant champion of law and order, resurrecting the battle, so long absent from the city, between the good guys and the bad.

On a frostbitten Sunday morning sixteen days after Ness's participation in the Harvard Club raid, residents of the Third Precinct along the twenty-three-hundred block of East Twentieth Street were awakened by the howling of a dog. Most concluded that the dog's agitation was due to the frigid temperatures. The city was in the midst of one of the most prolonged cold spells in its history. An unceasing arctic wind had kept Cleveland thermometers near zero for almost two weeks, with no relief in sight. It was no wonder that there was little movement on the streets. Neighbors, hearing the dog, preferred to remain in their beds with pillows over their ears.

At eleven o'clock, a black woman finally bundled herself up and braved the bitter cold to investigate the incessant howling. In an alley behind the Hart Manufacturing plant, she found the dog snapping at its leash and straining toward a bushel basket resting against the back wall of the factory a few yards away. After peering inside the basket, the woman walked to the end of the alley, where she met Charles Paige, a neighborhood butcher. She informed him that there was a basket in the alley containing "some hams." Thinking that his shop might have been burglarized and some meat left behind, Paige hurried to the basket to see for himself. He reached beneath a burlap sack covering the top, then drew back in horror as he pulled out a human arm.

Police arriving on the scene discovered more pieces of a neatly dismembered female body in the basket—both thighs and, inside a second burlap bag, the lower half of the torso. Some of the parts were wrapped in newspapers dated January 25, 1936 (the previous day) and August 11, 1935. Ashes, bits of coal, and chicken feathers were also found inside the basket.

Police were able to identify the victim through fingerprints obtained from the hand. She was Florence Genevieve Polillo, alias Florence Martin or Clara Dunn, a forty-one-year-old prostitute with a sporadic record of arrests. Her address was a rooming house at 3205 Carnegie Avenue, only a few blocks from where her partial remains were found.

Like Andrassy, Flo Polillo had been a familiar face to the cops of the Third Precinct. A short, squat, squint-eyed woman with several chins and almost no neck, a mop of stringy, dark brown hair turning gray, and liver spots covering her face and arms, Flo had frequented the bars and sleazy dives of the Roaring Third. Her first encounter with Cleveland police had been in December of 1930, when she was arrested for soliciting. The arrest report described her as "height 5 ft-7 with shoes on, 160 lbs, medium stout build, light complexion, dark chestnut hair (dyed red), dark chestnut eyes—All the upper and lower teeth are false . . . Irish-American descent." Another arrest had followed on June 14, 1931, for "occupying rooms for immoral purposes." Several times, she had been identified as an active participant in barroom brawls. Friends claimed that Flo had been a pleasant, passive woman except when she drank, at which time she became loud and abusive.

Homicide teams including Emil Musil with Orly May and Ralph Kennedy with Leo Duffin were assigned to the case. They discovered that almost all of the numerous people they interviewed had known Flo, but that no one seemed to know anything *about* her. Her police file listed Ashtabula, Ohio, as her hometown, but she had lived under such a vast array of aliases that detectives could not even be certain of her maiden name. She had been twice married, twice divorced. Nothing was known of the first husband. The second was Andrew Polillo, a postal worker in Buffalo. They had been married six years before Flo deserted him. About a year later, in 1930, she had turned up in Cleveland and spent the remaining five years of her life drifting through the seedy landscape of the Roaring Third.

Detectives attempting to trace her movements had a difficult time. Flo, they discovered, had changed names, addresses, jobs, and lovers with astonishing frequency. Once, she had left Cleveland and traveled to Washington, D.C., where she was arrested for prostitution on May 2, 1934. When she returned to Cleveland, she had been accompanied by a tall, blond, good-looking man she introduced as Harry Martin, her new husband. The investigators were unable to verify the marriage. Detectives Musil and May located a run-down hotel on Walnut Street where the couple had lived for several months. The manager informed the detectives that Martin had often beaten Flo. He also stated that just before Christmas, Flo had appeared in the company of a young Italian. Since that had been slightly over a month before her death, and also because the description of the Italian matched that of a reported friend of Edward Andrassy's, the police searched thoroughly for the man, but they could not find him. Neither could they locate Harry Martin.

A maze of trails led the investigators to an apartment Flo had occupied on East Seventy-eighth Street, a rooming house not far from Central Station where she had been known as Flo Davis, and yet another rooming house where she had lived as Flo Gallagher. They checked the places where she had been employed—usually as a waitress or barmaid—as well as whorehouses where she had occasionally operated. One madam reported that Flo had been "a good gal" who often had a rough time with her customers. A bartender who had known Flo well told police that he had seen her on crutches about three months earlier. Police also learned that in early January she had moved in with an older Italian who was on relief. The detectives looked for him and for another Italian she had seen regularly the previous summer; for an Italian bootlegger who had met with her just two days before she died; for yet another Italian, this one named Al, who had reportedly supplied her with drugs; for a cabdriver who had been a frequent lover; for a seaman who had often visited her; for a black woman, currently working as a singer, who had met Flo in jail; for a gambler who had pimped for her; for several prostitutes said to have been close to her; for a mysterious Dr.

Manzella to whom she had made a series of payments ranging from three to forty dollars; and for a peddler who had lived with her and who had allegedly boasted two weeks earlier that he was going to find her and "cut her all up." None of these people was ever found, though the lawmen searched diligently for each. There were also several black men said to have been her lovers. Police tracked down one, a character called One-armed Willie, who admitted having lived with Flo briefly but denied any part in her death.

Ultimately, the investigation led back to where the detectives had started—the apartment on Carnegie Avenue. The landlady, Mary Ford, showed detectives Flo's room and told them that Flo had lived there since May, paying her rent with relief checks. For the most part, Flo had been quiet and sociable. They had become friends.

"Her only bad habit," recalled Mrs. Ford, "was that she would go out occasionally and get a quart of liquor—bad liquor too—and drink it all by her lonesome in her room. When she was drinking she was pecky—quarrelsome, you know. She never talked very much, except about her mother, who died three months ago. I felt sorry for her, and drove her out to Pierpont, Ohio, for the funeral."

The last time Mrs. Ford saw her, Flo had been leaving her apartment at eight-thirty on Friday night, January 24. Mrs. Ford was the last to see her alive, or at least the last to admit it. There was a vague report that Flo had fought with a black man in a bar on Saturday night, but the coroner was certain that she had died by then, fixing the time of death to late Friday or early Saturday.

Meanwhile, the unseasonably cold weather had temporarily lifted. On the night of Thursday, February 7, police were summoned to the backyard of a vacant house on Orange Avenue, just a few blocks west of the alley on East Twentieth. There, a young mechanic cutting through the yard had spotted more pieces of Flo Polillo strewn in the melting snow along the back fence, as if the killer had stood on the opposite side and hastily tossed them over. The remains were close to two weeks old, and it was possible that they had been dropped the same night as the earlier deposit. Police found the upper torso, the lower legs, and the left arm and hand. Only the head was still missing. It was never found.

The frigid temperatures had kept the pieces well preserved. Coroner Pearse and his staff noted that the neck muscles were retracted, indicating that the decapitation had either been the cause of death or been performed immediately after death. The remainder of the body appeared to have been cut up much later, after rigor mortis began to set in. The torso was bisected between the second and third lumbar vertebrae; the head had been removed with several clean strokes between the fourth and fifth cervical vertebrae. The arms and legs were expertly severed at the shoulder, hip, and knee joints. Detectives debated the significance of an irregular gash along the pubic area, some concluding that it indicated the act of a pervert. The medical examiners, however, thought that the killer's knife had merely slipped as he sliced through the hip joint.

Detective Sergeant James T. Hogan, the newly appointed head of Homicide, refused to acknowledge a parallel to the four-month-old murders of Andrassy and his unknown companion, despite the unusual feature of death by decapitation. A tall, imposing figure with receding white hair, Hogan announced that the Polillo case would be regarded as a totally unrelated murder.

Leads in the case were rapidly evaporating. Mrs. Ford supplied police with a description of the clothes Flo had been wearing that Friday night when she was last seen—a black cloth coat with a gray fur collar, a black hat, and brown shoes. None of the articles ever turned up. Other detectives attempted to trace the pair of burlap bags containing the initial remains. The trail led first to a poultry dealer outside the city, then to the Cleveland Feather Company at 1838 Central Avenue, only several blocks east of where the remains had been discovered. The detectives learned that the bags had arrived with a delivery of chicken feathers on January 17. The premises were searched and the employees questioned, but no valuable clues surfaced until a peddler was discovered who claimed he had purchased some bags from the company at about that time. The peddler had sold the bags to a neighborhood junk shop, and some of them, in turn, had been sold to another junk dealer. The police suddenly had two separate locations from which the killer might have obtained the sacks. But neither shop owner could remember when he had sold the bags, or to whom.

And there, for the moment, the investigation of Flo Polillo's murder came to a grinding halt.

THREE

In the fall of 1796, a man named Moses led his people to the promised land. That, at least, is the colorful way that many Clevelanders describe the founding of their city. The man was General Moses Cleaveland, a Connecticut surveyor who brought a party of New England explorers to the place where the winding Cuyahoga River flows into Lake Erie. He chose the high ground along the east bank as the site for the town which would eventually bear his name (minus the initial *a*).

Unlike the biblical Moses, Cleaveland inspired no exodus to the new land. His community began with a modest population of three white settlers, growing to a mere seven by the turn of the century. Over the next few decades, Cleveland gradually took shape by fits and starts as pioneer families trickled into the Cuyahoga Valley and built homes for themselves around the wide, sunny meadow that is today Public Square.

With the completion of the Erie Canal in 1825 and the Ohio Canal in 1832, the trickle abruptly became a flood. On May 8,

1836, Cleveland was incorporated as a city with six thousand inhabitants. By the end of the year, nearly two thousand sailing vessels had visited her harbor, and the first railroad lines had arrived. In the next few years, the population increased by 464 percent. The transfiguration of the sleepy village into a bustling commercial port with a strategic location on the Great Lakes seemed to happen before anyone realized it.

The next century of Cleveland's history was one of prosperity and phenomenal growth. Business and industry boomed; immigrants poured in to supply the backbone of a labor force; and ships loaded with ore and oil kept coming. Monopolies were formed and fantastic fortunes made; the elegant homes of the wealthy stretched for miles along Euclid Avenue, which earned fame worldwide as Millionaire's Row. Slowly, a metropolis of concrete and steel rose upon the Lake Erie shoreline. A hundred years and nine hundred thousand people later, the city was still gasping for breath and struggling to catch up with itself.

The early years of the depression retarded but did not halt the city's incredible growth. Its people had time to pause and look at what a century of unrestrained expansion and industrialization had done to their community. Cleveland seemed to have everything any other big city had, yet it had somehow failed to develop its own identity, a distinctive flavor distinguishing it from the rest of America's big cities. There were many across the nation who regarded Cleveland as an overgrown country town wholly devoid of the culture and prestige of places like New York, Philadelphia, and Boston. Clevelanders wanted respect and recognition.

Nineteen thirty-six proved to be a key year in Cleveland history. With the worst of the depression behind, municipal leaders and prominent citizens were fully committed to promoting a positive image for the city. The Eucharist Congress the previous September had been only the first in a series of prestigious events which Clevelanders hoped would make their city shine brightly at a time when many others had grown notably dim. There were great expectations as Cleveland's centennial—May 8, 1936—approached. Exactly one month later, the Republican National Convention would come to town, and near the end of summer so would the American Legion Convention. But the most prodigious, bold, and eagerly awaited attraction was the Great Lakes Expo, officially titled the Northwest Territory Exposition, a miniature world's fair scheduled to open June 27 on Cleveland's lakefront.

The millions of visitors anticipated for these events would be pouring into the downtown area, which only recently had become the chief source of civic pride. Ambitious municipal development in the years just prior to the stock market crash had given the vicinity between Public Square and the lakefront a fresh, modern, even dazzling look. The centerpiece of the urban landscaping was the magnificent Mall, with its memorial fountain and gardens. Around the Mall, an array of exquisite edifices arose—Municipal Auditorium, the new city hall, the Federal Building, Municipal Stadium, the Plain Dealer Building, the public library, the Federal Reserve Bank Building, the county courthouse, and Cleveland College.

Head and shoulders above all was the fifty-two-story Terminal Tower, another brainchild of the neoeccentric Van Sweringen brothers. The project had been conceived in the early twenties as a downtown terminal for the Van Sweringens' transit system. But the brothers, never known to do anything on a small scale, had reasoned that since their beloved Cleveland was the largest city in Ohio, it should have the tallest building. Completed in 1930 at an estimated cost of $119 million, the ornate, regal-looking structure with its turrets and buttresses stands 708 feet from foundation to flagpole. It remains even today one of the most distinctive skyscrapers in the world, as well as a monument to a financial empire that was virtually obliterated a year later in the chaos of the depression. Terminal Tower is still the most outstanding landmark in the city.

The development downtown was almost enough to lead citizens to forgive, or at least overlook, the rotting tenements of the Roaring Third; the horrid, inexcusable pollution of the Cuyahoga River and the Lake Erie shoreline; one of the worst records of traffic control of any major American city; and the failure of city officials to address the nagging problems of rampant crime, widespread corruption, and an impoverished citizenry. In 1936, there was optimism that Cleveland would experience a renaissance. The city seemed to be on the right track, although it obviously had a long way to go.

Most agreed that one of the brightest prospects for the city was Eliot Ness, the man many believed would remove the stigma of lawlessness from Cleveland. His display of courage and determination in the Harvard Club raid had won the praise of the press and the public, and it had silenced a good number of his critics. Ness was rapidly becoming one of the most visible men in the city, somehow finding time in his hectic schedule to speak at business luncheons and to deliver law-enforcement lectures at Cleveland College. Even Mayor Burton seemed to have taken a back seat to his baby-faced safety director. But the mayor could not help being delighted at the results Ness obtained and the charisma he added to the new administration.

As in Chicago, the media greatly enhanced Ness's image. It was not just that Ness was a colorful, clean-cut, extremely newsworthy figure; many newsmen genuinely enjoyed his company. Ness was totally unlike the stodgy politicians usually occupying city hall. He was open and friendly with reporters, constantly involved in some fascinating work. He was seldom found in his office. Newsmen often had a rough time keeping up as they followed Ness through various meetings, inspections, and investigations. On occasion, they came along on raids, including one that spring that broke a policy racket and resulted in 150 arrests. A great part of Ness's appeal, no doubt, was that in a job consisting primarily of paperwork, he refused to be tied down to a desk. He seemed driven, instead, to be directly involved in the excitement of police work. Obviously, there was a lot of "Untouchable" left in the young safety director.

With the eyes of the city upon him, Ness launched his crusade to regenerate Cleveland's police force. He realized that any serious attempt to bring reform to the department had to begin with a purging of corrupt officers. Ness had the authority and the zeal for such an undertaking. What he initially lacked was information—names, details, and, above all, evidence. Although Ness had gained the respect and trust of many under his authority, policemen were by no means inclined to betray brother officers or hang out their dirty laundry before the safety director. The break that Ness needed would have to arise from outside the department.

It came, finally, in the person of a large, balding immigrant from Slovenia named Gus Korach, who one day in late March wandered into the offices of the *Cleveland Press* on the corner of East Ninth and Rockwell. Explaining that he had a story to tell about being swindled, Korach was shuffled between receptionists and staff before arriving at the desk of reporter Clayton Fritchey. Korach squeezed his huge frame into a chair and described in his thick eastern European accent how a fast-talking salesman had convinced him to invest in cemetery lots, assuring him that his money would double over a matter of months. Korach had purchased eighty lots at a cost of two thousand dollars, his life's savings. Many of his friends and neighbors had also been persuaded by the salesman's pitch. But after several weeks, Korach had started to grow suspicious about the too-good-to-be-true opportunity. Unable to enlist aid from county or city authorities in checking the salesman's company's legitimacy, he had come to the *Press*.

Fritchey, a sparse man with a bow tie and glasses, agreed to help, well aware that there was a state law prohibiting the sale of cemetery lots for profit. The next day, he accompanied Korach around the neighborhood to speak to other investors. Fritchey discovered an incredible record of abuse; people had bought anywhere from fifty to two hundred lots apiece at a total price of over eighty-six thousand dollars. Smelling a story as well as a swindle, Fritchey raced to the city editor, Norman Shaw, and asked to work full-time on the case. Shaw gave him the green light.

Extending his investigation across the city, Fritchey uncovered a widespread racket preying chiefly upon Cleveland's enormous immigrant population. Undeveloped real estate was acquired cheaply, then sold in sections as cemetery lots at inflated prices. One piece of land valued at a mere $6,000 had been dispensed, piece by piece, to the tune of $6 million. So many lots had been sold that Fritchey calculated they would suffice to bury Cleveland's dead for the next five hundred years.

With singular diligence, Fritchey sliced his way through a veil of fictitious names and companies to identify the actual ringleaders of the racket. He and his editor took the evidence to Prosecutor Cullitan, who, in turn, presented the facts to a grand jury. Indictments were returned against half a dozen individuals, some with known gangland connections. One committed suicide. Several others fled the city and escaped prosecution. But the rest stood trial and were convicted. The cemetery racket was successfully ended.

Fritchey, however, was not satisfied. Time and again in his probe, the name of John L. Dacek had surfaced among the prominent figures behind the scenes of the swindle. But the mysterious Dacek could not be located. Determined to find the racket's missing link, Fritchey spent days and nights searching in vain for some clue to his whereabouts. Late one night, the frustrated reporter grabbed a pencil and started doodling with the name. Suddenly, it struck him that by switching two pairs of letters, J. L. Dacek became L. J. Cadek, the police captain of Cleveland's Sixteenth Precinct. For over a decade, an unsavory reputation of alleged underworld ties had hung over Cadek, but so far none of the charges had stuck.

Armed with only a hunch and the unimaginative anagram, Fritchey this time went to Eliot Ness. The safety director listened intently and agreed that the matter was worth looking into.

Working together, Ness and Fritchey unearthed some startling facts about Captain Louis J. Cadek. They learned of four banks where Cadek had been depositing large sums of cash since 1921. His savings totaled $139,000; by contrast, his annual income on the force as of 1936 was $3,500, and it had been much less in years past. Ness and Fritchey also learned that Cadek owned two automobiles that had been gifts from a pair of notorious gangland figures. As they dug deeper, more evidence came to light revealing that the fifty-two-year-old Cadek had been in league with a number of local mobsters. During Prohibition, he had extorted tens of thousands of dollars from independent bootleggers in return for police protection. Ness spoke to as many of Cadek's shakedown victims as he could find. Some had reformed and were leading honest lives, while others were still engaged in criminal activities. There were plenty from both sides willing not only to talk but to testify against the police captain who had drained them of a good portion of their profits.

Although Ness and Fritchey failed to connect Cadek to the cemetery racket, they supplied Cullitan with ample evidence to bring the officer to trial on bribery charges. On May 26, 1936, Cadek was convicted and sentenced to a prison term of two to twenty years.

Ness and Fritchey congratulated each other on the success of their joint investigation. More than one observer commented that they made a good team. It was the beginning of a long and fruitful working relationship that was destined to blow the lid off corruption in the police department.

The Republicans were coming.

As the second week of June approached, they poured into Cleveland by plane, train, and car. Mayor Burton was delighted. The entire city, though long a Democratic stronghold, was proud to host the 1936 Republican National Convention, set to begin on Monday, June 8. There was a flurry of activity as Cleveland prepared for the arrival of distinguished delegates from each of the forty-eight states. With the 1932 assassination attempt on President Roosevelt still fresh in everyone's mind, Safety Director Ness spent most of the week before the convention supervising the preparations for police security.

At eight o'clock on June 5, a bright, balmy Friday morning, two black youngsters ages eleven and thirteen set out for a day of fishing, taking a shortcut through Kingsbury Run. Close to where the Kinsman Road bridge passes over the Run, the boys stopped when one of them spied a pair of pants rolled up in a ball and tucked beneath a willow bush. Suggesting that there might be money in the pockets, the older boy walked over and nudged the pants with his pole. The pants unrolled, revealing a man's severed head, its eyes open and staring back at the boys.

The pair ran, not stopping until they reached the house of the older boy. When his mother arrived home at five o'clock, they told her what had happened. She phoned the police. The two patrolmen who arrived first had no difficulty in finding the head. It was near the rapid-transit tracks a thousand feet west of the Kinsman Road bridge, about two-thirds of a mile up the Run from Jackass Hill. Apparently, the grisly object had remained unnoticed (except by insects) right where the youngsters had left it nearly nine hours earlier. The pants that had held the head were a dark brown cashmere and appeared new. Police found three shirts in a heap along-side the pants. One was a white, knit polo shirt bearing the label Park Royal Broadcloth; it was ripped and bloody at the collar and shoulders. There was also a pair of white undershorts striped with blue that were bloodstained and bore the laundry mark JD. About fifteen feet away were two badly worn, tan, size 7½ oxfords tied together by the laces. A pair of thick socks was stuffed inside. Some distance away, police recovered an old brown cap.

Early the next morning, as Clevelanders were reading about the gruesome discovery between the columns covering the impending convention, a pair of railroad workers in Kingsbury Run stumbled upon the matching body less than a quarter of a mile west of where the head had been found. Partially concealed under some sumac branches, it was sprawled in a patch of weeds between two sets of tracks near the East Fifty-fifth Street bridge, almost directly in front of the office of the Nickel Plate Railroad Police. To at least a few, it seemed that the killer was deliberately mocking the railroad detectives who regularly patrolled the Run. The body was nude and, except for the head, intact.

At the Cuyahoga County Morgue, the body rejoined its head and came under the scrutiny of Coroner Pearse and his staff. The victim was a well-nourished young man in his mid-twenties, five foot eleven, 155 pounds, with a fair complexion, slender build, small hands and feet, reddish brown hair, and blue eyes. He had a narrow, handsome face with high cheekbones, a strong jaw, and a slightly prominent nose. Pearse commented that the victim looked to be of Slavic or possibly Scandinavian descent. Five teeth were missing—one upper and three lower molars on the right side and a lower molar on the left. There were also six tattoos on the body: on the left forearm, the initials WCG with an arrow through a heart; also on the left forearm, crossed flags; on the right forearm, "Helen–Paul" with a dove beneath; on the right shoulder, a butterfly; on the left calf, the cartoon character Jiggs; and on the right calf, a cupid superimposed over an anchor.

Death had been recent. Pearse and his assistants fixed the time of the murder to late Wednesday night or early Thursday morning. In what was becoming a disturbing pattern, the young man had obviously been decapitated while alive. The decapitation had been performed by a large knife that had cut neatly between the first and second cervical vertebrae. The killer had used several strokes to complete the task, prompting the coroner to theorize that he may have allowed the victim to bleed to death after the first sweep of the knife. Yet the last stroke, like the first, had been clean and precise, and there were no other marks of violence on the body to indicate that the tattooed man had struggled or been bound like Andrassy. The autopsy revealed no trace of alcohol or drugs in the body. Police could only speculate that the victim had been over-powered and physically restrained by an unusually strong individual or, more likely, that he had been asleep or unconscious when the killer struck.

Detectives initially believed that the murder had occurred near the place where the remains were found in Kingsbury Run. The young man, living as a vagrant, could have come to town aboard a train and fallen asleep along the banks of the gully, as many hobos were known to do, to be murdered where he rested. The investigators searched long and hard for the telltale evidence of a pair of slashed jugular veins, but they found none. Once again, the eerie absence of blood on both head and body suggested that the killer had operated indoors, cleaning the remains and bringing them to the Run at a later time. A Nickel Plate detective told police that he was certain the head had not been under the willow bush at three o'clock on Thursday afternoon. The killer had probably deposited the torso that evening, having committed the murder (according to Pearse) the previous night. The area is accessible by car from Kinsman Road, and a railroad worker reported having observed a dark, late-model Cadillac sedan parked beneath the bridge not far from where the head was found around eleven o'clock Thursday evening.

Fingerprints failed to identify the victim. Nevertheless, the police were confident. The tattoos, the teeth, and the excellent condition of the remains were all promising prospects for an identification.

As Pearse was examining the latest Kingsbury Run torso that Saturday afternoon, Eliot Ness was receiving a visitor in his city hall office. Councilman Anton Vehovec wanted to see the safety director to complain that vice was rampant in his ward and that he believed police protection was involved. Ness was familiar with Vehovec, a boisterous politician known for his bellowing voice and his flair for dramatics. Ness was also aware that the councilman had a long-standing duel with Captain Michael J. Harwood, commander of the Fourteenth Precinct, which corresponded with Vehovec's ward. Only a week earlier, the two had clashed over a stretch of Lake Erie shoreline where a fence had been erected on Harwood's orders to keep out swimmers. Vehovec had loudly protested that the captain was overstepping his authority in sealing off a public beach. When Harwood ignored his complaint, the councilman himself had cut down the fence with a pair of wire cutters. Enraged, Harwood had threatened to arrest Vehovec before eventually reconsidering.

Now, Vehovec had come to Ness's office charging that the precinct captain was covering up a vast array of vice in his district. He had no proof, only rumors alleging Harwood's involvement. Ness was unimpressed until Vehovec stated that he knew of one establishment, the Blackhawk Inn on Ivanhoe Road, that fronted for a betting parlor. He claimed that Harwood had been alerted to the operation on several occasions but had done nothing.

Ness had never cared for politicians, and leaping into the middle of a municipal power play was one of the last things he wanted to do. Still, if Harwood was dirty, Ness wanted to know. "All right," he said, rising from his desk. "Let's take a look."

Ness recruited a single detective to accompany them. With a couple of reporters tagging along, the unlikely raiding party arrived at the Blackhawk Inn close to four-thirty. They found a legitimate restaurant operating in the front. Vehovec pointed out a door that he said led to the gambling room. Ness and the detective led the way through the door, loudly announcing, "This is a police raid."

A dozen patrons were captured. At least twice that many escaped with the employees out a back exit, but Ness was satisfied and Vehovec was elated. While the detective rummaged through papers and betting slips gathering evidence, Ness questioned the captives individually. About ten minutes after the raid had been sprung, a young, heavyset man walked in and demanded to know what was going on. "Who are you?" Ness asked.

The man identified himself as Edward Harwood, adding in an arrogant tone that his father was "the captain who runs this district."

"Well," Ness threw back, "I'm Eliot Ness. I run the police department in this town."

Harwood was allowed a quick phone call before Ness sat him down for an interrogation. Harwood admitted owning the building, but he claimed he had no idea that the back was used for gambling. The room was rented by a certain "Joe" about whom Harwood could give no further details. A few minutes later, Joe arrived on the scene; he turned out to be a short, stocky individual named Joseph McCarthy who supported Harwood's statement practically word for word. Ness informed them that the whole story sounded rather thin and that he believed the two had set up the tale on the phone a short time ago. Ness then took their keys and tried them in the room's doors. Harwood's fit the locks; McCarthy's didn't. "You're quite sure you want to take the rap on this?" Ness asked McCarthy.

McCarthy reluctantly nodded and was taken away by the detective. The rest, including Harwood, were released. Vehovec still maintained that Captain Harwood was behind the gambling operation, though they had found no evidence other than the obvious but unverifiable involvement of his son. Ness assured the councilman that he would pursue the matter.

That evening, Ness contacted Police Chief Matowitz and instructed him to relieve Harwood of his command of the Fourteenth Precinct pending an investigation of his reputed connection to vice in the district. Matowitz had also heard of Harwood's shady dealings, and he agreed that it was the right move. He asked who would lead the investigation. "I will," Ness replied.

New rumors of police corruption and a gruesome decapitation that hinted of a psychopathic killer at large in the city were not what civic officials had hoped would be the weekend prelude to the Republican National Convention, which opened Monday. The convention proceeded with all the pomp and pageantry expected. By week's end, the delegates had chosen Kansas Governor Alf

Landon as the candidate who would "win back the presidency" from Franklin Delano Roosevelt.

Long after the final gavel sounded, the efforts of Cleveland police to identify the tattooed victim and find his killer continued to make local news, despite attempts by the department to keep a low profile on the case. Several days of checking fingerprint files and dental records and circulating the murdered man's description drew nothing but blanks. It was decided to exhibit the head and body at the morgue. Two thousand people filed by the victim the first night, followed by thousands more over the next few days. The remains were buried on June 9 after a plaster death mask had been cast. Detectives armed with photos of the victim's face and each of his six tattoos canvassed tattoo parlors. The multiple tattoos, especially the one of an anchor, strongly suggested that he had been a sailor. Detectives took the victim's picture to local ports and sailor hangouts, checked naval records, and sent files to other Great Lakes cities. But no one claimed to have known or to have ever encountered the young man.

Even the tattoos, which detectives considered the best bet for identifying the victim, seemed to contradict each other. The initials WCG might have been his, but since they appeared next to a heart, they might just as well have been those of a girlfriend. The names Helen and Paul might have been those of the victim and his wife or sweetheart. Others suggested that they might have been the names of his parents. Neither Paul nor WCG agreed with the laundry mark JD found on the bloody underwear.

Had the young man simply been a wandering tramp who drifted into town just before his death? There was some convincing evidence to suggest he had not. With the exception of his shoes and cap, his clothing was fairly new, not typical hobo garb. He had been clean shaven and well nourished; the autopsy surgeon reported finding an undigested meal of baked beans in the victim's stomach that had been consumed no more than an hour before he died. (Andrassy's autopsy had also revealed the consumption of vegetables shortly before death.) Considering these facts, detectives gradually developed a theory that the killer befriended his victims, took them into his home, and fed, clothed, and cleaned them up before murdering them.

In the end, the exhaustive efforts of the police failed to identify the young man. Eventually, as numbers rather than names came to be used to designate victims in the case, the tattooed man became officially known as "No. 4."

Police, however, were still denying that a pattern existed; when one detective told newsmen that there was "a maniac with a lust to kill" loose in the city, he was instantly taken off the case. Sergeant Hogan of the Homicide Unit scoffed at the reports of a diabolical fiend stalking the citizens of Cleveland. He admitted that there were similarities between the murders of the tattooed man and the two Kingsbury Run victims discovered the previous fall, but he stated emphatically that the murder of Flo Polillo was totally unrelated.

There were no reported comments by Eliot Ness about the murders. Oddly, since the Blackhawk Inn raid, newsmen who had usually found him accessible and cooperative suddenly had a difficult time locating him. The reason was known only to a select few; what began as a routine probe into the background of Captain Harwood had mushroomed into a round-the-clock investigation that placed the entire police department under scrutiny.

Not long after the June 6 raid, Ness had spoken to the mayor about leading a full-scale review of the department's personnel. Their paths rarely crossed at city hall, but the two customarily discussed civic matters during their weekly racquetball game. It was most likely at one of those sessions that Ness had announced his plans. Burton had been enthusiastic about the project and had pledged his support. When Ness pointed out that there were no municipal funds available to finance the investigation, Burton had immediately contacted his friends in the chamber of commerce and the American Legion to raise the needed cash. Many were businessmen who had suffered directly or indirectly from police corruption, and they eagerly agreed to help. A special undercover fund had been formed to pay the expenses.

Ness zeroed in on every individual on the force suspected of corruption or misbehavior, from veterans to rookies and from prominent officers to patrolmen on the beat. He assembled a file on each that contained bits and pieces of solid evidence, anonymous tips, and mere rumors. The project, however, was not a witch-hunt. Determined to give every man a fair chance, the safety director set out to check each lead and its source, no matter how indisputable or trivial the information appeared.

The task proved enormous. Some legwork was delegated to trusted aides, but for the most part, Director Ness hit the streets and did his own investigating, much of it on his own time. He reportedly spent almost every evening through the summer of 1936 engaged in this quiet crusade, speaking to vagrants, prostitutes, and criminals in bars and alleys one night and meeting the city's wealthiest and most respected citizens the next.

It was almost too much for one man to do. Eventually, *Press* writer Clayton Fritchey joined Ness in his investigation, recruited by the safety director with the promise of an exclusive story when the facts were ready for presentation to the public.

One muggy mid-July evening, the pair visited a bar on the corner of East Eighty-second Street and Kosciuszko Avenue to gather some information on one of its suspects. Among the patrons was an on-duty patrolman who had stopped in for a couple of quick rounds. Instantly recognizing the safety director, he darted to the back and locked himself in the rest room. Giving no indication that he had observed the patrolman's hasty exit, Ness strode to the bar and asked to speak with the owner. The bartender stated that the owner had just left and would return in about an hour. "I'll stop back," the safety director said. "Tell him Eliot Ness wants to talk to him."

A customer seated nearby laughed out loud. "You're Ness?" he asked sarcastically, eyeing the youthful man standing next to him. "I suppose you're gonna tell us you're the safety director too, huh?"

"That's right," Ness replied.

"Listen, buddy, I got news for you. It just so happens the director's a friend of mine. And you ain't him."

Ness started to leave, then stopped and looked back. "If you really don't believe I'm Eliot Ness, I suggest you ask that policeman who's hiding from me in the back."

He turned and left the bar with Fritchey at his side and a wide grin on his face.

Cleveland is bisected into almost equal halves by the twisting, churning Cuyahoga River. The name is an Indian word meaning crooked, and one need only glance at a map of Cleveland to realize its appropriateness. The Cuyahoga makes a confusing dividing line, since the west shore is occasionally farther east then the east shore, and vice versa. Nevertheless, the river has always been recognized as the boundary that separates east and west Cleveland.

There is a traditional antagonism between east and west. Before Cleveland existed, the Iroquois dwelling along the eastern bank of the Cuyahoga were constantly at odds with the Hurons on the opposite side. The east-west enmity continued when white settlers began to build their city on the eastern side while various Indian tribes held onto the western shore. When whites came to occupy both sides, it was in separate, rival communities—Cleveland on the east and Ohio City on the west. The two competed for commerce and prominence. A bridge across the Cuyahoga even became the scene of a battle between Clevelanders and Ohio City residents. County authorities finally interceded and brought a shaky peace.

Cleveland eventually overshadowed and, in 1854, absorbed its western counterpart, inaugurating the intracity conflict between Eastsiders and Westsiders that has endured to this day. Eastsiders tend to look down their noses at the residents of the west, maintaining that the east side is the true Cleveland. Westsiders do not argue that point, but they are inclined to answer the bloated egos of the Eastsiders by claiming that their side is the quieter, the less complicated, and the safer place to live. Eastsiders fully agree, only preferring to use adjectives like dull and ordinary.

Despite its suburban character, the west side was by no means a spotless haven in the 1930s. There was one section in particular, centering around West Twenty-fifth Street, that was often regarded as the west side's Roaring Third, only on a much smaller scale. It was called Rowdy Row, a strip of dilapidated buildings and crumbling asphalt close to the river, populated by panhandlers by day and prostitutes by night. Many forms of vice operated openly throughout the region.

Eliot Ness did not limit his investigation of police corruption to the east side. The obvious failure of the Eighth Precinct cops to

control Rowdy Row's crime attracted his attention. What he uncovered was a situation in which payoffs from local criminals were
much in evidence.

On July 15, Ness and a few trusted aides staked out a gambling
parlor on West Twenty-fifth known as McGinty's. Ness's information indicated that the establishment had operated for ten years or
more with an annual income exceeding half a million dollars. All
that time, with all that profit, there had not been a single instance
of police interference. Ness wanted to get some men inside, but he
was reluctant to use regular cops for the assignment, still unsure of
whom to trust. He decided that since it was difficult to tell the bad
apples in the barrel from the good ones, it would be best to go
directly to the tree.

The previous week, Ness had sworn in a score of young rookies.
He now chose the five who had most distinguished themselves
during training and offered them the undercover assignment of
infiltrating McGinty's. Each one eagerly accepted. Posing as customers, the five rookies managed to gain entrance one or two at a
time and then to supply the director with a layout of the joint along
with descriptions of employees and gambling activities. After several days, Ness phoned the Eighth Precinct and ordered a raid,
curious to see what would happen. A pair of officers arrived, investigated the premises, and reported that they had found nothing
illegal. Two of the undercover rookies present at the time informed
Ness that before the policemen appeared, a set of lights had
flashed, warning those inside. The customers had been swiftly
evacuated and the gambling equipment stashed. It was clear that
McGinty's had some friends on the force.

Ness discussed the matter with Chief Matowitz. They agreed
that before conducting a proper raid they should speak with the
precinct captain of the Eighth, a stocky, twenty-six-year veteran
named Adolph Lenahan. On July 21, Captain Lenahan arrived at
the chief's office for the meeting and almost fell as he staggered in,
obviously intoxicated. Matowitz suspended him on the spot. When
Ness was informed of this development, he elected to spring the
raid that afternoon.

Once all five of his undercover rookies were inside, the safety
director and a raiding party of half a dozen handpicked men started

for McGinty's door. A lookout spotted the approaching lawmen and triggered the alarm. As soon as the warning lights began to flash, the rookies whipped out their revolvers and badges, covering the exits until Ness and the others burst into the room. Seven employees and over eighty patrons were taken into custody.

Despite the success of the raid, no tangible proof was obtained implicating any Eighth Precinct officers with the obvious protection that the establishment received. The investigators did, however, discover that three sons of Deputy Inspector Timothy J. Costello, another prominent figure of the Eighth, were employed at McGinty's. From the joint's records, they found evidence that local gambling chieftain Arthur Hebebrand, a co-owner of the Harvard Club with Jimmy Patton, was connected with the operation.

The next day, July 22, Cleveland's west side was still buzzing over the safety director's latest crusade when a much more shocking crime was discovered in its midst. That morning, a seventeen-year-old girl was hiking through some densely wooded terrain along Big Creek, slightly southwest of the city limits in the suburb of Brooklyn Village. As she tramped along a shallow gully just south of Clinton Road, a horrible sight greeted her—the naked, decapitated, badly decomposed remains of a man.

Her frantic call sent dozens of lawmen racing to the scene from different directions. Brooklyn Village police were joined by county officers, a horde of west-side cops, and Sergeant Hogan and several Homicide detectives from the east side. The corpse lay chest down in a secluded area about a hundred yards from where the tracks of the B & O swept through the region. Not far away, an abandoned hobo camp was found. A county officer confirmed the fact that vagrants often inhabited the vicinity, but none were found that day, and those discovered in the days to come claimed to know nothing of the murder or the victim.

The head, little more than a hair-covered skull, was discovered ten feet from the body. Beside it was a pile of ragged clothes which later proved to fit the dead man. There were a light blue polo shirt, a dark gray, single-breasted suit coat with the sleeves turned inside out and the right one slashed by a knife, matching trousers, a leather belt, a white undershirt, white undershorts, light blue rayon socks, black oxfords, and a dark gray cap with black stripes.

All of the pockets were empty; some had been turned inside out. The shirt and coat were horribly bloodstained. A pathologist accompanying the east-side detectives noted that a considerable amount of blood had seeped into the soil around the neck wound. He was certain that the man had died where he was found.

The extreme decomposition made for a difficult autopsy. Pearse estimated that the man had been dead a minimum of two months, possibly as much as a month longer. Pressed for a more precise time, the coroner assigned the murder to May 22, a date he most likely plucked out of the air. If Pearse was correct, the victim had been killed well before the tattooed man. The victim had been a small man, five foot five and 145 pounds, about forty years of age. He had brown eyes and a narrow, pointed chin. His hair was brown, slightly balding on top and unusually long on the back and sides. His teeth were in good condition except for a missing upper incisor and two lower molars. There were no marks on the body other than the single, skillful knife wound that had detached head from torso between the third and fourth cervical vertebrae.

Fingerprinting was impossible. The length of the victim's hair, his cheap clothing, and the area in which he had been found all suggested that he had been one of the nameless vagrants who rode the rails during the depression. One detective came upon a missing persons report of a WPA worker at Cleveland's airport who had disappeared about the same time the victim was killed. The airport was not far from where the body had been found, and the general description of the WPA worker matched that of the victim. But no further details about the WPA worker were forthcoming, even though detectives interviewed airport employees. Officially, the west-side corpse was listed merely as "No. 5."

Two significant features distinguished this murder from the previous ones and from the ones to follow. "No. 5" alone was found on the west side of the city, far from Kingsbury Run and the Roaring Third. Also, the murderer did not transport the remains of "No. 5" to another location as he had with all the others; he had left them at the scene of the crime. But by now the killer's trademark—his expert beheading of his prey with a large, heavy knife—was unmistakable. Even the most skeptical men on the force, including the dogmatic Sergeant Hogan, were beginning to put the pieces together and to see a terrifying pattern.

The press and the public were not yet fully aware of what was happening, which was how the police preferred it. The west-side victim, in fact, received almost no attention from the media; in the *Plain Dealer*, only a few paragraphs appeared on page 3, while the *Press* carried an even briefer story on page 12. There were simply too many exciting, positive things occurring in the city for people to notice the mysterious deaths of a few obscure and unidentified individuals.

Through the remainder of the week, the exploits of Eliot Ness continued to be the major news story. His raid on McGinty's had inspired a flurry of police activity. Before the week ended, ten more gambling raids were conducted, nine of them in the downtown area. Ness personally supervised several and had an active hand in the rest. Largely through his efforts, the web of police protection purchased by local vice lords was rapidly eroding. Corrupt cops were severing their ties with Cleveland's underworld; good cops, frustrated for years, were reawakening to their duty. Citizens began to get involved, phoning in tips and showing a new willingness to identify criminals and testify in cases.

On July 26, the Sunday edition of the *Plain Dealer* included an editorial praising the safety director's relentless quest to clean up the police department, stating in part, "Eliot Ness, with his boyish face and enigmatic manner, is well aware of what is going on in the department, and attending to one matter at a time. The cops at first were inclined to scoff at him, but by now they are aware he knows his business. It is fairly obvious that he considers his business the rebuilding of a police force which had gone badly to seed. His greatest handicap is that he must investigate by himself, and can trust so few others."

In the background of all this, the Great Lakes Expo had been in operation for a full month, capturing the hearts of Clevelanders and the attention of northeastern Ohio. It provided a marvelous diversion from the hard times at a reasonable price, as well as giving the city's economy a tremendous boost. The unemployed found work first in constructing the sprawling exposition on the lakefront and then in general employment after its opening. Visitors began to pour in from all over the country, including President Roosevelt in a much-publicized appearance on August 14. Cleveland merchants and hotel owners were ecstatic.

Among the exposition's many and varied attractions were an International Village filled with ethnic shops and restaurants, an Aquacade featuring swimmers Johnny Weismuller and Esther Williams, exotic displays and exhibits showcasing scientific wonders, and spectacular daily shows parading the talents of actress Eleanor Holm, dancer Sally Rand, and composer Billy Rose.

There was also a police exhibit sponsored by the city and organized in large part by Director Ness. The displays told the story of the history of criminology, described the newest crime-fighting techniques, and emphasized the need for citizens to support and aid their lawmen. In one corner of the exhibit stood a glass case containing what appeared to be a disembodied head. It was, in fact, a replica of the death mask of the tattooed victim found in Kingsbury Run. It had been fitted with natural-looking hair to enhance its lifelike quality. A white sheet was tucked snugly under the chin and around the neck. A sign informed the public that the display was a cast of "an unidentified individual and suspected murder victim found earlier this year in the city." Anyone with "information about this person or his identity" was urged to contact the Cleveland police.

Hundreds of thousands of people viewed the display during the following months. There was not a single person who could tell the authorities anything about the dead man.

FOUR

Shortly before noon on Thursday, September 10, 1936, Jerry Harris, a vagrant from St. Louis, was leaning against a steel girder of a water tower near the East Thirty-seventh Street bridge, his eyes fixed upon a slow-moving eastbound freight rambling along the rails toward him. Harris had drifted into town aboard a train several days earlier, and he had come to Kingsbury Run Thursday morning hoping to leave Cleveland in the same manner, stationing himself strategically near the tracks and watching intently for the railroad bulls. Seeing none, he scrambled for one of the boxcars. Nearly stumbling over something in his path, he stopped abruptly as he realized that the object was the upper half of a human body without the head and arms. Forgetting the train, Harris ran to an oil company tank station and found a storage clerk, Leo Fields, who agreed to phone the police. Within minutes, lawmen were pouring into the area about midway between the Flats and Jackass Hill.

The lower portion of the trunk, its legs amputated at the hips, was discovered nearby. Both halves had apparently emerged from a sewer near the bridge. The foul waters emptied into a large, fetid pool, which in turn drained into a narrow stream along the rocky bottom of Kingsbury Run. A search was immediately begun for the missing pieces. The entire length of the stream was examined, but nothing was found. The attention of the searchers then centered upon the stagnant pool from which the two torso halves had evidently floated. Some chunks of flesh found clinging to the sides of the pool suggested that more body parts might be discovered in the waters.

By midafternoon, the scene in Kingsbury Run began to take on a circus atmosphere. Hundreds of curious spectators crowded into the region, some of them the ragged occupants of a hobo jungle on the opposite side of the bridge. Newsmen and photographers were all over, swarming around the policemen at work. Most of the officers gathered around the pool to discuss ways to explore its fifteen-foot depth. Others including Detective May searched along the weed-covered banks of the gully. About 175 feet away, they discovered some blood-spattered newspapers dated September 8 and two articles of bloody clothing—a torn, blue denim shirt with the collar partially sliced away (perhaps in the act of decapitation) and a pair of faded green undershorts bearing the laundry mark JW. Inspector Joseph M. Sweeny, head of the Detective Bureau, found an old, gray, size 7¼ hat nearby. The label inside read "Loudy's Smart Shop, Bellevue."

At the morgue, Coroner Pearse and his staff went to work on the remains. Their preliminary examination determined that the victim was a white male age twenty-two to twenty-eight with brown hair and a muscular build. He had been dead about forty-eight hours. Despite the missing parts, they were able to estimate the victim's height at five foot nine or ten and his weight at close to 150 pounds. The head had been removed between the third and fourth cervical vertebrae, the trunk bisected between the third and fourth lumbar vertebrae. The coroner reported that the edges of the skin had been sharply cut, that few hesitation marks were displayed at the neck, and that the heart and the major vessels were empty of blood. He further noted that undigested kernels of corn were present in the victim's stomach. The dead man had also been emasculated.

There could no longer be any doubt that a maniacal killer was at large in the city. The latest Kingsbury Run corpse confirmed that the previous murders had all been the work of the same man. Among the common features of "No. 6" were the emasculation, as with the first two victims nearly a year earlier; the exact same pattern of dismemberment performed upon Flo Polillo, including the intricate severing of the lower torso; and the skillful beheading, which had apparently been the cause of each victim's death. Newspapers began to refer to the unknown slayer as the Torso Murderer, the Mad Butcher, the Horrible Headhunter, and the Phantom of Kingsbury Run.

At first light the next morning, police resumed their search at the Kingsbury Run pool assisted by a detail of firemen dispatched by Safety Director Ness. Standing on planks placed across the pool and using grappling hooks, officers managed to dredge up the thighs and the lower legs of the victim as a crowd of about six hundred looked on. Other policemen explored the maze of sewers running beneath the ravine. There were numerous locations where the killer might have deposited the dismembered parts. Some, however, suggested that the pieces might have been dumped directly into the pool, a theory that took on a measure of credibility when a switchman of the Nickel Plate Railroad informed police that he had observed a green Ford truck parked by the pool at quarter after ten on Wednesday night. The clothing found nearby also supported the contention that the body parts had been deposited directly into the pool.

Twenty-five detectives, the majority of them from Hogan's Homicide Unit, were placed full-time on the case, the most assigned to any single investigation in Cleveland history. Some worked on missing persons reports, including that of a thirty-one-year-old railroad worker who had vanished on August 31 (and who was later found alive and well). Detectives Ralph Kennedy and Leo Duffin canvassed the run-down neighborhoods bordering Kingsbury Run and uncovered a number of notable suspects. One was a thirty-seven-year-old Mexican who lived a couple of blocks north of the Thirty-seventh Street bridge. People in the area accused him of acting strangely and carrying knives. One rumor claimed that the Mexican had a collection of skulls in his basement. The two detectives found no skulls but did discover a considerable quantity of drugs. The Mexican admitted being an addict, but when questioned about the murders, he vehemently denied that he had ever harmed anyone. Another suspicious character nabbed by Kennedy and Duffin was a squat, bowlegged Oriental they found living in a condemned building and carrying a long knife. Both suspects, though jailed on other charges, were quickly exonerated of the Torso killings.

The most promising clue proved to be the hat discovered near the bloody shirt and undershorts. The label led detectives to a clothing shop in Bellevue, Ohio, a small town sixty miles west of Cleveland. Mrs. Charles Hoffman, a Bellevue housewife, recognized the hat as one she had given to a young hobo who had appeared at her door about two weeks earlier. Her description of the vagrant came remarkably close to the Torso victim. In addition to the hat, Mrs. Hoffman had furnished the young man with a brown tweed coat and a pair of white shoes, neither of which ever turned up.

The latest Torso murder continued to blacken headlines and dominate conversations throughout Cleveland on Saturday, as the examination of the pool entered its third day before another multitude of morbid onlookers.

Citizens were becoming uneasy; quite a few, it seemed, were reporting flimsy suspicions to the police. Detectives were bogged down following trivial leads about husbands, neighbors, friends, relatives, doctors, butchers, mailmen, and numerous others. Most of these tips came to nothing. A few, such as one that led to a bloody knife in a pile of rubbish not far from Kingsbury Run, were seriously considered by the investigators. One call led a pair of detectives to a mysterious trunk in a Third Precinct basement. They unfastened the snaps, and both leaped back with a gasp as an artificial arm tumbled out. The detectives looked at each other and laughed.

A shudder rippled through the suburb of East Cleveland when two boys unearthed a large box containing a human skeleton. Coroner Pearse joined the detectives who raced to the scene, a vacant lot behind Wymore Street, just a block off busy Euclid Avenue. A large crowd gathered around the site, and police began to speak of victim "No. 7" until a neighborhood man came forward and explained that the skeleton was an old family "keepsake" that he had abandoned there.

The paranoia sweeping the city was particularly evident in Kingsbury Run after nightfall. Railroad employees began to work in teams; some armed themselves. The latest murder inspired a mass exodus of hobos from the region. Those who remained appeared jumpy and fearful, tending to congregate more than usual. The railroad police of the Erie and the Nickel Plate intensified their patrols and allowed their detectives more overtime than ever before. The same vagrants who usually ran at the sight of the bulls suddenly seemed almost happy to see them.

On the night of Saturday, September 12, a *Press* reporter covering the Torso case went to Kingsbury Run for a nocturnal look at the Mad Butcher's favorite hunting ground. On the East Thirty-seventh Street bridge, he met a pair of neighborhood youths who offered, for a small fee, to act as guides. Following the boys, the newsman descended into the blackness of Kingsbury Run, a world where the bright lights and the sounds of metropolitan traffic curiously failed to penetrate.

The boys pointed out a dark, silent hobo camp; the reporter spied a few grizzled inhabitants, one sleeping in a large cardboard box. The pool where pieces of the latest victim had been discovered was not far away, the area cordoned off by police barricades with warnings not to trespass. No policemen could be seen that night; the reporter told himself that even the cops knew better than to come to the Run after dark. Farther along, his young guides showed him a narrow side gully turning off toward the southeast and the barren, triangular slope known as Jackass Hill, where the first two bodies had been found. Up the Run and around another bend to the northeast were the East Fifty-fifth Street train yards, where the torso of the tattooed man had been discovered.

The reporter had seen enough. The ambience of Kingsbury Run was sufficient inspiration for his story. He thanked the boys, paid them, and asked them almost as an afterthought why they seemed unafraid of the killer. "The Torso Murderer?" one of the boys asked. "Nah, he doesn't bother us. Everyone says he only cuts up the bums."

The Great Lakes Expo, entering its seventy-eighth day, prepared to greet its three millionth visitor. At Municipal Stadium that Sunday, September 13, a huge, exuberant crowd watched the Indians win a doubleheader from the Philadelphia Athletics. In the first game, a rookie pitching sensation named Bob Feller registered seventeen strikeouts for the Tribe. And in Kingsbury Run, more than five thousand spectators gathered to observe a professional diver hired by the city enter the putrid waters of the pool in search of the head, arms, and genitalia of the unidentified sixth victim.

Plainclothesmen circulated among the onlookers on the chance that the killer might be among them. A number of spectators were taken aside and questioned; a few were whisked away to Central Station for a more careful examination. The diver made several attempts but failed to find anything. The disappointed crowd began to disperse.

That evening, Eliot Ness learned that security around the search area had been relaxed. He immediately sent fifteen uniformed officers to the site with orders to seize all vagrants lurking about the region. Even if the officers failed to catch the killer, Ness told Assistant Safety Director John R. Flynn, they might at least remove some potential victims. A steady stream of tattered, destitute figures passed through Central Station that night. One tramp had a remarkable story to tell. The previous week, a man had approached him as he rested alone on the edge of a hobo camp in the Run. As the stranger crept closer, the tramp had seen that he held a large knife. The tramp had leaped to his feet and escaped. He provided a vivid description of the stranger, claiming he had been dressed entirely in black, with black leather gloves. Detectives, however, doubted the story, one stating to reporters that the tramp "saw too much in too little time."

Along with the hobos, more than a few respectable citizens were brought in for questioning, usually on the strength of vague suspicions reported by neighbors or acquaintances. Sergeant Hogan learned that an elderly west-side doctor had been jailed merely because a woman informed police that he was "acting strangely." He instantly ordered the arresting officers to apologize and return the doctor to his home.

The morning edition of Monday's *Plain Dealer* featured a large photograph of Director Ness on its front page under the headline, "Ness Probe Hits Police Officers." The story of Ness's diligent undercover investigation had leaked out prematurely. Every reporter in the city was aware by then that the safety director had been collecting information about Captain Harwood and others. The revelations were the extensiveness of the search and the fact that virtually the entire department had come under scrutiny.

Facing newsmen, Ness stated that the story was "embarrassing" to him, and he refused to confirm or deny reports of the expected shake-up. "I've said all along," he declared, "that when my activities were completed, I would present my findings to the proper authorities. Until then, I have nothing to say."

He did, however, agree to talk about the Torso murders, denying a recent rumor that he had taken control of the case. Nevertheless, Ness said that he planned to be involved as much as possible. "Like everyone else," he told the reporters, "I want to see this psycho caught. I'm going to do all I can to aid in the investigation."

Some of the reporters expressed bewilderment at the safety director's sudden about-face. What had prompted Ness to be drawn into this strange case? The most realistic answer seemed to be that the murder cycle had only begun to reach the front page in the past few days. But a few newsmen shrewdly considered the fact that on Friday, the day after "No. 6" had been discovered, Ness and Mayor Burton had met for one of their racquetball sessions. Rumors circulating through city hall suggested that the mayor had requested that Ness put aside his police probe for the moment and get involved in the Torso case.

At eight o'clock that evening, Ness was one of the thirty-four individuals who attended a special meeting about the murders. The select group met in the police laboratory on the third floor of Central Station. Present were Coroner Pearse; Police Chief Matowitz; Inspector Sweeny; Sergeant Hogan; County Prosecutor Cullitan; Lieutenant David L. Cowles, the department's ballistics expert; Dr. Reuben Strauss, the county pathologist who had participated in all six autopsies; three outside medical consultants; and most of the detectives assigned to the investigation. The meeting began when Sergeant Hogan rose from his seat and announced,

"Gentlemen, we are right where we were the day the first bodies were found."

Coroner Pearse, the principal organizer of the meeting, took the lead. Standing before the group, his thumbs plucking at his suspenders, he carefully reviewed the medical evidence and the similarities among the remains of the Torso victims. Hogan and some of the detectives broke in regularly with details from the investigative side of the case. Seated in front, Eliot Ness listened intently with his arms folded, saying little. With his suit coat buttoned and his tie neatly straightened, he was a curious sight in the overheated room, where all the others had removed their jackets, loosened their collars, and rolled up their sleeves.

After considerable discussion of all the evidence, a list of seven conclusions was agreed upon:

1. *All six Torso killings were the work of a single individual operating alone.* Several other murders were mentioned as candidates for the Torso series. Among them was the dismembered Lady of the Lake, whose partial remains had washed up at Euclid Beach and North Perry a full year before the two Jackass Hill corpses were found. The coroner pointed out some startling features of the remains of the Lady of the Lake, including almost the exact same disarticulation as that of Flo Polillo and the latest victim. There was also the same discoloration of the skin as with Andrassy's unknown companion. Nevertheless, all present agreed that the murder had been too early and too far away to be regarded as the work of the same maniac, a view that would change very soon. They also discussed an unsolved 1929 decapitation murder. The body of an unidentified black male had been found in a vacant lot at East Fortieth Street and Woodland Avenue, only four blocks north of Jackass Hill. As with Flo Polillo and the body in the pool, the black man's head had never been located. But that murder, too, was declared to be unrelated. In the end, only the six sure victims discovered over the last year were considered to belong to the Torso series.

2. *The killer, while obviously demented and psychopathic, was not recognizably insane.* Some present, in fact, believed that he might lead a perfectly normal existence when he was not murdering. The

majority were also convinced that the killer was a sexual pervert, citing his butchery of the bodies and especially his emasculation of three of the five males. One of the medical experts disagreed; sexual psychopaths were known to mutilate their victims, he said, but he had never encountered a case where decapitation and methodical dismemberment of bodies represented "a pattern of perversion." Ness, for one, agreed with the doctor. It seemed more likely, the safety director stated, that the killer carved up his victims to prevent their identification or to make it easier to transport their remains. Most of the detectives were still convinced that the Butcher was a homosexual, despite the fact that one of his victims had been a woman.

3. *The killer possessed a definite knowledge of human anatomy and some surgical skill, but he had not displayed evidence of any actual medical training.* While admitting that the decapitation and disarticulation of the victims were unusually skillful, the medical experts present were adamant in refuting a theory popular among the police that the murderer was a doctor with surgical training. The murderer's knowledge of anatomy was agreed to be more akin to that of someone with considerable experience as a butcher or hunter.

4. *The killer was "large and strong."* The bodies of the first two victims—and probably that of the tattooed man as well—had been carried, not dragged, some distance by the murderer. It was obvious, Director Ness remarked, that the Torso Murderer was "a big man with the strength of an ox." Pearse agreed that all the knife wounds had been executed by "an exceptionally strong individual." Since at least three of the victims had been conscious or at least alive when they were beheaded, the suggestion that the killer overpowered his victims reinforced the belief that he was a physically powerful man.

5. *The killer probably lived in or near the Third Precinct or another area close to Kingsbury Run.* It was certain that he operated in the district and that he must have spent considerable time there. Andrassy and Flo Polillo had frequented or inhabited the Roaring Third. The burlap bags found with Polillo had been obtained from a local merchant. Only the west-side victim led the trail away from the Roaring Third, and he alone had been killed where he was found, in an isolated, uninhabited region. There were no such

secluded spots in the densely populated Third Precinct. Even along the desolate stretches of Kingsbury Run, vagrants and vagabonds roamed all night while railroad workers on the graveyard shift performed their duties up and down the ravine. Each of the east-side victims had been murdered and cut up somewhere else—most likely indoors—and had then been transported to where they were found. All of this suggested that the killer felt at ease moving through the Roaring Third and Kingsbury Run and that he must have been familiar with the movements of the railroad police. His apparent confidence also indicated that he was someone who would not look out of place if observed. A railroad worker? A policeman? A hobo?

6. *The killer probably kept a private "workshop" or "laboratory" in which he conducted his butchery.* Such a workshop would very likely be in the murderer's own home, a place where he could lure his victims, kill them, and cut them up without fear of detection or interruption. Some present, including Ness, commented that such a room would have to be elaborate. The severed jugulars of live victims would make an incredible mess. The evidence in several of the cases indicated that the remains had been drained of blood and then cleaned up by the killer.

7. *The killer preyed upon individuals of the "lower classes."* There was certainly no shortage of destitute people in the Third Precinct or around Kingsbury Run, a world inhabited by drunks and hustlers, like Andrassy and Flo Polillo, and by drifters and vagrants, as police believed the last two victims had been. Not only were victims plentiful, they were extremely accessible, and they might easily be won over with promises of food, drink, sex, temporary shelter, companionship, or an opportunity to lift themselves from the gutter. There was little doubt that the Butcher had befriended his victims and gained their trust before killing them. Perhaps he was a familiar figure, someone they had known for weeks or months, even years; perhaps his personality or his profession put his intended victims at ease and won their confidence. Many people of the Third Precinct were the type who would not likely be missed if they suddenly vanished. They were, as Inspector Sweeny put it, "perfect victims," easy prey. All agreed that a mass murderer with a minimum of intelligence could select his victims

from the inhabitants of the Roaring Third and be remarkably successful.

How, then, could such a psychopath be captured? That was the final question addressed by the assembly of police and medical officials Monday evening. Various ideas were discussed; few sounded even remotely practical. When Pearse suggested that the best method might be to dress policemen as hobos and offer them as bait, there was a burst of laughter in the room, especially from Hogan and his detectives. Ness and several others thought that a better way to find the killer would be to locate his bloody laboratory, even if it meant conducting a building-by-building search.

After two and a half hours, the meeting ended. Newspapers called it "the Torso Clinic." Clevelanders read how the best police minds in their city had gathered to analyze the string of brutal murders. Instead of reassuring citizens, the newspaper summaries of the meeting generated sensationalism about the killer. The officials, even with their seven conclusions, seemed to have raised more questions than they answered. Many misinterpreted "facts" like the murderer's unusual strength as suggesting superhuman or phantomlike qualities. Even the active involvement of Safety Director Ness was viewed by many as an indication of how serious the case was.

For eight days, the story of the most recent Torso murder stayed on the front page, until the American Legion Convention opened in downtown Cleveland and stole the news coverage with the raucous, almost riotous behavior of its participants. Eventually, the Kingsbury Run pool was flushed out—a process consuming sixteen hours and the pumping of three million gallons of water—and was found to be empty. The head, arms, and genitalia of "No. 6" were never found. Without a face or fingerprints, identification proved to be impossible.

To many in the police department, Detective Peter Merylo seemed a humorous figure. He was a huge, hulking man with a notable stomach, a beefy face, big ears, sagging jowls, a large nose, and a perpetual grin. His ties were a particular source of amusement, as they were usually bright, gaudy, out of date, and sloppily knotted. But most of all, Merylo was known for his hats. There were two of them—at least that's all anyone ever saw. On rainy or wintry days, he wore a broad, black hat pulled down snugly, like that of a movie gumshoe. On warm, sunny days, he always showed up for work wearing a common straw hat that some thought made him look like W. C. Fields.

Few police officers knew Merylo except by sight. Working out of the Detective Bureau, he and partner Martin Zalewski spent virtually all their time on special assignments away from the mainstream of law enforcement. Merylo's superiors, however, knew his record. They looked beyond his face and recognized the keen investigative abilities and the singular tenacity that made Merylo one of the finest, most resourceful detectives in the city.

About a week after the sixth victim was found, Director Ness contacted Inspector Sweeny and asked for two of his best men to follow new leads in the Torso case. He was given Merylo and Zalewski.

A special hot line was set up at city hall. Ness initially oversaw the project, but after several days he left the two detectives on their own and asked only for daily reports from them. Most of the calls pouring in were the flimsy hunches and suspicions of a paranoid public. Merylo and his partner investigated as many of the calls as possible. The pair found themselves digging up backyards and basements, rummaging through trash cans and dumps, searching apartments and houses, interrogating local eccentrics and perfectly respectable individuals denounced by neighbors, and crawling through rat-infested sewers. People were suddenly finding bones all over the city. Usually, they proved to be the remains of animals left in a pile in an alley or park, the meal of some hobo. The most promising call brought the detectives to a dump just south of Kingsbury Run where a human foot had been discovered amid the rubbish. The appendage turned out to be a discarded medical specimen.

Eager to return to his investigation of the police department, Ness did all he could to bring about a swift solution to the Torso murders. When it didn't come, he ordered Assistant Safety Director Flynn to spend time on the case. Ness wanted to know if any similar murders had occurred elsewhere. Flynn, a tall, broad-shouldered man with a mustache and a lantern jaw, reported that there had been two. One had produced the decapitated body of an unidentified white male a few weeks earlier along the train tracks near Haverstraw, New York, a small town on the Hudson River twenty miles north of New York City. The details strongly resembled those of the Cleveland murders except that the killer had used a saw to behead the Haverstraw victim. The second case had involved the discovery of a nude, headless corpse in the train yards outside New Castle, Pennsylvania. After examining the cases, Ness and Flynn agreed that there was sufficient evidence to warrant a closer look at the New Castle crime.

On September 16, Flynn, Sergeant Hogan, and several detectives journeyed to the little town about ninety miles southeast of Cleveland. New Castle was almost the halfway point along a direct train route between Cleveland and Pittsburgh. Close to the New Castle train yards was a swamp with a malevolent reputation. There, in the dank, weedy marshes of the Mahoning River, the remains of six beheaded men had been discovered more than a decade earlier.

Chief of Police Ralph Criswell met the Cleveland lawmen and told them the story of the Murder Swamp. In the spring of 1923, two beheaded skeletons had been discovered. Both victims had been dead about three months. A search had been launched for the heads immediately. To the shock of the tiny community, the head of a middle-aged victim dead only a couple of weeks had been discovered. The middle-aged victim's body and the two missing heads were never found. The next year, a dog had led its owner to the site of another rotting, decapitated corpse. Again, a search of the swamp turned up a fresher head. Several months later, another headless skeleton unrelated to any of the previous remains had been discovered. No clothing was found with any of the six victims, and none of the victims was ever identified.

Criswell shared his theory that the remains were those of victims of gang murders and that the swamp was used as a dumping ground by mobsters. Flynn and the others could not argue with the chief's view; it was infinitely more plausible than believing that the twelve-year-old killings had been the work of the same maniac now terrorizing Cleveland.

The recent New Castle murder was quite another matter. On July 1, 1936, a railroad car inspector had found a body on the floor of an old boxcar, one of a string of twenty-three cars that had been sitting idle in the yards since 1930. The dead man was naked; his head had been neatly removed with a knife stroke at the middle of the neck and was nowhere to be found. Underneath the victim were pages of two newspapers, the *Cleveland Plain Dealer* and the *Pittsburgh Press*, both from July of 1933. The victim, though badly decomposed, had been dead only ten days to two weeks. The body had not been present when inspectors checked the car on June 10, but a local farmer had noticed birds flocking around that particular boxcar not long afterwards. Some bloody underwear had been discovered about a hundred yards away near the edge of the swamp, and the garment was traced to a store in Piqua, Ohio, a town near the Indiana border, on the opposite side of the state from Cleveland. The underwear had not helped in identifying the victim.

Returning to Cleveland, Flynn and Hogan conferred with Ness. Despite the amazing similarities between the cases, they announced to the press that there was nothing definite to link the New Castle slaying to the Torso murders. Unofficially, Ness told the others to keep an open mind and to closely monitor any reports coming from the little Pennsylvania town. He was learning, as were others around him, that there was nothing in the case that could be regarded as certain.

On the morning of October 6, Ness arrived at the office of Prosecutor Cullitan and presented him with an eighty-six-page report detailing his investigation of corruption in the police department. Twenty officers were named, including a deputy inspector, two captains, two lieutenants, and three sergeants. The scope of the safety director's probe was reflected in the fact that the tainted officers were from almost every precinct in the city. Most of the offenders had been found in the Tenth, Fourteenth, and Fifteenth precincts, Cleveland's more affluent and peaceful districts. The report also contained abbreviated statements from sixty-six witnesses willing to testify against the officers.

Eight of the policemen were immediately suspended. It came as no surprise that one was Captain Harwood. "I am the most misjudged man in Cleveland," Harwood protested. In arguing his innocence, he failed to explain how, on a salary ranging from forty to seventy dollars a week, he had amassed a small fortune that included property valued at close to two hundred thousand dollars. Ness's report supplied the details of how the captain had accepted bribes and extorted money throughout his twenty-four years on the force. It also contained testimony linking Harwood to various gambling operations like the Blackhawk Inn. One witness Ness had uncovered supplied an account of a meeting in a restaurant between Harwood and his son a few hours after the raid on the Blackhawk Inn. The witness revealed how the captain had angrily told Edward that he was "a damn fool" for allowing Ness to catch him in the establishment. The report went on to describe the intimate contact Harwood enjoyed with gangland figures, detailing how he had once raised twenty thousand dollars to help finance an east-side nightclub, the Green Derby.

The story hit the newsstands with a great deal of sensationalism. The *Press* scooped the other papers with an eight-column streamer, an extra, and the inside story under Clayton Fritchey's by-line. There was talk that Ness and Fritchey had shrewdly withheld their findings until the most appropriate time; the Great Lakes Expo, the major recipient of the city's attention, had ended just two days earlier. It was even alleged that the pair had been set to release their report three weeks earlier but had decided to hold off due to the publicity over the sixth Torso murder.

Such accusations were part of an attempt by Ness's and Mayor Burton's enemies to counter the safety director's evolving mystique in the city. The critics portrayed Ness as a self-centered official interested only in his aggrandizement, a charge very similar to the mild censure he had received in Chicago as leader of the Untouchables. It was obvious that Ness enjoyed the flattering publicity he had attracted. And it was common knowledge that he had a number of friends on the staffs of local newspapers who guaranteed that his coverage would be favorable. But it was also clear that

Ness, whatever his motivation, had won the hearts of Cleveland's law-abiding citizens with his daring raids and his example of honesty.

If Ness had timed the presentation of his report to insure maximum publicity, he didn't spend any time basking in the spotlight. At his office, he told reporters, "Any action now is up to the prosecutor. I'm going on vacation."

And with that, Ness withdrew to his suburban home and vanished from public view for the next two weeks. His home life was the one area where Ness did not welcome any intrusions, and his friends in the press respected his privacy. At home, the safety director enjoyed quiet evenings with his wife and their cats. His favorite pastime was stretching out on the floor while listening to opera and reading classical works. Occasionally, the childless couple took cruises on Lake Erie or visited the city's best restaurants. But for the most part, Eliot and Edna were homebodies who shared their time together in a modest world of suburban security.

Back at city hall, the furor over the Torso case was subsiding and the trivial tips were tapering off. Detective Merylo was growing weary of the hot line assignment, and yet at the same time, he was becoming increasingly fascinated with the case. He decided to take advantage of Ness's absence by asking Inspector Sweeny to allow him and his partner to conduct their own investigation of the murders free of the interference of the safety director and others. Sweeny seemed reluctant at first, but he finally gave his consent.

On their own, the two detectives operated out of their offices at the Detective Bureau, on the streets, and in their homes. When most officers were finishing for the day, Merylo and Zalewski were usually just starting. Dressing as tramps, they lived for days at a time among the hobo camps of the Flats and Kingsbury Run, listening to the hobo grapevine. Sometimes, they took turns offering themselves as bait for the Butcher, the approach scoffed at by the police officials at the Torso Clinic. As one pretended to sleep in the open, the other would vigilantly watch from cover nearby. At the office of the Nickel Plate Railroad Police near the East Fifty-fifth Street bridge, the pair interrogated the vagabonds pulled by the dozens from the trains each day. There were times when a single freight was found to be carrying more than two hundred destitute men.

Some evenings were spent in prowling the streets of the Roaring Third. Over the years, Merylo and Zalewski had recruited a number of informants there, and they now called on them to report any unusual individuals in the area. One of the difficulties was that the Third Precinct was a breeding ground for bizarre behavior. From prostitutes came accounts of some of the oddest personalities imaginable—sadists, sodomites, masochists, and deviates with queer fetishes of all kinds. Merylo and Zalewski disregarded the ones who appeared to be mere degenerates and concentrated on those who displayed a penchant for violent acts of perversion.

One character in particular surfaced as an intriguing suspect. He was well known among Third Precinct prostitutes as "the Chicken Freak." According to police reports, the suspect could only "receive sexual satisfaction" while observing the beheading of a live chicken. The man, described as big and muscular, had often been seen entering brothels with chickens under each of his arms; he also brought along a large butcher knife. The prostitutes would undress and then behead the chickens as the man looked on and masturbated. If this failed to satisfy him, he would instruct the prostitutes to rub the dull side of the bloodied blade back and forth across his throat until he finished.

Merylo and Zalewski spent several weeks tracking the Chicken Freak, but he proved to be elusive. A prostitute finally supplied the pair with a license number that was traced to a husky truck driver. In custody, the man freely admitted his perversions, even confessing that he had engaged in intercourse with chickens. But when the detectives confronted him about the Torso murders, he insisted that he could never harm a human being. When the Chicken Freak was shown morgue photos of the Butcher's victims, he was visibly repulsed. Merylo concluded that the man was innocent—at least of murder—and ordered him released.

October is special in Cleveland, a month when the landscape along the Cuyahoga River and Lake Erie comes alive in hues of burnt orange, deep brown, brilliant red, and gold. But winter winds arrived prematurely in 1936, stripping the trees of their lavishly colored leaves. There was a change in the mood of the city as well. In the hobo jungles, tramps hovered close to their fires and eyed each other suspiciously. Everywhere, even in the safe, sprawling suburbs, children were admonished to stay close to home, and many adults felt uncomfortable venturing out after dark. The Torso Murderer was beginning to occupy Clevelanders' thoughts.

FIVE

Prosecutor Frank Cullitan wasted no time in making use of the massive report compiled by Eliot Ness. He introduced the evidence to a grand jury headed by Mrs. Luca McBride. Two earlier grand juries examining police corruption had whitewashed the picture, but not this one. On October 29, indictments were returned against the eight suspended officers on charges of bribery and graft.

The indictments, like Ness's report, seemed well timed. Election day, Tuesday, November 3, was just around the corner. To no one's surprise, Cullitan was reelected by a mammoth margin. What was astonishing, at least to some, was the fact that Eliot Ness campaigned vigorously for the Democratic prosecutor. The safety director made no apologies to his fellow Republicans. Cullitan, he maintained, was simply the best candidate. Despite their political affiliations, the two worked well together and had become best friends since the Harvard Club raid.

There was one genuine upset in the election. Arthur J. Pearse, running on the Republican ticket, was defeated in his bid for reelection to the office of county coroner. His Democratic successor was Dr. Samuel R. Gerber, a diminutive, sallow-complexioned bachelor of thirty-nine with a small, thin mustache and wavy hair prematurely flecked with gray. Gerber's dapper, unpretentious appearance made him look curiously at home hunched over a microscope or puttering around a laboratory. In a crowd, others seemed to tower over him.

Gerber was born in Hagerstown, Maryland, of Lithuanian descent. He was well educated and possessed an intense energy, intelligence, and diligence; he was the kind of person who became totally absorbed in his work. After moving to Ohio with his elder sister, Gerber had pursued a number of scholarly fields with remarkable success. While still in his early twenties, he had served as the mayor of Scott, a small Ohio town. In Cleveland, he had been appointed to the medical staff of the Warrensville Workhouse, where Edward Andrassy had briefly been an inmate. Gerber held a degree in law as well as in medicine; he had a keen interest in criminology and psychology, an ideal quality for a coroner. Gerber had already expressed a fascination with the Torso case, and, following his election, he spent considerable time studying the police and medical records of the murders.

The legal machinery, meanwhile, had begun to descend upon the indicted policemen. One by one, they were brought to trial between December of 1936 and March of 1937, providing the public with more than enough courtroom dramatics to take their minds off the bitterly cold Cleveland winter and the equally chilling reality of the mass murderer in their midst.

Looking proud and confident and very handsome for a man in his mid-fifties, Michael Harwood strode into court accompanied by two of Cleveland's finest lawyers. Local newsmen called him "the cop who couldn't be broken." Witnesses were intimidated, and there were attempts to bribe jurors. But the evidence supplied by Ness and presented by Cullitan was overwhelming, especially the testimony of former bootleggers who related how Harwood had forced them to pay for "the privilege to run booze" in his district. On December 16, Harwood was found guilty and sentenced to two to twenty years in the Ohio State Penitentiary. His wife spat vehemently at the safety director as she left the courtroom. Ness told a reporter standing next to him, "Nobody is above the law."

More trials and convictions followed in rapid succession. Lieutenant Thomas J. Brady pleaded guilty and received a suspended sentence. But Deputy Inspector Edwin Binns, a twenty-four-year veteran; Lieutenant John H. Nebe, a twenty-year officer; Sergeant James E. Price; and a pair of patrolmen all received terms of one to ten years behind bars.

The undercover investigation and the convictions drew applause from near and far. Clayton Fritchey and the *Press* were jointly awarded the Pulitzer Prize Citation for Civic Achievement. Director Ness was presented the Veterans of Foreign Wars Medal as Outstanding Citizen of Cuyahoga County. Chief Justice Carl V. Weygandt of the Ohio Supreme Court praised Ness for the "outstanding completeness and care with which he assembled evidence against the police officers."

Ness was only getting started. There were more suspensions, and five additional policemen were ultimately brought to trial. Along with exposing corruption, Ness went after officers with records of misconduct or negligence on the job. Some were transferred to different precincts with a warning to shape up, a procedure used with officers of the Fourteenth Precinct, the former command of Harwood, where Ness cleaned out the entire staff and scattered it across the city. Others were forced to resign—nearly two hundred of them over the next few months, including Captain Lenahan of the Eighth Precinct.

At the same time, Ness took steps to insure that new recruits coming into the department would be honest and efficient lawmen. He raised the standards for entrance and instituted more rigorous examinations. More than half the recruits accepted that year were college graduates. Late in 1936, Ness founded a training school for all new officers, an institution that later evolved into the Cleveland Police Academy. Rookies were instructed in new, scientific methods of crime detection along with martial arts and marksmanship, and they were even required to take a typewriting course.

Gradually, Ness selected a band of "new Untouchables" from the ranks of the force, most of them young, collegiate types like himself with outstanding records. Ness trained them in many of the undercover methods he had employed against the Capone mob in Chicago—wiretapping, cultivating informants, tailing suspects, staking out the locations of illegal activities, and much more. The safety director used the squad for special investigations and difficult assignments. Newspapers dubbed them Ness's "Minute Men." The best known of the group proved to be Lieutenant James M. Timber, who, under the director's spirited leadership, raided and closed down over forty gambling operations in the city.

With the consent of Mayor Burton, Ness formed another band of special assistants that came to be called "the Unknowns," a small group of undercover investigators whose identities he never revealed. They operated in complete secrecy, regularly feeding the safety director information about which cops and politicians were dirty, what illegal activites were going on, where they were happening, and who was behind them. The Unknowns were paid with the special undercover fund provided by the mayor. It wasn't until many years later that the general public and even the press learned of the existence of such outstanding investigators as Tom Clothey, Sam Sagalyn, and Keith Wilson.

During this time, there was a brief, minor sensation when Ness's assistant, John Flynn, suddenly submitted his resignation. The gossip at city hall was that Flynn had been eased out because of his politics and because of some critical comments he had reportedly made about Ness's police probe. Another story alleged that Flynn was a good friend of Captain Harwood's and that he deeply resented Harwood's conviction. Publicly, Ness praised Flynn for his work and wished him luck.

Ness wasted no time in finding a replacement. His choice was Robert W. Chamberlin, a personable young lawyer and an officer in the Ohio National Guard who was well known and well liked around Cleveland. He was also Ness's landlord and neighbor in Bay Village. Chamberlin and his wife became close friends of Eliot and Edna's. As the new assistant safety director, Chamberlin proved to be a zealous official, developing a great working relationship with Ness. Phillip Porter, city editor of the *Plain Dealer*, observed that "the two stuck together like glue." As a friend, Chamberlin convinced Ness to occasionally take time off to unwind, a triumph that no one else, not even Edna, had been able to accomplish. Chamberlin was a great football enthusiast, having been a star player at Lakewood High and the University of Michigan. He got Ness interested in the sport, and together they attended as many games as their hectic schedules allowed.

And in the midst of all this, the Torso Murderer struck again.

Late in the afternoon on February 23, 1937, police were notified that a portion of a human body had washed ashore at Euclid Beach, the very same stretch of sand where the Lady of the Lake had been cast up nearly two and a half years earlier. Sergeant Hogan, eight miles away in the center of the city, raced to the scene and managed to be the second officer on the frigid, deserted beach. Robert Smith, a middle-aged man from East Cleveland, was also there, shivering in his hat and overcoat. Smith had come to the area to collect driftwood for his stove and had spotted an unusual object rolling in the waves just offshore. "I thought it was a dog or some dead animal," he informed the policemen. "But after taking a closer look, I knew I should call."

Hogan and the other officer waded into the icy waters and retrieved the piece, which proved to be the upper half of a woman's torso, minus the head and arms. It was immediately wrapped in a blanket provided by Smith and taken in Hogan's car to the county morgue. The new coroner and Dr. Strauss went to work at once. As usual, the dismemberment was exceptionally skillful. The arms had been removed cleanly at the shoulder joints. The killer had bisected the trunk with only two precise, powerful strokes, one slicing through the abdomen in front and the other cutting through the first lumbar vertebra in back. The woman had been decapitated just below the seventh cervical vertebra, slightly lower than the previous victims. Also unlike the others, it was apparent in this instance that the act of beheading had not caused death. Strauss commented that the blood clots he discovered in the heart left no doubt that the organ had stopped beating before the head was taken off. The exact cause of death, however, could not be determined.

The torso had been in the water about forty-eight hours, and the victim had died one to two days before that. The examiners estimated her age in the mid-twenties, her height at five foot five to five foot seven, and her weight at 100 to 120 pounds. The victim had been a slender, small-boned woman with a fair complexion and light brown hair. She had given birth at least once, possibly twice. From the condition of her lungs, Coroner Gerber and Dr. Strauss felt certain that she had lived most or all of her life in a large, industrial city like Cleveland. There were no traces of alcohol or drugs in the body. Gerber and Strauss detected sand from the lake and, oddly, fragments of weeds on the body, indicating that the remains had temporarily rested on the ground after or perhaps during disarticulation.

"He gives us one regularly every five months," observed Detective May to reporters. The investigating officers, already weary and confused from the many dead ends encountered in the previous killings, were beginning to show the strain. There was sharp dissension among them over the latest discovery. Since the victim had died before decapitation, some were eager to reject her as a legitimate Torso victim. Others like Hogan not only accepted her but, because her remains had been discovered at Euclid Beach, suggested that the Lady of the Lake be added to the Torso murder cycle. Officially, the Lady of the Lake remained an unrelated case. There was even disagreement over how the victim's torso could have come to appear where it did. One theory was that the Butcher had dumped the dismembered pieces either in the river or in the sewers around Kingsbury Run that drained into the Cuyahoga. Others argued that the torso could not have floated such a distance in only two days and suggested that the killer must have disposed of the remains directly into Lake Erie.

Hoping to settle these disputes as well as to locate the remainder of the woman, the lawmen assigned to the case explored the Erie shoreline with the aid of civilian volunteers. The search was a grueling and painful one. The bonechilling north wind whipping in from the lake brought more than a few cases of frostbite, while the treacherous footing on the ice-covered rocks resulted in some bruises and cuts. Merylo and his partner located a sewer pipe emptying into the lake not far away. Thinking it possible that the remains had come from there, the pair descended into the pipe with only a small flashlight to guide them. Zalewski emerged claustrophobic and frozen after several minutes, while the diligent Merylo continued to the end of the pipe, finding nothing.

Searching through the neighborhood, Merylo and Zalewski discovered a trail of blood in the snow that zigzagged through streets and backyards and ended at the beach. It appeared to be a substantial piece of evidence until it was learned that the blood had been left by an injured dog. A few of their fellow detectives poked fun at them, but Merylo and his partner had the last laugh. Several local residents reported having observed two men in a small boat near the spot where the upper torso had washed up the following day. Homicide detectives went on record saying that they believed the men had been the Butcher and an accomplice. Merylo and Zalewski investigated, and they discovered that the men in the boat had been nothing more than a pair of high school boys trying out a homemade canoe. Interestingly, the youths said that they had noticed debris in the water that could have been more parts of the victim. Police continued to search the beaches and drag the lake, but they failed to find anything.

Efforts to identify the victim proved equally frustrating. Two recent missing persons matched the general description. One was a Canton, Ohio, woman who had vanished during a visit to Cleveland but who reappeared just as abruptly back at her home a few days later. The second was an East Cleveland mother of two who had been reported missing by her father the day before the remains of "No. 7" turned up. The father suspected foul play. Detectives Kennedy and Duffin were certain that she was the victim, and they considered arresting her estranged husband, thinking that he had murdered his wife and hacked up the corpse to look like a Torso victim. The theory collapsed when the woman walked into Central Station and announced that she was quite alive. No other missing woman whose description corresponded to the victim was ever reported. One team of detectives spent several weeks attempting to track down a rumored abortion clinic operating in the area that some believed might have been responsible for the remains. But such an establishment, if it ever existed, could not be found.

While the investigators struggled over the latest victim, Coroner Gerber undertook an extensive review of all the medical facts related to the case. He recorded his conclusions in a five-page report that he submitted to the Homicide Unit on March 1.

Gerber disregarded the earlier Euclid Beach victim because she had been found "too long ago" and because "too few details" were known. He was firmly convinced that the other seven cases were the work of the same individual. "The possibility of a different operator having entered the series is slight," Gerber wrote. "It is particularly the peculiar dissection of the bodies which groups these seven cases together. All cases show that the heads were severed from the bodies through the intervertebral discs. . . . Cases No. 3, 6, and 7 showed further that the bodies were cleanly dismembered at the shoulder and hip joints apparently by a series of cuts around the flexure of the joints and then by a strong twist wrenching the head out of the joint cavity and cutting the capsule. The torsos were further sectioned through the abdomen, the knife being carried in cases No. 3 and 6 through the intervertebral discs."

Elaborating further on the bisecting of three of the victims, Gerber noted that the killer had accomplished the difficult task by cutting anteriorly "down to the vertebral spines" and then flipping the bodies over and completing the sectioning "from behind in all cases." The purpose of this extreme form of dismemberment, Gerber thought, was "to facilitate transportation and disposition" of the bodies.

The direction of the knife marks indicated a right-handed individual. In every instance, Gerber continued, "all the skin edges, muscles, blood vessels and cartilages were cut squarely and cleanly, apparently by a long sharp knife such as a butcher or heavy bread knife. There was relatively little hacking of the tissues and relatively few hesitation marks." The coroner felt certain that the killer was someone "highly intelligent in recognizing the anatomical landmarks as they were approached, or else, as is more likely, by a person . . . with some knowledge of anatomy." Gerber thought that the most suitable candidate would be a doctor "who performs the crime in the fury of a long drinking bout or derangement following the use of drugs." Other suspects, in order of likelihood, were medical students, male nurses, orderlies, butchers, hunters, and veterinary surgeons.

Gerber found the motivation behind the murders "difficult to evaluate." In contrast to Merylo and almost every other detective on the case, Gerber was certain that the killings were not sexually motivated. He argued that a sexually depraved maniac would se-lect either males *or* females as his victims, but not both, as the Butcher had done. He also pointed out that classic sex killers like Jack the Ripper usually mutilated their victims with mad slashing rather than deliberate, detailed disarticulation. But while taking considerable time to discredit the sexual theory, Gerber failed to present another plausible motive for the slayings.

"In conclusion," Gerber wrote, "it must be admitted that though many isolated facts are known, and a few conservative inferences are drawn here, there is yet much to be desired before the final solution is realized."

Only fragments of the coroner's conclusions were printed in newspapers for the eyes of the general public. Part of the reason may have been the influence of Safety Director Ness, who, in the wake of the seventh victim, exhorted his journalistic friends to tone down their coverage of the killings. Gerber's lengthy recapitulation of the medical facts—depicting the Torso Murderer as a methodi-cal, efficient killing machine on a rampage of motiveless murder— was just the sort of thing Clevelanders did not need at that point. Some of Ness's comments got back to Gerber and infuriated the new coroner.

It is possible that Ness's view of the matter was misread or distorted. It certainly seemed hypocritical that the man who so cherished publicity should suddenly have disapproved of the me-dia sensation surrounding the case. Actually, Ness's chief concern was the investigation. During the front-page furor following the discovery of "No. 6," he had seen the entire department become paralyzed by the deluge of hysterical calls that poured in. If the Headhunter was to be caught, the police needed to concentrate on legitimate leads.

There were also a few who interpreted Ness's attitude to mean that he regarded the Torso case as too unimportant to merit his immediate attention, an accusation that gained considerable mo-mentum over the next few months. Not true, claimed his assistant, Bob Chamberlin, who quoted Ness as declaring that the capture of the Mad Butcher was "a major priority" of the safety director's office. But like everyone else on the case, Ness's Minute Men and his Unknowns searched the streets, scrutinized suspicious characters, and checked local mental hospitals, only to report that they had made no progress.

More than two months later, on May 5, the lower half of "No. 7" surfaced near the foot of East Thirtieth Street. A worker at the exposition grounds spotted the piece bobbing in the choppy waters just offshore and notified police. A Coast Guard boat recovered it. The lake was still cold enough to have kept the remains fairly well preserved. Even so, the lower half provided no new clues. Its discovery some seven miles west of Euclid Beach and less than two miles from the mouth of the Cuyahoga did reinforce the belief that the murderer had discarded the body parts in the river rather than in the lake. The legs, arms, and head were never found. No identification was possible.

Long after the other police investigators had returned to their regular duties, Merylo and Zalewski remained on the case, following leads, examining and reexamining bits of information, tirelessly exploring even the most trivial clues. When they were not on the streets, the tenacious pair spent hours searching police files for likely suspects, often making lengthy lists and checking each individual the following day.

There were three men in the records about whom Merylo was especially curious. All were at large in the Cleveland area, though they could not be easily located. The first was a convicted murderer paroled in 1934 and reported to have a mania for drinking blood. The second was a forty-two-year-old black "Voodoo Doctor," a former suspect in the 1929 decapitation murder. Third and most promising was a fifty-year-old escaped mental patient originally from Butler, Ohio, who was described as a violent man who suffered from hallucinations and extreme paranoia. In 1934, the suspect had been arrested in Akron carrying a bloody razor, and he had been placed in the state hospital at Athens, Ohio. He had broken out in early September of 1935, about a week before the first two Torso victims were found. Since that time, the suspect had been spotted sleeping in the fields near the Trumbull Street bridge. He had also been seen running about with a knife in his hand. Merylo learned that the man had visited some relatives on their farm in eastern Ohio, a farm that was just across the state line from New Castle, Pennsylvania.

Each was a prime suspect in Merylo's book, and most of his energy that spring was spent in tracking them. He finally traced the Voodoo Doctor to a Third Precinct apartment building and arrested him there. The other two were eventually captured by Cleveland police. Merylo and his partner questioned each suspect for days at a time; but although they were jailed for other crimes, they could not be connected to the Torso murders.

Many more suspects were uncovered in the following months. Among them were a "mad Russian" who carried a machete and hung around Calvary Cemetery on the extreme south side of the city; a "crazy Greek" who wandered the streets of the Roaring Third with knives concealed in his overcoat; an alcoholic former butcher living in a cave near the tracks of the Erie Railroad south of Kingsbury Run who reportedly "chased people with a large knife"; and yet another cave dweller in some wooded terrain off East Forty-ninth Street who was hovering over a fire and eating raw corn when police nabbed him. Then there was the twenty-six-year-old unemployed chef living on Fowler Avenue about a mile south of Kingsbury Run who went berserk one night with a meat cleaver, terrorizing neighbors and wrestling with four policemen until one of them finally knocked him unconscious with a mop handle. There seemed no end to the bizarre, perverted personalities brought in for questioning about the murders. Any, conceivably, could have been the killer; perhaps one of them was and slipped through the nets. The investigators had strong suspicions about many, but the arrest reports always ended with the words, "Released . . . no connection."

In Kingsbury Run, the Nickel Plate Railroad Police continued to scrutinize the hundreds of hobos discovered daily in "shaking the trains." The more suspicious among them were sent to Central Station for questioning by Merylo and the Homicide detectives. Overseeing the Nickel Plate operation was Captain J. C. Van Buren, who had assisted the city police and investigated the case on his own since the first bodies were found. Like Merylo and Zalewski, Van Buren and his detectives occasionally disguised themselves as hobos in the hope of attracting the Butcher. One night, the stocky captain was feigning sleep beneath a willow tree near Jackass Hill when a large stranger appeared and started toward him. In the same instant, a rat crawled onto Van Buren's stomach; he managed to remain motionless, but the stranger passed by.

Two Nickel Plate detectives, Anthony Kotowski and Paul Troutman, regularly checked the hobo camps in the Run and listened to the stories. Many tramps talked about a strange vagrant dwelling beneath the Lorain-Carnegie Bridge in the Flats. He was described as a big, powerful man. It seemed that all the hobos were afraid of him. Kotowski and Troutman found the vagrant's nest near an embankment, surrounded by heaps of rubbish he had collected. The man apparently had a keen interest in women's shoes, as several hundred pairs were scattered about. Kotowski and Troutman watched for the man vigilantly but were never able to get a look at him. When they returned the following day, they found evidence that he had been there—a size-twelve footprint and more piles of assorted junk.

A trash-strewn field only a few yards from the mysterious vagrant's nest became the scene of tremendous activity on Sunday afternoon, June 6, 1937. Fourteen-year-old Russell Tower had spent the morning by the river watching Coast Guard boats search for the victim of a drowning. Tower passed beneath the huge Lorain-Carnegie Bridge on his way home, kicking rocks and cans until he suddenly spied a human skull in his path.

Next to the skull, police found pieces of a skeleton stuffed inside the rotted remnants of a burlap bag tied with a piece of hemp. Also in the sack was a page from the *Plain Dealer* dated June 5, 1936. Twenty feet away were a cream-colored wool cap, fragments of a dress, and some tangled strands of black hair.

The coroner and his staff had their work cut out for them. Gerber estimated that the remains were a year old. (If he was correct, the murder had occurred not long after the tattooed man was slain.) Traces of lime were detected that might have hastened the corpse's deterioration. The victim had been neatly dismembered, a fact confirmed by an anatomy professor at Western Reserve University who examined the remains under a microscope. The bones of the arms and legs were missing, but the rest were present except for a single rib. According to Gerber, the remains were those of a petite black female about thirty-five years of age who had stood no taller than five foot one and weighed about a hundred pounds.

With five fresher bodies still unidentified, there was little optimism that this latest victim—no more than a pile of bones—would be identified. The victim's teeth, however, had some distinctive features. The first upper molar on either side was missing; the wisdom teeth had been extracted; and several other teeth were badly decayed. There were also two gold crowns and a gold bridge of three teeth on the upper left. A check of local dentists drew a blank, but a vague communication was received about two weeks later claiming that a Cincinnati dentist long since deceased had performed the work upon a woman named Rose Wallace.

Most of the investigators working on the case considered the tip dubious at best. Merylo, however, decided to explore the report. He discovered that a Rose Wallace had in fact lived in the Third Precinct; she had vanished on August 21 of the previous year and had not been seen again. She had been about forty years old, and her general description matched that of the victim.

A friend of Rose Wallace's told Merylo that she had last seen Rose leaving her home at 2027 Scovill Avenue on her way to meeting a man at a neighborhood bar. Merylo located the tavern at East Nineteenth and Scovill and learned that Rose had left that night with a white man named Bob, reportedly headed for a party on the west side. Bob was described as having a dark complexion; he was presumably an Italian or a Greek. Another woman stated that she had seen Rose riding in an automobile with three white men a short time later. That was the last anyone had seen of her.

As Merylo dug deeper into Rose's past, he noted some startling similarities to the Flo Polillo case. Rose, like Flo, was a known prostitute. The two had lived close to each other and frequented some of the same places, including the bar that Rose had visited the night she disappeared. Though Merylo did not find evidence that Rose and Flo knew each other, the two women had shared some of the same acquaintances. Among them was One-armed Willie, one of Flo's black boyfriends who, it was discovered, had also been a live-in lover of Rose's. The burlap bag containing the remains of the latest victim was almost identical to the sacks that had been wrapped around the pieces of Flo Polillo, and the Lorain-Carnegie Bridge was only blocks away from where Flo had been found.

Despite Merylo's findings, many were unconvinced that Rose Wallace was victim "No. 8." Coroner Gerber flatly rejected the identification, primarily due to the fact that Rose had disappeared two and a half months after he believed the victim was killed. The other detectives remained skeptical. Eliot Ness, in a comment made later, also claimed to have doubts. The *Plain Dealer* declared in an editorial that the identification was "no more than a good guess," pointing out that aside from the ambiguous letter about the Cincinnati dentist, there was no sure evidence. Merylo, nevertheless, was convinced. Not only did Rose's description match that of the dead woman, but the dress Rose had reportedly worn the night she vanished was similar to the one found near the remains.

Perhaps the most convincing evidence that Rose Wallace was the eighth victim was the simple fact that after her disappearance she was never seen again.

Tension and unrest characterized Cleveland in the summer of 1937, despite the gala reopening of the lakefront exposition with record-breaking attendance. The perpetual failure of police to solve the Torso case continued to have an unsettling effect on citizens. Democrats, looking to discredit the mayor before the November election, began to use the murders to criticize the administration in general and Ness in particular, labeling him "Burton's alter ego." They charged Ness with wasting time and taxpayers' money in prosecuting "cops who had taken $25 ten years ago" instead of devoting the department's resources to capturing the mass murderer at large in the city.

Another source of intense political controversy was the violent upheaval between local industrialists and union workers in the Flats. A strike sanctioned by the Congress of Industrial Organizers pulled thousands of laborers from their jobs and threatened to shut down major factories. The companies brought in nonunion help to keep the plants producing at a reduced rate. The resulting clashes were chaotic and often bloody, with beatings, brawls, broken windows, overturned trucks, and minor riots. The companies appealed to the city for greater police protection.

Mayor Burton called a special meeting with Ness and Chief Matowitz to discuss the crisis. A strike detail headed by Inspector Sweeny was formed to keep order. The presence of police only added fuel to the fire. Strikers continued to clash with nonstriking workers, and both sides battled with police.

In the background of this riotous activity, some prominent labor figures accused Burton and Ness of being pawns of the industrialists who were intent on destroying the unions. Several months earlier, Ness had begun a new undercover project involving the investigation of union racketeering in the city. At least a few of the voices that now filled the air with inflammatory allegations against the mayor and the safety director belonged to those who felt threatened by Ness's probe.

The violence, meanwhile, continued to escalate. In one flare-up alone, over a hundred people were injured. Ness was forced to send in reinforcements armed with clubs and tear gas to disperse the tumultuous crowds. Ness set up barriers around some of the factories, creating a sort of no-man's-land between the picketers and the plants. But even these measures failed to resolve the conflict. Finally, on July 3, Burton called in the National Guard to restore order. With their uniforms and helmets, toting rifles with bayonets, the guardsmen made sections of the Flats look like a war zone.

At five-thirty on the morning of Tuesday, July 6, one of the guardsmen on stike duty wandered onto the West Third Street bridge and watched a tug pass lazily underneath. A white object floating in the brown, murky water just offshore caught his attention. The guardsman thought that it looked like part of a store mannequin until it rolled over in the tug's wake; he then realized that it was the lower half of a man's torso. The young private ran and found two fellow guardsmen and the bridge tender, John Haggarty. The four men fished the gruesome object from the river, then phoned police.

By the time officers arrived, more pieces of the body had appeared in the oily Cuyahoga. The two halves of the left leg, neatly separated at the knee, were found floating nearby. Police pulled a burlap bag from the water. According to the label, it was supposed to contain a hundred pounds of Purina chicken feed. Inside, wrapped in newspapers, was the upper part of the torso. One of the patrolmen on the scene spotted the right thigh wedged among some bridge pilings. A Coast Guard boat joined the search and found the upper left arm some 250 feet west of the bridge. Detectives Musil and May commandeered a police boat and spent the remainder of the day cruising up and down the river looking for more parts; they found only the lower half of one of the victim's lungs.

News of the latest Torso killing swept through Cleveland with uncanny speed; by early afternoon, the whole city was talking about the Mad Butcher and expressing horror and indignation. That evening, a middle-aged customer in an east-side restaurant reportedly boasted to the other patrons that he knew "all about the Torso murders" and that he was "good at cutting people up." A woman slipped away and phoned the police. Minutes later, over a dozen officers burst in and pounced upon the man. At Central Station, it was revealed that the man was a former ambulance driver who was more than a little intoxicated. He could not even remember his statements the next morning. A brief check cleared him of any connection to the case.

At dawn, the search for the remainder of "No. 9" resumed, with Coast Guard and police vessels exploring the water while officers and volunteers combed both banks of the river. By day's end, the searchers had found both forearms with the hands attached. Three days later, on July 10, the upper right arm was recovered; on July 14, the lower right leg and foot appeared almost a mile upriver.

All of these parts—like pieces of a grisly anatomical jigsaw puzzle—were assembled by the coroner and his assistants into a complete body except for the head, which was never found. Gerber estimated that the man had been killed late Saturday or early Sunday. As usual, death appeared to have been the result of decapitation. "The killer leaves his signature every time," Gerber commented, noting that most of the dismemberment had been performed with the previous expertise. But this time, for reasons known only to the murderer, his carving of the corpse had been much more extreme and erratic. In removing the right arm, he had left numerous "hesitation marks" and done considerable hacking, as if he had been nervous or hurried. His cuts in bisecting the torso were also uncharacteristically crude and jagged. He had even sliced off the bottom of one of the lungs, the piece recovered by Musil and May. The police and medical experts pondered these unusual findings. Perhaps the killer had been interrupted or had grown intoxicated by the blood lust of his dissection. Or the findings may only have indicated that his knife was growing dull.

But there was more. The body of "No. 9," unlike any other, had been disemboweled. The entire abdomen had been split open and its contents gutted. The heart had also been removed; the killer had cut through the chest with a single, decisive stroke and ripped out the organ with his hand. None of the internal organs were ever located.

The victim, according to Gerber's best guess, had been thirty-five to forty years old, five foot eight, 153 pounds, with coarse, dark brown hair. There was a scar on the right thumb and a peculiar cross-shaped mark on the calf of the left leg. The cross was two inches long and vivid blue in color, prompting some to conclude that it was a tattoo. Gerber, however, determined that the mark was scar tissue from an infection. The man had been muscular, well nourished, and in good physical condition except for a slightly arthritic spine. His fingernails were neatly groomed, strongly implying that he was *not* a vagrant. But just who the victim was remains a mystery to this day. His fingerprints could not be found in local files or in those of the FBI.

Aside from the body itself, two of the three pieces of physical evidence left for the investigators were the burlap bag and the three-week-old newspapers found with the upper torso. Lieutenant Cowles scanned both with ultraviolet light in the hope of turning up the murderer's fingerprints; there were none. The bag itself was reportedly "at least three years old," and it could not be traced. Oddly, a woman's taupe-colored silk stocking was also discovered in the sack. Cowles found two hairs in the stocking—one long, black-and-white strand presumed to be that of a dog and the other short, blond, and definitely that of a human.

On the streets, there was the usual flurry of flimsy reports. A night watchman had heard groans from inside a garage on the night of the fourth; another bloodstained knife was found in a trash can; there were tips from informants and concerned citizens who had seen something, heard something, or suspected someone. No matter how thorough and determined the investigators were, none of these leads brought them any closer to the killer.

Another barrage of criticism followed, aimed at the police and at Eliot Ness. Once again, Ness's special investigations were blasted; it was alleged that the director was too involved in his "witch hunts" to properly perform his duty in making city streets safe. Ness responded in his usual mild-mannered fashion, quoting some convincing figures showing that in his first eighteen months in office, from December of 1935 to June of 1937, Cleveland's crime had diminished by 25 percent while arrests and convictions had increased by 20 percent. The police force, he proudly reported, was more efficient, and the influence of the mobs had been substantially weakened.

Ness said little about his ongoing investigation of union racketeering. On one hand, the project was certainly timely. Labor unions were young, just beginning to realize their vast potential under the supportive administration of Franklin Delano Roosevelt. Many unscrupulous men, some with criminal pasts and connections with the underworld, had foreseen opportunities for power and wealth in organized labor and were beginning to acquire positions of influence in the unions. It was Ness's goal to ferret out the crooks and put them behind bars. At the same time, he realized that in blue-collar Cleveland, with the prevailing labor turmoil, he would be walking on eggshells. There were reports that some of the mayor's men attempted to persuade the safety director to abandon or at least postpone his project. But Ness would not be deterred.

The investigation began as a cleanup of an extortion ring preying upon farmers and producers at the Northern Ohio Food Terminal. By early June, Ness and his Minute Men had amassed enough evidence to indict two well-known union leaders, Harry Barrington of the Carpenters' Union and Harry Wayne of the Kosher Butchers' Union, on charges of extortion. Released on bail, Barrington fled to California, where he was captured by federal agents and extradited to Cleveland. At his trial, Barrington pleaded guilty and was sentenced to three to fifteen years. Once the prison doors slammed behind him, Barrington suddenly became talkative. He sent for Ness and announced that, for a deal, he would tell all he knew about labor racketeering in Cleveland.

Barrington's information helped Ness to zero in on Donald A. Campbell and John E. McGee, two of the most powerful and feared union bosses in the city. Their notoriety was widespread. For years, newspapers and even national publications had called Campbell and McGee "Cleveland's bad boys," a term hardly sufficient to describe the city's archterrorists.

Campbell was president of the Painters' District Council and the Glaziers' Union, as well as a prominent figure in other locals. McGee was head of the Laborers' District Council and the Window Washers' Union. Physically, they seemed a mismatched pair—the thirty-nine-year-old Campbell was short and stubby, while the forty-three-year-old McGee was tall and lanky. But they had similar pasts filled with arrests. Campbell especially had a lengthy criminal record that included imprisonment for petty theft, burglary, and carrying concealed weapons. After supposedly going straight by entering organized labor, Campbell had faced half a dozen more arrests but no convictions for employing terrorist tactics in building his empire. McGee had once operated a protection racket; his alliance with Campbell proved fruitful. After assembling a small army of strong-arm men and professional bombers, the duo had become masters of the art of extortion.

Campbell's lofty status in the locals endowed him with the power to rule over Cleveland's glass industry like a tyrant. No glass could be installed anywhere in the city without his permission. Businessmen were forced to pay shakedown fees to acquire workers, and they were also forced to purchase their glass from Campbell alone. Often, Campbell ordered work halted in the middle of a project and demanded another payment to finish. Another common practice was inducing proprietors to sign a contract to employ workers from McGee's Window Washers' Union. If any proprietor dared defy the pair by hiring nonunion workmen, performing his own work, or refusing to pay, a well-aimed brick or a baseball bat turned his windows into a million fragments. To make a harsher statement to merchants who proved especially stubborn, enforcers

Eliot Ness, public safety director, city of Cleveland.
Cleveland Public Library

Ness with two of his Untouchables.

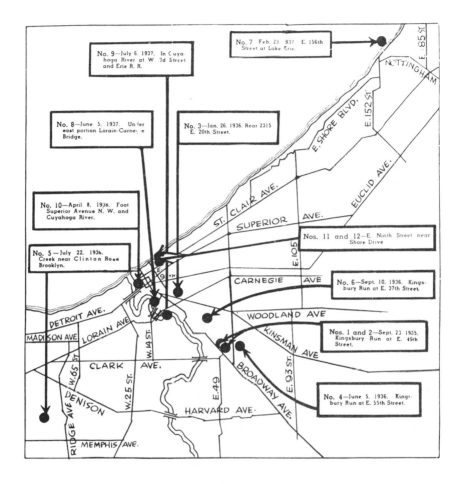

Discovery sites of the Torso victims, as published
on August 17, 1938, the day after "No. 11" and "No. 12" were found.

THE PLAIN DEALER, Cleveland Ohio

Torso victim Edward Andrassy.
This is one of the four photographs discovered by
Detectives Merylo and Zalewski in 1938, more than two years after Andrassy's murder.

THE PLAIN DEALER, Cleveland Ohio

The two burlap bags containing the partial remains of
Flo Polillo, found in an alley off East Twentieth Street on January 26, 1936.

Cleveland Public Library and The Bettmann Archive

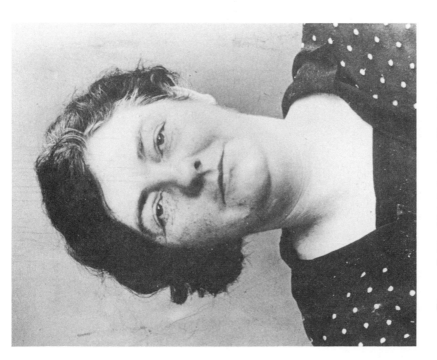

Florence Polillo, third victim of the Torso Murderer.
THE PLAIN DEALER, Cleveland Ohio

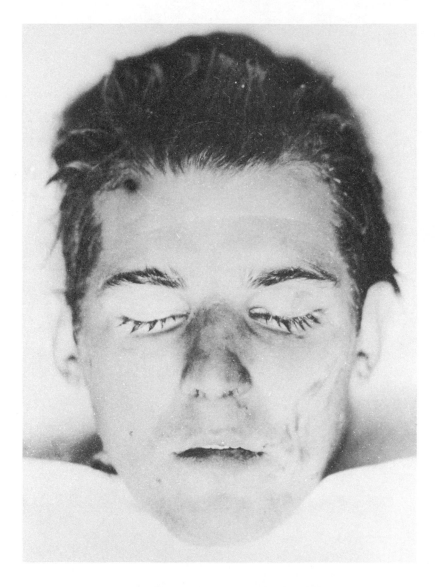

The severed head of the tattooed "No. 4," as displayed
at the Cuyahoga County Morgue with the victim's body.

THE PLAIN DEALER, Cleveland Ohio

Officers searching the Kingsbury Run pool for the
remains of victim "No. 6" on September 11, 1936,
with part of the estimated crowd of six hundred looking on.

THE PLAIN DEALER, Cleveland Ohio

Detective Peter Merylo.
THE PLAIN DEALER, Cleveland Ohio

Robert Smith of East Cleveland at the Euclid Beach site
where he spotted the remains of "No. 7" on February 23, 1937.

THE PLAIN DEALER, Cleveland Ohio

Fourteen-year-old Russell Tower at the site beneath
the Lorain-Carnegie Bridge where he discovered the remains
of the victim tentatively identified as Rose Wallace on June 6, 1937.

Cleveland Public Library and The Bettmann Archive

The West Third Street bridge, beneath which the
dismembered remains of victim "No. 9" began to surface on July 6, 1937.

One of the burlap sacks containing the partial remains of victim "No. 10" found floating in the Cuyahoga River on May 2, 1938. The initial discovery had been made almost a month earlier, on April 8.

Cleveland Public Library and The Bettmann Archive

The mob scene on August 16, 1938, as the remains of
victims "No. 11" and "No. 12" were discovered on the lakefront in full view of city hall.

Cleveland Public Library and The Bettmann Archive

Officers and spectators looking at the head of victim "No. 11,"
as discovered by twenty-one-year-old James Dawson and his fellow scrap-iron collectors.

Cleveland Public Library and The Bettmann Archive

Detective Merylo searching the Scovill Rag & Paper Company in his attempt to trace the patchwork quilt wrapped around the torso of "No. 11."

THE PLAIN DEALER, Cleveland Ohio

The patchwork quilt.

Cleveland Public Library and The Bettmann Archive

Cuyahoga County Coroner Samuel Gerber with the skeletal remains of victim "No. 12."
THE PLAIN DEALER, Cleveland Ohio

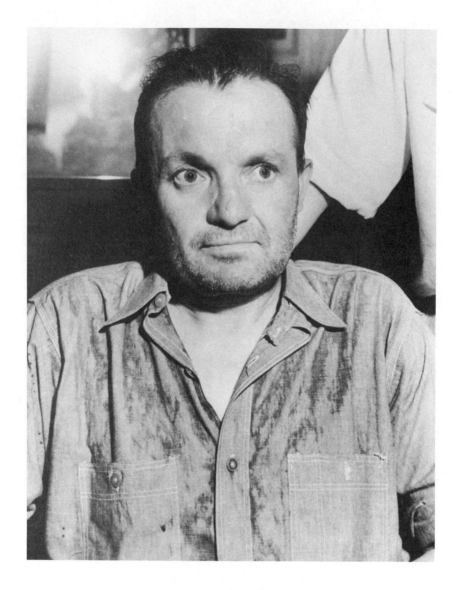

Torso murder suspect Frank Dolezal shortly after
his grueling interrogation by county authorities.

THE PLAIN DEALER, Cleveland Ohio

The decomposed remains of one of the three murder
victims discovered at McKees Rocks, Pennsylvania,
on May 3, 1940, showing the cryptic word *NAZI* carved
into his chest. The pattern of dismemberment
strongly resembled that practiced by the Torso Murderer.

THE PLAIN DEALER, Cleveland Ohio

Ness campaign poster from
the Cleveland mayoral election of 1947.

Cleveland State University

threw acid, planted dynamite, or hurled stench bombs into their establishments.

The cops and the courts seemed powerless to halt the reign of terror. Many Cleveland businessmen had complained about the situation, but none were willing to testify. Campbell and McGee made no attempt to conceal their ill-gotten affluence, openly scoffing at the efforts of lawmen to build a case against them. The frustrated police had finally placed the pair under twenty-four-hour surveillance. Wherever the two union bosses went, a pair of plainclothesmen observed their every move.

Before long, Campbell and McGee had realized that they were being tailed. At first, they played with the detectives, taking them on long, pointless, high-speed rides through the countryside or zigzagging through city traffic and laughing at the lawmen's attempts to keep up. Eventually, they had devised a brazen scheme to publicly ridicule the police. At precisely noon on May 26, 1934, thousands of pedestrians along Euclid Avenue had stopped in their tracks to gaze at the sight of a three-car caravan moving slowly down Cleveland's principal street. In the center vehicle, an expensive, chauffeur-driven touring car with its top down, sat Campbell and McGee in tuxedos and silk top hats, waving to the throngs of spectators. Leading the procession was another topless touring car carrying a small band playing "Me and My Shadow." Bringing up the rear was their police tail—two detectives, faces red with humiliation, dutifully following the labor leaders in their dilapidated sedan.

Clevelanders called it "the Big Parade." With amazing audacity, Campbell and McGee had displayed to the entire city that they were above the law, and they had made the police look like buffoons in the process. The pair continued their terrorist tactics over the next three years and remained completely untouchable. During that period, police estimated that more than ten thousand Cleveland windows were smashed by Campbell-McGee hoods.

Like every other lawman in the city, Eliot Ness had heard a great deal about the two racketeers, and he had often expressed his disgust at their smug effrontery. His personal interest in the case came about through a social acquaintanceship with two brothers, Vernon and Gordon Stouffer, the owners of a chain of restaurants.

The Stouffers shared with Ness how they had experienced labor difficulties in the summer of 1936. Six weeks before the scheduled opening of the Stouffers' new $125,000 restaurant on Euclid Avenue, painters and glaziers had suddenly walked off the job and refused to return. Campbell had contacted the brothers, claiming he could resolve the problem for a fee of $1200. After considerable discussion with their father and friends, the brothers had consented to pay. Vernon had delivered the payoff in cash to McGee.

Ness had asked his friends if they would be willing to tell their story in court. The brothers were understandably fearful and reluctant. A little later, after Harry Barrington had begun to share his knowledge of the Campbell-McGee operation, Ness spoke again with the Stouffers and made them an offer; he would call on them only if he had gathered at least a couple of dozen others who pledged to testify against Campbell and McGee. Ness offered safety in numbers and police protection. The brothers agreed to testify.

Using Barrington's information, the safety director sought out local businessmen who had been extortion targets. Most were too terrified to talk despite Ness's assurance of security. Only a handful—a butcher, an ice cream parlor proprietor, a clothing store owner, and several department store owners—were willing to take the stand. Desperate to find more witnesses, Ness began to trace victims who had moved from the Cleveland area. He found them as close as Youngstown, Ohio, and as far away as Evanston, Illinois. The operation consumed the late summer and the fall of 1937 partly because Ness, a man revered for his courage, was intensely afraid of flying and preferred to make his trips by car or train. His time and efforts were ultimately rewarded. Almost all of the transplanted Cleveland merchants promised to testify against Campbell and McGee.

Ness was still deeply involved in the investigation when the November election arrived. John McWilliams, the Democratic candidate for mayor, and his chief supporter, Congressman Martin L. Sweeney, made much in the press of the "Ness-Burton failure to solve the horrible Torso crimes." What Cleveland needed, McWilliams claimed, was not "a G-Man from Chicago" serving as safety director, but a local lawman who would display the proper concern for the city. In a close contest, Burton was re-elected.

Celebration of the victory ended abruptly for Ness on November 7, when a phone call from his brother, Charles, a prominent businessman in Indianapolis, informed him that their seventy-three-year-old mother had died in Chicago the previous day. Ness and his wife journeyed to the Windy City for the funeral, a modest ceremony in which Emma Ness was laid to rest beside her immigrant husband, Peter, who had died five years earlier. It proved to be Eliot's final visit to his hometown.

Back in Cleveland, Ness immediately plunged back into his extensive inquiry into the shady affairs of Campbell and McGee. It was early December before the safety director was able to obtain indictments against the pair and two of their henchmen. Cleveland's bad boys appeared unworried. "We welcome this investigation," Campbell arrogantly informed reporters. "Let them do their damnedest."

As 1937 drew to an end, there were no new breaks in the Torso case, but there were no new bodies either. Sergeant Hogan often sat alone in his office studying the reports written by his detectives, sifting through mountains of material collected in the course of the investigation. Like many of his men, Hogan was haunted by a nagging hunch that the answer to the mystery was right in front of him—perhaps a trivial clue or a piece of information that had been disregarded.

Never in his thirty-one years on the force, Hogan confessed to a reporter from the *Press*, had he been involved in such a lengthy, exasperating case. In the last two years, over three hundred suspects had been examined. Since the sixth victim, the murders had received national attention. More than five hundred letters and telegrams had poured in from every state in the country. Some of the authors claimed to know the identity of the killer; many more thought they knew the victims, especially the tattooed man. One recently received, typed postcard addressed to "One Interested in Justice" alleged that the tattooed victim was Charles Griffith, a tire salesman from Phoenix. Another letter was from a Philadelphia housewife whose sailor-husband had been missing for two years. Even the most insignificant tips had been checked thoroughly, but they had failed to provide answers to the investigators' many questions, let alone any clues to the identity of the Torso Murderer.

There had also been phone calls. "Thousands," Hogan told the reporter, wearily shaking his head. "I don't even want to think about 'em all." Still, the Homicide chief remained confident. "It's been a night-and-day job since the first torso was found, and it would seem like a pretty hopeless situation. But the cards are stacked against anyone who has killed ten persons. We'll get him."

SIX

Nine months passed uneventfully. By the spring of 1938, the city seemed to be breathing easier. Many were convinced that the mysterious killer had, for reasons unknown, ended his two-year murder spree. Others like Merylo and Zalewski who were not so sure continued their search for the Mad Butcher.

The undisputed sensation of the winter months was the trial of Donald Campbell and John McGee. From the very beginning, there was controversy, as the ever-resourceful Eliot Ness uncovered evidence of an attempt to bribe a prospective juror. The twelve finally selected were all union men or the wives of union workers.

Prosecutor Cullitan began his case with the testimony of the Stouffer brothers. They told how Campbell had guaranteed "peace and quiet" for their establishment for the sum of twelve hundred dollars and how McGee, acting as Campbell's "representative," had received the payment. The Stouffers' story was immensely damaging. In the days that followed, forty-three more witnesses enlisted by Ness took the stand for the prosecution. Each told an account of how Campbell and McGee had bullied or terrorized him into surrendering shakedown fees. About midway through the parade of witnesses, one of the defense attorneys made a motion to have Ness barred from the courtroom, claiming that the director was "impressing" the witnesses and jurors merely by his "presence." Judge Alva R. Corlett denied the motion.

The defendants remained smug and confident. Campbell and McGee had raised a thirty-thousand-dollar defense fund; at least part of that sum was used in a smear campaign against the safety director that centered around the claim that Ness's objective was to break the unions. The Cleveland Federation of Labor, voting unanimously to give "moral and financial support" to Campbell and McGee, denounced Ness's investigation as "a vicious attack on organized labor." The defense lawyers presented thirty-seven witnesses, most of them respected Cleveland labor figures or prominent union officials from around the nation, who testified to the honesty, integrity, and sterling character of Campbell and McGee.

The end came on March 8, 1938. The jury returned a verdict of guilty. Referring to the defendants as "cunning thugs," Judge Corlett sentenced them to one to five years in the state penitentiary. Bail was denied. Looking shell-shocked, Campbell and McGee were taken immediately to prison to begin their sentences.

Conviction of the labor racketeers propelled Ness into the national spotlight again, bringing him greater acclaim than he enjoyed even in his Untouchable days. Publications like *Newsweek* praised the director for his "cleanup campaign" in Cleveland. At the same time, the antilabor image propagated by Ness's critics continued to follow him. A team of investigators from the American Federation of Labor arrived from Washington to examine the charges against the safety director. After thoroughly reviewing the evidence, they were satisfied that Ness was interested only in law and order and in ridding the unions, as well as the city, of its racketeers.

Local newspapers, to no one's surprise, also rallied behind him, further exalting the safety director before the Cleveland public. According to one editorial, "Director Ness . . . lifted fear from the hearts of honest men. . . . Cleveland is a better, cleaner, more wholesome place, . . . a safer place in which to do business."

Far removed from the fanfare Eliot Ness was enjoying, Detectives Merylo and Zalewski continued to hunt for the Torso Murderer. Their investigation took them to virtually every corner of the city and many outlying areas. They visited every hospital and slaughterhouse in Cuyahoga County in search of suspects. By March of 1938, the pair had interviewed no fewer than fifteen hundred persons in connection with the case.

The Butcher's inactivity since the discovery of "No. 9" had left a cold trail. With no fresh victims or clues coming in, Merylo decided to backtrack through the murder series and examine each case in detail. Of the ten sure victims (Merylo, like Hogan, considered the first Euclid Beach torso part of the cycle), he felt that four merited close review—Edward Andrassy, Flo Polillo, the tattooed man, and Rose Wallace, whose identity as the eighth victim was still disputed by many.

After several weeks, the two detectives began to focus exclusively on Andrassy. Since Andrassy had been murdered long before anyone realized a serial killer was on the loose, Merylo was convinced that a more extensive investigation at the time would have resulted in the Butcher's capture. Gathering all the original reports, now over two years old, Merylo and Zalewski contacted as many of those who had been questioned as they could locate. They also uncovered many people not previously spoken to—some of Andrassy's cronies in the Roaring Third, others who had known him in the workhouse, and even people he had gone to school with. They learned many new sordid details of Andrassy's bisexual behavior and his swindles, but nothing that led to his killer.

Merylo and Zalewski talked at length with Andrassy's parents and relatives. With the permission of his mother, they examined the personal effects he had left behind, and they discovered four negatives that had apparently been ignored by the original investigators. When developed, the prints revealed four poses of Andrassy in a bedroom wearing a dark, double-breasted suit. In two of the shots, he was standing; in the third, he was seated and smoking a cigarette, his right arm resting on a nightstand; and in the fourth, he was stripped of his suit coat and reclining on a bed. Merylo and Zalewski scrutinized the details of the room captured in the photos. It had flowered wallpaper, a neatly made bed with a headboard of blond wood, a Japanese lantern dangling from the ceiling, and a heavy vase squatting upon a small table. None of Andrassy's family and friends recognized the room, and neither did any of the Homicide detectives. It seemed like the most solid clue yet. Merylo suggested that the unknown bedroom might be the Torso Murderer's workshop.

Cleveland newspapers printed the photos and asked the public to help identify the room. A young man arrested for selling obscene literature informed his jailers that he knew the place and could lead police there. Merylo and Zalewski talked to the young man. He told them that the room in the pictures was a second-floor bedroom at 1734 West Twenty-eighth Street that he had visited several times about three years earlier. On each occasion, the owner, an older man who had befriended him, got him intoxicated and "made improper advances." When the detectives reached the address, Merylo was surprised and slightly embarrassed to find that it was a house he had visited before while checking another suspect. He had even been in the bedroom, but he hadn't recognized it in the pictures because it had been remodeled.

The former occupant was traced to a house on Fulton Avenue only a few blocks from Andrassy's home. He was a short, sparse man of fifty-six with a sharply bent nose and dark, piercing eyes who lived with his two elder spinster sisters. Under questioning, the man was cooperative and even affable with the detectives. He freely admitted that he was a homosexual and that he had known Andrassy; they had met eight years earlier at Brookside Park and become good friends. The suspect described Andrassy as "a nice boy" but claimed that Andrassy had not interested him sexually. He had taken the photographs as "a favor" for the young man.

A search of the suspect's current residence produced some interesting discoveries. The detectives found a trunk in the attic containing love notes from various men. Digging deeper in the trunk, they came upon a butcher knife with a six-inch blade wrapped in a towel. On the floor next to the trunk were stains that appeared to be dried blood. Elsewhere, the searchers turned up numerous articles of bloody clothing and sixty-seven pieces of silverware taken from various Cleveland hotels. Most interesting of all was a photograph of a handsome young man in a sailor's uniform who looked remarkably like the tattooed man. Merylo placed the suspect under arrest.

At Central Station, the questioning became a formal interrogation. The suspect retained his calm, confident manner, continuing to deny that he and Andrassy had been more than friends. He said he knew nothing about Andrassy's death or any of the Torso murders. A fingerprint check revealed that the suspect had once been convicted on a charge of petty larceny in Buffalo. He claimed he was innocent and that a woman he had worked with framed him out of spite when he had refused her sexual advances. Concerning the sailor in the picture, he assured investigators that the photo was twenty years old. The young man in the sailor's uniform had been an acquaintance who worked as a bartender in Cleveland. The suspect had not seen him for years. "I don't think you'll ever find him," he told the detectives.

"If he's dead," Merylo reportedly shot back, "I don't suppose we will."

The photograph was printed in newspapers, but the sailor was never identified. And although photographic experts were certain that the print was not as old as the suspect claimed, they determined that it was not a picture of the tattooed victim. Lieutenant Cowles examined the stains in the attic and concluded that they were not blood. The suspect explained the bloody clothing by asserting that he had frequent nosebleeds, a fact corroborated by his sisters and their neighbors. The butcher knife was tested, but no traces of blood were found on it. In short, evidence to connect the suspect to the Torso murders was just not there. Merylo remained suspicious and succeeded in having the man jailed on a charge of sodomy, commenting that the best way to determine his guilt or innocence was to wait and see if another body appeared.

Despite a nine-month lapse since "No. 9" and the incarceration of a likely suspect, there were some unsettling indications that a fresh Torso victim was in the making. On January 17, a pile of women's clothing—an imitation chinchilla coat, a black felt hat, and undergarments, all in good condition—was found in a vacant lot near East Sixty-fifth Street not far from Kingsbury Run. Clevelanders held their breath expecting a body to follow, but it never turned up. Oddly, the garments were similar to the clothing, never found, reportedly worn by Flo Polillo on the night she was last seen almost two years earlier.

At 8:40 on the evening of March 3, an attendant at a Sohio refinery pump house near Kingsbury Run noticed an expensive-looking automobile halt midway across the Jefferson Street bridge. A man stepped out and tossed a heavy bundle over the railing; a thud and then a splash followed. The attendant told police that it had been too dark to note any details of the car or the man. Investigators discovered a sizable dent in the metal roof of a building directly beneath the bridge, indicating that a large object had struck it and then toppled into the river. But again, the expected remains never appeared.

Instead, there were bodies, or at least pieces of them, turning up elsewhere. In Sandusky, Ohio, that same month, a dog trotted out of a swamp dragging a human leg. The local coroner stated that the limb was fairly fresh and that it had been severed with "professional" care. No other parts of the body were found. About that same time, the nude, headless body of a woman washed ashore at Lake Ontario near Oswego, New York. The following month, a man's arm and leg were fished out of the Mohawk River near Albany, New York. Albany medical examiners declared that the pieces belonged to a heavyset, middle-aged man of medium height. The amputations were "a clean job." Merylo and other lawmen studied the reports of such discoveries and noted similarities to the Cleveland murders, but they could do little more than wonder if the Torso Murderer was again at work.

And then, suddenly, the scene shifted back to Cleveland when, on April 8, the lower half of a woman's left leg came floating down the flood-swollen Cuyahoga. A young factory worker in the Flats spotted it caught against a tree limb along the east bank near Superior Avenue at quarter after two that afternoon; he thought it was a dead fish until he drew closer. Only the shin, skillfully severed at the knee and ankle joints, was found, but it was enough to reawaken the city to the fact that the Torso Murderer was still at large.

Even more alarming was the coroner's announcement that the piece was only three to five days old. There were a few, unwilling to believe that the Mad Butcher was back in action, who attempted to contest Gerber's conclusions. One was Eliot Ness. Like everyone else in Cleveland, he had hoped that the partial limb was old, perhaps the remains of a previous victim. On the instructions of his chief, Bob Chamberlin brought in an eminent pathologist from Western Reserve University to confirm the time of death. Gerber indignantly refused to allow the pathologist to examine the limb. Ness and Chamberlin denounced the coroner to the press, even suggesting that Gerber was deliberately withholding evidence that might help resolve the case. Despite the criticism, Gerber stood his ground, remaining officially within his right as county coroner to do so.

In the days that followed, the feud between the safety director and the coroner came to typify the kind of pressure felt among municipal officers. As the public and press reasserted their outrage, many at city hall and Central Station blamed each other for the continuing failure to capture the killer. Some of the detectives, fed up and frustrated with the investigation, began to quarrel among themselves. A few requested reassignment.

Sadly but not surprisingly, the tensions of the case finally struck the two men working the hardest to catch the Butcher. A dispute erupted between Merylo and Zalewski over the suspect who had occupied the Twenty-eighth-Street bedroom where Andrassy's picture was taken. Merylo was intent on keeping the suspect behind bars, while his partner argued that they should release him and keep him under surveillance. Their disagreement intensified until, on April 13, Zalewski informed Inspector Charles Nevel, acting head of the Detective Bureau, that he wanted off the Torso case. About a week later, Zalewski asked to be reinstated. Although he occasionally worked with Merylo again in the hunt for the Butcher, they were no longer the same inseparable pair.

Against the background of bickering and buck-passing, police desperately sought clues concerning the latest discovery. Some argued that a single partial limb hardly constituted a murder victim. Gerber could only estimate that the leg belonged to a woman in her late twenties or early thirties. Its length, thirteen inches, suggested a petite stature, perhaps five foot two. The leg was shaven, but Lieutenant Cowles found six long strands of blond hair on it and suggested that they might have come from the victim's scalp.

One group of detectives checked for missing persons matching the partial description of the victim, while others investigated the usual flood of reports. There were two that seemed plausible. First was the report of a pair of construction workers in the Flats who told police that several days before the leg turned up, they had witnessed a heavyset individual entering the storm sewer beneath the High Level Bridge. Since the bridge was close to where the leg was found and since the sewers drained into the river, it seemed possible that the man the construction workers had observed was the Torso Murderer. Unfortunately, the two men had been standing some distance away and could supply no details other than that the suspect appeared to be over six feet tall. There was also a report from a deckhand aboard a dredge who claimed to have seen a human head sweeping past him in the surging waters the same afternoon that the leg was discovered. Inspector Sweeny and six detectives searched the river banks and the sewers for several days but found nothing. The bloated condition of the Cuyahoga, the result of the spring thaw and recent heavy rains, left little hope of finding the remainder of the victim. After three weeks, investigators concluded that the other body parts had been swept away.

They were wrong. On Monday, May 2, Albert Mahaffey, the bridge tender at the West Third Street bridge, spotted two burlap sacks floating in the water. (Six days earlier, a tugboat captain had reported seeing two sacks upriver, but police had been unable tofind them.) Inside the bags, officers discovered the two halves of a woman's torso along with both thighs and the left foot. Merylo spent the rest of the day circling the area in a rowboat, but he failed to locate any of the remaining pieces.

At the morgue, Gerber and the medical examiners matched the lower leg with the newly recovered remains. With the additional evidence, they were able to establish that the victim had been a short, slender, flat-chested woman, twenty-five to thirty years old, five foot two or three, between 115 and 120 pounds, with brown hair and tiny feet, size five narrow. Her appendix had been removed by legitimate surgery. The victim had given birth twice, once by cesarean. As usual, the body had been drained of blood, but for the first time with any of the Torso victims, the presence of drugs was detected. Gerber pointed out that the victim had not necessarily been drugged by her killer, but that she may have been an addict, as might have been confirmed by the missing arms.

As with the previous victim, the dismemberment was unusually erratic—skillful one moment, sloppy the next. The killer had used a number of cuts to remove the head, the first one rather jagged and apparently the cause of death. The last stroke had sliced between the fourth and fifth cervical vertebrae. For the first and only time, the Headhunter had failed to cut completely through the back of the neck and ended up ripping the head off the rest of the way. He appeared to have experienced difficulty in severing the arms; his incisions around the shoulder joints were "cruder and more irregular" than in previous cases, it was reported. The sectioning of the trunk between the ninth and tenth dorsal vertebrae showed numerous hesitation marks, and the killer had snapped several of the lower ribs to complete the task. Upon both thighs, there were deep, jagged slashes unrelated to the surgery that were quite uncharacteristic of the usual cool, methodical dismemberment performed by the Butcher.

Detectives managed to identify the two burlap bags as potato sacks that had been shipped to the Cleveland area from Maine. The bags had come through two different distributors located in the Third Precinct. One operated at the corner of East Forty-ninth and Woodland, where the headless corpse of the 1929 case had been discovered. Neither wholesaler could help the investigators, each reporting that he received fifteen hundred to two thousand such bags of potatoes every year, which were then distributed to markets all over the city. The killer could have picked them up anywhere.

Other detectives searched diligently for an identity to match the remains. There were twenty women listed among the missing persons from the beginning of the year, but none fit the victim's description. Although the vital statistics of the victim were published widely and repeatedly, no one came forward who claimed to have known her. The head, arms, hands, and lower right leg and foot were never found. Before long, the victim became simply

"No. 10" on the growing list of Cleveland's nameless, headless dead.

As one citizen sarcastically commented in an April letter to the *Plain Dealer*, it seemed that everyone in northeastern Ohio was hunting the Torso Murderer except Eliot Ness. Despite the public outcry and the derisive charges of critics, the safety director had maintained a curiously detached position since the discovery of the sixth victim. In a statement to a *Plain Dealer* writer that April, however, Ness indicated that his office was still actively involved in the case. "We have been doing intensive work for almost a year," Ness said, "but very quietly. I hope it will lead us to the end of the chain of killings." He revealed that his assistant, Bob Chamberlin, kept him posted on any fresh developments in the investigation. Occasionally, Ness ordered a sweep through Kingsbury Run to roust the transients and to arrest any suspicious characters found in the area. But the hobo camps had thinned out greatly in the wake of the murders, and the practice accomplished little more than harassing the few pathetic souls discovered there.

The plain truth behind Ness's reluctance to devote time and energy to the Torso investigation was that he was at a loss to find a way to catch the elusive killer. Shortly after the discovery of the tenth victim, he spoke with detectives working on the case and reportedly told them, "I don't know how we're going to do it, but we'll have to come up with something."

Ness's frustration was evident in interviews, when he usually evaded questions put to him about the murders. Once, when pressed for a comment, Ness stated that it was obvious the killer had "great cunning." He added that "he certainly doesn't leave many, if any, clues. About all we have to go on is that one of the victims we have been able to identify was a pervert and another was a prostitute. This man seems to specialize in the sort of people nobody is likely to miss." The man who had helped smash the Capone mob, cleaned up and rejuvenated Cleveland's police force, and battled top racketeers seemed baffled as to how to proceed in the Torso case. Some wondered if Eliot Ness had met his match.

Though Ness acted as if he had better things to do than pursue the Butcher, his critics could hardly accuse him of being idle. After two and a half years in office, Ness remained as mercurial and restless as ever, working on a dozen different projects simultaneously. Among his priorities through the late spring and early summer of 1938 was the modernization and mobilization of the police department. Ness also initiated and vigorously supervised a prodigious campaign for traffic reform in the city. But one of his greatest, yet least recognized, achievements during this time was in addressing the critical problem of juvenile delinquency, a task he undertook largely in his free time.

Vandalism, street gangs, and teenage crime had risen to alarming numbers, especially in Cleveland's worst sections like the Roaring Third. Ness visited the troubled areas with social workers and met with gang leaders. He campaigned to divert municipal finances for the erection of gyms, bowling alleys, playgrounds, basketball courts, and baseball diamonds. He also organized one of the greatest promotions for the Boy Scouts ever witnessed, recruiting scoutmasters from the police and fire departments, enlisting the sponsorship of local merchants, and providing municipal buildings for meetings. Before year's end, Ness became the principal founder of Cleveland's Boys' Town. To deal with less compliant youths, he created a special juvenile bureau that handled only youth-related cases.

Surprisingly, Ness came under fire from a critical few who accused him of coddling young punks. Statistics, however, proved the success of his youth programs—there was an astonishing 80-percent decrease in juvenile crime. "Keep them off the streets and keep them busy," Ness remarked years later. "It's much better to spend a lot of time and money starting and keeping them straight than it is to spend even more time and money catching them in the wrong and then trying to set them straight."

Such accomplishments, which quietly took a sizable bite out of Cleveland crime, did little to alleviate the tension, anxiety, and helplessness Clevelanders felt over the Torso killings. It was difficult for citizens to appreciate the efforts of the safety director while a murderous madman was on the loose. The Mad Butcher was rapidly becoming a thorn in the side of Eliot Ness.

In contrast to Ness, Coroner Gerber was becoming an increasingly prominent figure in the case. His fascination with the Torso slayings was almost as obsessive as Merylo's. Gerber spent considerable time in writing lengthy reports on the case, discussing the evidence with newsmen, and sharing his theories with detectives. At a national coroner's convention, he spoke at length about the murder cycle and won considerable acclaim for his findings. Letters and phone calls concerning the killings poured into his office, nearly as many as were received at the Homicide Unit.

Unlike his predecessor, Arthur Pearse, who may have downplayed the anatomical knowledge of the Butcher, Gerber seemed convinced that the murderer possessed some type of medical training. Gradually, from Gerber's frequent comments, the image of a mad doctor who conducted insane experiments upon his victims gained momentum in the minds of the public. Detectives working on the case began to focus on physicians as their primary suspects. Merylo traced down-and-out doctors who frequented Third Precinct dives. Some were drug addicts and others perverts; a number of "pin artists" survived by performing abortions upon prostitutes and other women.

Among the assorted characters Merylo came across was an elderly physician who boasted that he had invented a death ray. Exploring the physician's room, Merylo discovered a makeshift operating table of bloody, knife-scarred boards. There was also a bed rigged with electrical wiring and covered by bloody sheets. At first, it appeared that the tenacious Merylo had caught the Torso Murderer in his laboratory. But further investigation proved the suspect to be an aged crank who performed experiments on animals in his attempt to find a cure for cancer. Merylo tracked down numerous others with medical pasts, some dispensing drugs from the flophouses where they lived. While each one was a prime suspect in Merylo's book, none turned out to be the Butcher.

One of the strangest stories to cast suspicion on a doctor during the summer of 1938 surfaced not on the streets of Cleveland but from a tip received from Chicago. A police sergeant who had worked with Ness during his Untouchable days contacted the safety director and told him of a former vagabond who had spoken of a time in Cleveland a couple of years earlier when he had almost fallen victim to the Torso Murderer. The sergeant thought that Ness should hear the story, but he explained that the vagabond plainly refused to talk to police about his experience. Ness asked the sergeant to try to detain the man. "I'll send a couple of men to pick him up," Ness said.

Ness gave the assignment to Merylo and Musil. The pair traveled to the Windy City and took charge of the reluctant witness, Emil Fronek, a big, muscular longshoreman who protested that he would lose money and perhaps even his job if he returned to Cleveland. Only a few blocks from the police station, Fronek suddenly leaped from their moving vehicle. Merylo and Musil abandoned their car in midtown traffic and took off after Fronek through the Chicago streets, finally catching him several blocks away. When they returned to their car, one on either side of Fronek, Merylo and Musil found themselves facing half a dozen policemen with drawn revolvers. It took a few nervous moments for the breathless lawmen to explain that they were not kidnappers.

Back in Cleveland, Fronek was brought to the safety director's office, where Ness and the detectives finally convinced him to cooperate. Fronek proceeded to tell a remarkably detailed story. In the late fall of 1935, Fronek, living as a drifter, had come to the Roaring Third and been befriended by a short man who claimed to be a doctor. The "doctor" had invited Fronek to his office, a second-floor apartment on East Fifty-fifth Street, promising him a meal and a pair of shoes. But as Fronek ate, he felt himself growing faint and sick to his stomach. Realizing he had been drugged, Fronek lunged for the door and escaped, the doctor shouting after him that he should come back and have more to drink. After staggering through the streets for what seemed like hours, Fronek found an empty boxcar along the Flats and crawled inside. When he awoke, Fronek discovered that three days had passed. A group of hobos had then taken him in and shared their food with him. After regaining his strength, Fronek had hopped a freight and left the city vowing never to return.

Over the next few years, Fronek had heard stories of the Torso killings, and he surmised that he had been one of the lucky ones. While living among the hobos, he came across a tramp who alleged to have escaped from a Cleveland "doctor." Their descriptions of the man were identical—five foot six, 150 pounds, about forty years old, with a light complexion and sandy hair turning gray at the sides.

After listening for more than an hour, Ness and the detectives bombarded Fronek with questions until they were satisfied that he had spoken of an actual experience. The pieces seemed to fit. At the time, Fronek had been the type of homeless drifter the Headhunter apparently preyed upon. The investigators agreed that the killer probably drugged his victims. (Since only the latest body had revealed the presence of drugs, the theory was that the Butcher used something undetectable.) They also agreed that the longshoreman's account provided the most valuable lead so far in the case. Ness promised Fronek that he would be compensated for his time if he remained a few more days to help them. Fronek agreed.

The next day, the team of Musil and May was accompanied by Merylo and Detective Robert Carter in escorting Fronek to the neighborhood where he had encountered the doctor. Fronek was certain that the office was on East Fifty-fifth Street near the intersection of Broadway, but he failed to pinpoint the exact location among the dilapidated, nondescript buildings. The lawmen questioned local residents about a doctor answering the description provided by Fronek, but no one remembered such a man. Neither could the alleged office be found, though the detectives searched every second-floor flat in the area. Once again, a promising clue had led nowhere.

About that same time, Detective May came across a Third Precinct bartender who told him about an unusual character claiming to be a doctor who had been a daily patron nearly two years earlier. The bartender remembered him as a jovial, talkative, well-dressed, well-mannered fellow who had seemed strangely out of place. The doctor had been friendly with the bums hanging out near the bar and had frequently bought them drinks. Each night, the doctor let it be known that anyone needing a lift could count on him. Another regular at the bar during that time was Flo Polillo. Only several days before Flo's death, the bartender had seen the doctor with her, buying her drinks. He was unable to recall, however, if Flo had left with the doctor. Shortly after that, the unknown physician suddenly stopped attending the bar and was never seen again.

Musil and May and other detectives looked long and hard for the doctor but were unable to either locate him or learn more about him. Oddly, as one detective noted, the brief description supplied by the bartender matched the remains of "No. 9" in almost every detail. Was the man they were searching for a suspect or a victim? It was little wonder that the investigators were baffled and maddened in what was becoming the longest, largest manhunt in Cleveland history.

Even prominent doctors came under police scrutiny. In a few cases, respected physicians were discovered in such sordid behavior as visiting Third Precinct brothels or participating in homosexual affairs. One detective who had obviously been working on the case too long suspected Coroner Gerber of the Torso murders and kept him under surveillance until an irate Sergeant Hogan found out. Yet the detective's suspicions about Gerber were no more outrageous than many of the leads lawmen were working on. It was clear that the Cleveland police were grasping at straws.

As the investigation dragged into the summer, the weary detectives, critical newsmen, and jittery citizens realized that the case would soon be entering its third year with no solution in sight. No one, of course, could foresee that the Cleveland murder series was about to officially end as it had begun, with the discovery of the remains of two victims killed at different times.

SEVEN

August 16, 1938, was a hot, hazy, humid Tuesday in Cleveland. For nearly two weeks, citizens had languished under sweltering temperatures. In their attempt to escape the heat, people lined up three and four deep at soda fountain counters, jammed into air-conditioned theaters, and thronged on the beaches.

The downtown portion of Cleveland's lakefront was undergoing an extensive face-lift. At the foot of East Ninth Street, in the shadow of city hall, Municipal Stadium, and the Coast Guard station, were several acres of undeveloped land that were a particular eyesore. The rock-strewn landscape was crowded with all kinds of debris left behind by the exposition and by the excavation of scenic, newly constructed Shore Drive. And it was there, shortly after five o'clock in the afternoon, that three black men scavenging through the refuse in search of scrap iron stumbled upon the dismembered remains of a woman.

Police raced to the scene from Central Station, only a few blocks away. They arrived to find the region already overrun with hundreds of spectators. Homebound motorists were stopping along Shore Drive and backing up the rush-hour traffic for miles. Uniformed officers attempted to control the crowds and get traffic moving while Sergeant Hogan and his detectives crowded around the discovery site, which was just twenty-five feet off Shore Drive. One of the black men, twenty-one-year-old James Dawson, told the officers that he had been poking through the rubbish when he spied a patchwork quilt with rocks piled on top of it. Inside, Dawson had found a female torso swathed in a ragged, dark blue suit coat and dark brown wrapping paper of the kind used by butchers. The victim's head, arms, and legs had been removed in the usual fashion, but the trunk was intact, not bisected as the remains of Flo Polillo and the last five victims had been. The head, also wrapped in brown paper, was found only a few feet away. Nearby was a handmade cardboard container fashioned from a pair of larger cartons. Opening the container, police discovered the victim's arms and legs in wrapping paper neatly fastened with rubber bands.

The detectives were optimistic about the prospect of tracing the victim and her killer. For the first time in more than two years, they had a complete body to work with. Decomposition was evident, but the remains seemed recent enough to offer a good chance for identification. Hogan instructed his men to examine every bit of trash in the area that might be related to the crime.

Pressing the crowd back, officers cordoned off the region as detectives probed the entire site, overturning rocks and peering into crevices. Just beyond the eastern barricade nearly two hundred feet away, Todd Bartholomew, a tall, rawboned machinist, stood with his wife and a friend watching the lawmen work. Around seven o'clock, the three began to notice a terrible stench rising from a nearby rubbish heap. Kicking aside some rocks, Bartholomew saw what appeared to be human bones; he hastily informed the nearest policeman, Sergeant William Miller.

Hogan and several detectives rushed over. The spectators were moved back again; many must have shuddered at the thought that they were standing on a Torso graveyard. As the grisly pieces were sifted from the rubble, Hogan snatched up a large tin can he thought suitable for holding the remains. He casually pried back the lid and almost dropped the can as he found himself staring at a slack-jawed skull.

With light fading, the searchers tried to recover as much of the remains as possible. In less than an hour, over forty bones, including twenty-two ribs, seven dorsal vertebrae, three neck vertebrae, and two pelvic bones, were collected. Some of the fragments were wrapped in brown paper. One detective lifted a slab of concrete and discovered the bones of the arms and legs.

"He's changing his technique," Detective Merylo, a late arrival on the scene, observed to a *Press* reporter. "For the first time since the first bodies were found, he's left two victims together. He also left behind the heads." The man who had spent more hours and energy than anyone else in hunting the elusive psychopath pushed back his straw hat and folded his arms across his chest. Perhaps the killer was becoming too brazen. Why would he bring the remains of his victims here, to the lakeside, barely ten minutes' walk from Public Square, the heart of downtown Cleveland? "He's smart but he's gonna slip up," Merylo told the newsman. "I know it."

When it was too dark to continue, Merylo and the other detectives departed. Thirty-seven of them volunteered to resume the search at dawn, hoping to find more clues but praying that they wouldn't uncover another body.

About the same time police were finishing at the lakeside dump that evening, Coroner Gerber and his staff began their examination of the latest two Torso victims.

The Butcher had performed some of his neatest, nastiest work upon the woman found by the scrap collectors. As usual, the head had been taken off with little more than a single stroke, severed between the third and fourth cervical vertebrae. The victim's limbs had been amputated with expert surgical cuts at the hip and shoulder joints. Curiously, the left leg had been divided at the knee but the right had been left intact. In like manner, the right arm had been separated at the elbow while the left had been only partially severed. Again the evidence suggested that the killer was interrupted or hurried in his work or that he had simply lost interest.

Gerber found it difficult to determine the time of death despite the relatively good condition of the remains. The pieces, he noted, were dried and hardened, as if the murderer had kept them refrigerated for some time. Gerber finally concluded that the corpse was about six months old, give or take as much as a month. His best estimate placed the killing sometime in the month of March, prior to the murder of the tenth victim. Gerber believed that the remains had been at the dump no more than two or three weeks.

The victim had been a healthy woman in her mid-thirties with long, light brown hair, large feet (size nine), and small hands. She had stood five foot four and weighed 120 to 125 pounds. No one close to that general description was among the missing persons reports. Fingerprints were obtained from the left thumb and three fingers of the right hand. An exhaustive check by Lieutenant Cowles of over a hundred thousand prints in the victim's classification failed to produce a match.

The best bet for identification seemed to be the teeth, which were in notably bad condition. Two upper and two lower molars were missing. Two others were silver filled, and a third was false. All the dental work was poor in quality. Police checked every licensed dentist in the Cleveland area, but they found no record of the woman. She remains forever "No. 11."

An even greater challenge awaited the medical examiners when they turned to the skeletal remains of the victim found two hundred feet away. A hairpin the searchers had discovered with the bones prompted an early report that the victim was also a woman, but it was quickly determined that the remains were those of a male dead anywhere from seven to nine months—well before the murder of "No. 10" and possibly as early as mid-December of the previous year. The hands and feet, along with two ribs and several vertebrae, were never found. Microscopic examination of the bones revealed cuts at the neck, hips, shoulders, wrists, and ankles.

The dead man had been small boned and sparse, about five foot seven and 135 to 140 pounds, probably in his middle or late thirties. Gerber attempted to reconstruct the face. The jaw was wide and the forehead slightly sloped. The nose had been broken at some time and was bent to the left. Strands of long, wavy, dark brown hair still clung to the skull. One of the examiners believed that the features indicated a Negro, but Gerber and the rest agreed that the man had been a Caucasian. All the victim's teeth were present and in fairly good condition.

The prospects for identifying "No. 12" seemed bleak. Several detectives thought they had a good lead, however, recalling a story told by a married couple who had been swindled by Edward Andrassy. A few months before Andrassy's death, the husband had seen him with a companion. Andrassy had introduced his friend as Eddie, who, he said, worked as a chauffeur for a wealthy woman in the western suburb of Lakewood. According to the husband, Eddie had looked like an Italian or a Greek in his late twenties, five foot six, 150 pounds, with good teeth and a "pushed-in nose."

The resemblance between the dead man and the mysterious Eddie, based on a description three years old, seemed startling. It appeared a golden opportunity not only to identify a victim but to connect him to another victim as well. But the investigators, desperately trying to learn something about Andrassy's friend and certain that he was a critical piece in the puzzle, ran into another dead end. The twelfth victim remained unidentified.

The next morning, August 17, Cleveland awoke to another hot, muggy day made even hotter by the furious public outcry over the Torso murders. The *Press* and the *Plain Dealer* fueled the fire with front-page editorials demanding a swift end to the Butcher's killing spree. "When will the slayer's madness cause the mistake that will bring about his detection and capture?" cried the *Press*. "When will the madman's hand lose its cunning?"

It seemed obvious that conventional methods would continue to fail. "Unusual means must be taken to bring the detection of one of the most horrible killers in criminal history," stated the *Press*, which urged that a ten-thousand-dollar reward be posted by the city. A cash reward had been proposed by a city councilman after the discovery of the sixth victim nearly two years earlier. Since that time, city officials had argued over the legality and the wisdom of such a move. The debate lingered, and as a result, a reward was never offered.

At the lakeshore dump, thousands showed up despite the heat and the threat of rain to watch nearly sixty police and civilian volunteers explore the undeveloped acreage along Shore Drive and the tracks of the Pennsylvania Railroad. From the foot of East Ninth, where the bodies had been found, the searchers scrutinized the area as far as East Twenty-sixth, but they failed to find either human remains or evidence relating to the murders.

Standing near city hall that morning, Safety Director Ness briefly watched the police search. Later in the day, he was spotted with various police officials including Chief Matowitz at Central Station and with Mayor Burton at city hall. A few reporters suspected that something newsworthy was in the works, but they were unable to catch the suddenly elusive Ness.

The scheme in the works would later be termed "a grandstand play," a raid in the old Untouchables style designed to supply the needed break in the Torso case. Ness selected his men, most of them detectives and young patrolmen who had served with his Minute Men, and scheduled a meeting at ten o'clock that evening to discuss the plan.

Just after midnight, a caravan of eleven squad cars, two police vans, and three fire trucks left Central Station and headed into the Flats. The vehicles halted along Canal Street at the place where the river twists behind Public Square, the same spot where the leg of "No. 10" had been found. In the distance, beneath the Eagle Street ramp, was the largest of Cleveland's so-called shantytowns, a wretched cluster of thirty makeshift shacks serving as the homes of hobos and derelicts. Ness, hatless and carrying an ax handle, took charge of a group of twenty-five lawmen, among them Bob Chamberlin, Lieutenant Cowles, and Detective Lloyd Trunk. The officers moved silently toward the dark shacks while Ness, in a hushed voice, instructed them to fan out over the area. A second squad of ten men, led by Sergeant James McDonald, covered the six possible exits. When all the officers had crept into position, Ness took a powerful flashlight and shined it across the landscape, the signal to move in. It was 12:40.

The fire trucks lurched ahead with engines roaring, their gigantic floodlights illuminating the area. At the same moment, Ness and his men scrambled toward the shanties, stumbling down the slopes through the weeds and rubbish. Mongrels howled and tramps cursed. In the blinding glare of the floodlights, the raiders battered their way into the hovels and prodded, dragged, or carried out the inhabitants. In the midst of the bedlam, one bearded giant staggered out swinging a shovel, coming within inches of the safety director's head. Ness threw himself to the ground as two of his men ran to his aid, beating the man to the ground with their clubs. At almost the same moment, a dog lunged at Detective Trunk. He managed to strike the animal with his ax handle, sending it yelping into the night. Some of the ragged figures attempted to escape, with officers, swinging their clubs, in pursuit. Most ran into McDonald's men and were hustled into the waiting police vans. When it was over after a chaotic half hour, thirty-eight shantytown residents had been rounded up and taken to Central Station.

Ness and his raiders moved farther down the Flats. At quarter of two, they descended upon another set of shanties beneath the Lorain-Carnegie Bridge, close to where the eighth victim had been discovered. Ten more hobos were captured. One young tramp protested that he had just gotten a job and would lose it if he went to jail. Ness assured him that if he could prove his employment he would be released. Next, the safety director led his men into Kingsbury Run and stormed the hobo jungle near the East Thirty-seventh Street bridge, close to where "No. 6" had been found, rounding up another fifteen vagrants.

At Central Station, sixty-three men were questioned, finger-printed, and locked away. Eleven had criminal records and were handed over to the FBI. Of the rest, those who proved they were employed or had family were released. The others were held for what Ness called "relocation and rehabilitation"—in reality, they were sent to the workhouse.

At dawn, police and firemen diligently searched the shanties and the debris for evidence of the Mad Butcher. All they found were two dogs, three kittens, and the pathetic belongings of the rabble that had dwelt there. Then, on the orders of Director Ness, the shacks were set on fire and burned to the ground.

The razing of Cleveland's shantytowns and the ungracious treatment of their inhabitants backfired miserably for Eliot Ness. He had hoped that the raids would produce some vital clue to the Torso Murderer's identity. Failing that, he had felt assured that removing potential victims and ridding the city of its hovels would aid police and reassure the public that he was indeed working to catch the killer. But instead, citizens expressed outrage. The newspapers, normally Ness's most ardent supporters, were especially critical, charging that the safety director and his raiders had done little more than vent their frustrations over the Torso case upon hapless hobos. The *Plain Dealer* declared Ness's tactics "brutal." The following day, August 19, the *Press* printed a scathing editorial entitled "Misguided Zeal":

> Safety Director Eliot Ness' personally supervised raid upon the packing box homes underneath the Eagle Street ramp may contribute something toward the capture of the torso killer. We doubt it.
>
> Certainly, there was little justification for detaining all day the men arrested in the raid, preventing them from collecting their tattered belongings before firemen razed the miserable huts and set fire to the debris. The men were still being held today.
>
> Director Ness himself did not believe that any of the transients arrested in this raid and two similar ones was the butcher who has slain and dismembered 13 persons. He said he was convinced that it was from such transients that the killer selected his victims and that he hoped that the fingerprinting of those arrested might aid in the identification of possible future victims.
>
> Police have known all along that it was from the ranks of the homeless that the killer has taken his toll. To most of us, the arrest of the mad butcher would seem more important than the completing of arrangements for the identification of a possible corpse. . . .
>
> That such Shantytowns exist is a sorrowful reflection upon the state of society. The throwing into jail of men broken by experience and the burning of their wretched places of habitation will not solve the economic problem. Nor is it likely to

lead to the solution of the most macabre mystery in
Cleveland's history.

While Ness was weathering the storm of public criticism, Homicide detectives were devoting long hours to the material evidence collected with the lakeside bodies: the tattered quilt composed of triangular gingham patches that had been wrapped around the woman's torso; a ragged, man's blue-striped coat with two buttons missing; a piece of a striped pillowcase; a page torn from a magazine eventually identified as the March 5 issue of *Collier's*; the cardboard container that had held the woman's arms and legs; the tin can that had contained the man's skull; a bloodstained sugar sack discovered nearby; and the wrapping paper found with both victims.

All in all, it was the best collection of tangible clues yet assembled. After Lieutenant Cowles had applied his forensic expertise to the items and failed to find any useful evidence, Hogan assigned a team of detectives to each of the articles. The investigators were confident that if one or more of the items could be traced to its source, the Torso Murderer would be revealed in the process.

Detectives Musil and May went to work on the makeshift cardboard box. They were joined by Merylo, who considered the box the most intriguing clue. It had been put together, presumably by the murderer, from parts of two larger cartons. One had been a case containing three hundred pounds of frozen fish, the other a carton containing crackers. The trio discovered that both cartons had come from wholesalers located at Central Market in the heart of the Roaring Third. The fish box had been one of fifteen received by a dealer on Bolivar Road on June 8, 1938. The owner, Jacob Katz, told the lawmen that he had merely tossed the boxes onto the curb once the contents were unloaded; anyone could have taken them before they were picked up by garbage collectors.

The detectives turned to the cracker case. They learned that it had been part of a shipment of seventy-five arriving from Grand Rapids on June 17. The cases had remained in the warehouse until July 15, when ten had been sent out. Merylo and his partners traced each of the ten and finally narrowed the field to a pair of cases that had been discarded at the back of a store. Two employees of the store told the detectives that they had observed a local scavenger named Gus carrying away one of the boxes. Gus was described as a huge, husky eccentric, a familiar figure around Central Market who prowled through trash bins and occasionally washed windows or scrubbed floors for meager wages. The detectives regarded Gus as a likely suspect until they managed to track him down. He turned out to be a harmless character with the mind of a child. The carton was still in his possession and still intact. No one the officers talked to had seen the person who took the other box.

On August 22, the *Press* printed a photo of the patchwork quilt in the hope that someone would recognize it. The next day, Charles Damyn, a barber, informed police he was certain the quilt was the same one he had sold to a local peddler in early July. Damyn did not know the peddler's name, but he provided a detailed description. Detectives Herbert Wachsman and Ted Carlson stationed themselves at the corner of Rockwell Avenue and East Twelfth, studying the endless parade of scavengers and street people. Finally, they spotted the peddler—a short, swarthy, shabbily dressed character of about fifty who was pushing a cart overflowing with junk—and immediately arrested him.

The peddler identified himself as Elmer Cummings. One of the popular theories about the Torso Murderer was that he was a junk man, yet the detectives could hardly believe that the nervous little man in front of them was a mass murderer. Cummings admitted that he had acquired the quilt from Damyn, but he swore he had sold it to the Scovill Rag & Paper Company. A team of detectives went to Cummings's house. They questioned his neighbors, his wife, and even his children. Then they searched his home, spending hours rummaging through junk heaped in his cellar and backyard. They found nothing that suggested Cummings was anything but an honest, if unconventional, citizen.

A second group of detectives led by Merylo visited the Scovill Rag & Paper Company, located only a few blocks from where the dismembered remains of Flo Polillo had been discovered and in the same area where Rose Wallace had vanished. The detectives spoke to the owner, William Blusinsky, who did not remember the quilt. Neither did any of his employees. While this did nothing to support Cummings's claim, it did not discredit it either. The number of scrap pieces received into the company's warehouse was often great, and individual pieces usually went unrecorded. If his company had acquired the quilt, Blusinsky insisted that it must have been stolen, since there had been no rag sales for several months. Merylo and the others conducted a painstaking search of the warehouse, then searched the homes of Blusinsky, his salesman, and five workers. None of the men had a criminal record, and each appeared to live a normal, quiet, honest lifestyle.

And there the investigation reached another dead end. The detectives could only conclude that the quilt was stolen from the receiving platform shortly after Cummings had sold it to the Scovill Rag & Paper Company. But stolen by whom? It was hard to imagine that someone as cunning as the Torso Murderer could be stupid or daring enough to risk arrest while snatching such a worthless object. The odyssey of the patchwork quilt from the hands of Elmer Cummings to the headless trunk of "No. 11" remains one of the most baffling mysteries of the Torso case.

Detectives attempting to trace the blue coat, the tin can, the brown wrapping paper, the pillowcase, and the sugar sack all experienced the same fruitless results. Their time and efforts seemed wasted except for one significant fact—the trail kept leading to the Roaring Third, reinforcing the belief that the killer either dwelt or spent considerable time there.

Eliot Ness, still smarting from the backlash over his shantytown raids, met with police officials that weekend and shared his personal conviction that the Mad Butcher resided in the Third Precinct and that an extensive search might turn up his bloody laboratory. It was an idea Ness had proposed two years earlier at the so-called Torso Clinic, where it had been rejected as too impractical. Now, with every conventional method of catching the killer exhausted, Ness had little trouble organizing the project. Absolute secrecy was maintained; only a handful not directly involved knew what was going on. Ness divided the ten square miles of the Roaring Third among six search teams. From the ranks of the Detective Bureau, he chose six men—Merylo, Zalewski, Musil, May, Carter, and Trunk. Ness's status as safety director enabled him to pair the detectives with fire wardens, who did not need a warrant to inspect a premises.

The search lasted five days, from Monday, August 22, to Friday, August 26. The lawmen explored every building, house, and hovel within the sprawling, decaying precinct. They found firetraps galore, people sleeping on floors, vagrants dwelling in abandoned buildings, whole families jammed into a single room, and houses without toilets or water. But amid the squalor and misery, they found no trace of the Torso Murderer or his laboratory.

Perhaps the investigators somehow missed the Butcher's lair in their diligent sweep of the Roaring Third. It is not impossible that they actually visited his abode and noticed nothing irregular. Ness and many others held to the belief that the murderer's workshop was elaborate and gruesome. In all probability, the searchers had expected to find a room ankle-deep in blood, with gore-spattered walls and a collection of heads and assorted limbs scattered about. Actually, a number of murderers less clever and careful than the Cleveland Headhunter have demonstrated that a victim can be killed and cut up with little evidence left on the scene.

There was also the possibility that the killer did not reside in the Third Precinct, as popularly believed. There were a few who speculated that he lived on the west side, where Andrassy had lived and where the fifth victim had been found. Others suggested that the killer lived on the near south side beneath Kingsbury Run or on the far east side, where the pieces of two victims had washed up at Euclid Beach. Some even theorized that the Butcher dwelt in one of the city's affluent suburbs. And then there was the possibility that the killer, like at least some of his victims, was a transient who lived among the hobo camps, a theory that had helped to prompt Ness's shantytown raids. But if the killer was a hobo, then it was pure speculation as to where he performed his methodical dismemberments, some of which must have taken the better part of an hour. With the exception of "No. 5," it seemed inescapable that the Torso Murderer killed his prey indoors and almost as certainly transported the remains by car.

Rarely has any American city witnessed a manhunt as massive as that in Cleveland during the aftermath of the discovery of the lakeside torsos. The systematic search of the Roaring Third was only one of the extraordinary measures undertaken by Ness and the city police. One of the oddest—and certainly most useless— was the enlistment of the National Guard's 112th Observation Squadron in making four reconnaissance flights over the city to take aerial photos. Meanwhile, amateur detectives attracted by the proposed reward came to Cleveland in droves. Experts in criminology also arrived at the invitation of the police.

The public outrage over the Torso killings remained fierce well into the months of autumn. Newspaper commentaries continued to reflect the horror and the paranoia of citizens and the exasperation of Cleveland officials. The *Press* declared that the Mad Butcher "must be caught for the peace of mind of the city and its good name abroad." The latter concern, like the former, was well founded. The story of the latest Torso discoveries appeared on the front page of every major newspaper in the nation. In Nazi Germany's propaganda publications, *Beobachters* and *Tageblatts*, Joseph Goebbels commented on the Torso murders, asserting that such atrocities were typical of America's crime-infested cities; Goebbels, of course, said nothing about contemporary German mass murderers like Fritz Haarman, "the Butcher of Hanover," and Peter Kurten, "the Düsseldorf Vampire."

At the same time Clevelanders were worrying about their city's international infamy, Eliot Ness must have been concerned over his own public image. The furor over the murders generated considerable blame-passing, and much of the indignation was directed at Ness. It was a golden opportunity for his enemies among the police, the politicians, and organized labor, who had been waiting for him to fall flat on his face. As the criticism gained momentum, Bob Chamberlin and others complained that the safety director was being used as a scapegoat in the Torso case.

But the sudden erosion of Ness's popularity was not just the result of unfavorable publicity and the accusations of his critics. For nearly three years, the people of Cleveland had looked to Ness as their champion of law and order. They simply could not understand his repeated failures in the Torso case, from his apparent reluctance at becoming involved in the early stages of the investigation to his overzealousness in the shantytown raids. Unreasonable expectations about the safety director had been shattered. It was obvious that the honeymoon was over.

Other factors added to the public's disenchantment with Ness. Early in September, a week after the unsuccessful search of the Third Precinct, the *Plain Dealer* revealed that Eliot and Edna had been separated for the past five months and were seeking a divorce. With his usual analytical style, Ness told reporters, "It was a mutual decision. We both realized a mistake was made, and we set out to correct it."

The conservative, largely Catholic population of Cleveland was startled by the breakup and by Ness's matter-of-fact tone on the subject. Ness's squeaky-clean image as a family man began to crumble that fall as it became evident that he had adopted a new and flashier lifestyle. Instead of retiring to his suburban home or working late on his special projects, the safety director patronized the city's night spots, usually in the company of a pretty young lady. Two of Ness's favorite places, the Vogue Room at the Hollenden Hotel and the Bronze Room at the Hotel Cleveland, always kept a table beside an exit reserved for him. Even some of his good friends at the newspapers began to wonder if he was growing complacent.

Yet Ness was on the verge of some of his most spectacular achievements. The public scorn surrounding the Torso killings proved to be a minor issue that sparked controversy but only moderately undermined the city's confidence in Ness. Many remained convinced that if there was anyone in Cleveland who could catch the Mad Butcher, it was Eliot Ness.

EIGHT

Sometime after dumping the pieces of "No. 11" and "No. 12" on the lakefront, the phantomlike killer apparently departed Cleveland, some say never to return. He left the city in a state of unparalleled anxiety—citizens jumping at shadows, newspapers attacking public officials and theorizing endlessly over the murders, and detectives wondering what they were doing wrong and pondering over the thirteen victims, ten of them anonymous.

Unaware that the butchery had stopped, the investigation continued to consume countless man-hours as police checked out crank calls and fruitless leads. It was business as usual at the Homicide Unit. Clevelanders may have feared the Headhunter, but they were also fascinated with the case. Everybody had an opinion about the murders, and the detectives, as a result, were flooded with useless reports. Each one, no matter how silly it appeared, was tirelessly examined.

Pranksters were having a field day. A "skeleton" in an east-side basement proved to be a collection of unrelated bones. A "severed leg" found dangling from a tree was only a discarded artificial limb. Merylo and other lawmen began to receive jeering phone calls from a man claiming to be the killer. A large package addressed to Coroner Gerber arrived at the county morgue. It contained a grotesque papier-mâché torso. Police regarded it as no more than a macabre joke, but the fact that the object was wrapped in potato sacks identical to the ones found with "No. 10" prompted a few to wonder if it had been sent by the Butcher.

And then, the day after Christmas, there arrived at Central Station a typed letter postmarked Los Angeles that has remained a source of debate to this day. Some consider it a vital piece of evidence in the case; others dismiss it as the work of a crank.

Dec. 21, 1938

Chief of Police Matowitz,

You can rest easy now as I have came out to sunny California for the winter. I felt bad operating on those people but science must advance. I shall soon astonde the medical profession—a man with only a D.C.

What did their lives mean in comparasion to hundreds of sick and disease twisted bodies. Just laboratory guinea pigs found on any public street. No one missed them when I failed. My last case was successful. I know now the feeling of Pasteur, Thoreau and other pioneers.

Right now I have a volunteer who will absolutely prove my theory. They called me mad and a butcherer but the "truth will out."

I have failed but once here. The body has not been found and never will be but the head minus features is buried in a gully on Century Blvd. between Western and Crenshaw. I feel it is my duty to dispose of the bodies I do. It is God's will not to let them suffer.

(signed) X

The typing, like the spelling, was crude, perhaps deliberately so. The writer was offering nothing new in hinting at religious fanaticism in his reference to "God's will" or in presenting himself as a maverick scientist on the verge of some nebulous medical breakthrough. The mad doctor theory, in fact, had become a popular notion in Cleveland following Gerber's declaration that the killer's surgical skills were much keener than previously believed.

The fact that there was nothing original or revealing in the letter was taken by the authorities as sufficient reason to refute it as actual correspondence from the Butcher. Even less credibility was attached to the letter after Los Angeles police, at the request of Cleveland lawmen, searched the designated area on Century Boulevard and found nothing. The general public was of a different mind, however, and the controversy began when the existence of the letter became known in early January. The press had already likened the Torso Murderer to a twentieth-century American version of Jack the Ripper. Since the Ripper had boasted of his butchery in writing, the letter from the alleged Torso Murderer only inspired further comparisons. The Cleveland public ate it up.

Was the letter genuine? Despite its wide acceptance by Clevelanders, it seems extremely doubtful. Yet the best argument for its validity was not realized until later—the writer appeared to know that the Butcher had taken leave of Cleveland for good. Though the letter arrived six months after the discovery of the last victims, it was still a time when almost everyone expected another body to turn up; it should also be remembered that nine months had passed between the discovery of the ninth and tenth victims. Even so, such "evidence" is far from convincing. The skeptical Merylo conducted a search for the anonymous author but never found him. The letter remains another piece that fails to fit comfortably into the puzzle.

All things considered, 1938 was a bittersweet year for Cleveland's safety director. Ness's celebrated triumph over labor lords Campbell and McGee in the early months brought him not only local acclaim but national recognition as well. Many compared his crusade in Cleveland to the cleanup campaign of another young Republican, Thomas Dewey, in New York City. What might have been Ness's finest hour was followed by a wave of unfavorable publicity—allegations of antiunion activities, the disintegration of his nine-year marriage to Edna, and his handling of the Torso case. During the aftermath of the discovery of the lakeside bodies, Ness's critics widely discredited him with charges of complacency, instability, self-centeredness, shallowness, and arrogance.

But by year's end, Ness rebounded remarkably. He did it primarily by returning to the slam-bang style of law enforcement that had originally brought him fame. Organized crime had adopted a low profile in Cleveland since Ness's first year, when his relentless crusade virtually swept the lucrative gambling establishments from the city and shattered the intricate ring of police protection the underworld enjoyed. Nevertheless, lucrative mob activities in Cleveland still included prostitution, narcotics trafficking, and even sophisticated charity rackets.

On October 3, 1938, Ness and his Minute Men, acting on a tip from an informant, raided a private residence on East Thirty-sixth Street. Inside, they arrested a dozen individuals presiding over the largest numbers operation ever uncovered in the city, worth an estimated $5 million a year. After some prodding and offers of deals by the safety director, a few of the suspects talked. Their testimony, plus two trunks full of evidence collected from the house, implicated a number of local mob figures.

The message was clear. Eliot Ness was back in action, serving notice that he was resuming his war on Cleveland ganglords. During the next few months, he and his new Untouchables gathered evidence, sprang raids, and generally harassed known mobsters. In a much-publicized appearance before a grand jury, Ness presented the testimony of seventy witnesses, and on April 26, 1939, twenty-three Cleveland gangsters, most of them members of the notorious Mayfield Road Mob, were indicted for an array of crimes. Among those charged were Charles Pollizi, Big Angelo Lonardo, Little Angelo Scirrca, and John and George Angersola.

At the same time he was gunning for mobsters, Ness was supervising the most zealous campaign for traffic reform in Cleveland history. Prior to Ness's appointment, the city had been ranked by the National Safety Council as the second worst city in America for traffic-related deaths and injuries; only Los Angeles topped Cleveland's average of nearly 250 fatalities a year. Almost a quarter of the victims were pedestrians. "Cleveland's number one killer is the automobile," Ness was quoted as saying. "We must reduce the slaughter going on in our streets."

Almost single-handedly, Ness set out to salvage the crumbling municipal system of traffic control. He brought sweeping reforms to a traffic division known among policemen as Siberia, where the least competent cops were sent. Ness reversed that philosophy by cleaning out the undesirables and replacing them with officers with favorable records. Among the changes he fought for in the department and in the courts were on-the-spot examination of suspected drunk drivers and immediate arrest of those found intoxicated; severe disciplinary action for any officer caught taking bribes and for any officer discovered fixing tickets for friends, relatives, or public officials; the establishment of a court that handled only traffic cases; harsher penalties for violators who failed to pay fines or appear in court; arrest warrants for drivers guilty of multiple unresolved offenses; and tougher automobile inspections to reduce accidents due to improper vehicle care.

Ness was also the major force behind the creation of the Accident Prevention Bureau, which promoted traffic safety through a vigorous campaign for public awareness of responsible driving and the dangers of jaywalking. In 1938, over nine thousand public addresses were made in and around the city, with eighty thousand posters displayed and more than a million pieces of literature distributed. Safety contests that pitted the city's wards against each other were introduced, and a solemn service commemorating those who had died in traffic accidents was conducted in Public Square. Ness enlisted the aid and sponsorship of newspapers, radio stations, merchants, and various civic groups for his saturation campaign.

Yet another Ness-inspired project was the Cleveland Emergency Patrol. In an era when ambulances were mere shuttles to the nearest hospital and when paramedics were unheard of, Ness introduced a unit of twelve trucks manned by pairs of police officers specially trained in first aid and equipped with the latest lifesaving instruments. The vehicles were assigned to specific geographical areas and were constantly on patrol, and they were able to reach an accident site anywhere in the city within two minutes.

The fruit of Ness's reforms was nothing short of spectacular. In 1938, traffic-related deaths dropped to 130, qualifying Cleveland (along with Milwaukee) to be recognized by the National Safety Council for the greatest reduction in automobile accidents and fatalities. The following year, traffic deaths dropped to 115, and Cleveland was awarded the title of "safest city in the U.S.A."

Of all his colorful achievements, Ness later confessed that "this is the work of which I'm the proudest." The public seemed to agree. Director Ness was praised for his leadership near and far. He was invited to share his formula for success at speaking engagements across the country. National magazines paid handsomely for a series of articles he wrote on public safety.

Money was also saved as a result of Ness's efforts. Local insurance rates dropped as much as 50 percent, saving the Cleveland community an estimated $3.5 million over the course of a single year. At the same time, revenue from traffic fines almost doubled. Ness used his influence with the mayor and the city council to have a large chunk of the cash put back into the police department. Since becoming safety director, Ness had noted the need for improvement in the areas of mobilization and communication, but he had until then lacked the necessary funds. Police vehicles, Ness claimed, were too few and too old, and they were embarrassingly ill-equipped for a city of Cleveland's size and needs. The department's vehicles did not have two-way radios, and communication between precincts, let alone with other cities, was poor at best.

In December of 1938, Ness unveiled a fleet of thirty-two tricolor Ford squad cars and thirty Harley-Davidson motorcycles. Each was equipped with a modern RCA two-way radio system. Ness himself designed and instituted a patrol system that consolidated the communications of the entire department in a single nerve center at Central Station. The new system provided the public with a single number to phone for police assistance. By increasing the number of police vehicles on the streets and assigning each to a specific zone, any call could be answered within sixty seconds. Ness also introduced a new teletype system that provided Cleveland police with immediate exchange with other cities.

There were a critical few, as always, who denounced the director's advancements as a frivolous waste of taxpayers' money. In particular, they ridiculed Ness's new squad cars, which were painted a garish combination of red, blue, and light cream. ("And if you cannot see them coming a mile away," commented the *Plain Dealer*, "it will be because you are blind.") But if the colors marked an attempt by the safety director to enhance police visibility, then they worked. Suddenly, wherever one turned on Cleveland streets, it seemed that the new squad cars were cruising past, making citizens feel safer and criminals more uncomfortable. Statistics also vindicated the costly improvements Ness instituted. In a single year, overall crime diminished by 38 percent and robberies by an impressive 50 percent.

While Ness's triumphs as safety director won him a resurgence of favorable publicity, his personal life kept him at the center of controversy. Still boyishly handsome at thirty-six, Ness was suddenly the city's most eligible bachelor and one of its most provocative figures. It had become a nightly ritual for the safety director to make the rounds of Cleveland night spots with his friends, drinking and dancing until the early morning hours. Such behavior by a public official—especially the number one representative of law and order in the city—had tongues wagging. Ness's critics tried to make the most of the situation, some implying that the former Prohibition agent was a drunk. On the contrary, Ness's friends admitted that Eliot often sipped drinks all night, but they insisted that he rarely showed any effects.

There was also a good deal of gossip about his womanizing. Since his divorce, Ness had dated frequently, and he seemed to find an array of young ladies attracted by his charm, his gregarious nature, and his good looks. But the affairs never lasted long, one woman even suggesting that Ness lacked "the essentials" to keep a relationship going. Nevertheless, by the summer of 1939, he had settled into a steady romance with twenty-seven-year-old Evaline McAndrew, an attractive, honey-haired fashion illustrator and former model originally from Union City, Ohio. Evaline had spent two years studying at the Art Institute in Chicago, where, rumors claimed, she and Ness first met.

Very little of the scandalous talk was ever printed in Cleveland, largely because Ness's closest after-hours companions were newsmen like Ralph Kelly at the *Plain Dealer* and Clayton Fritchey at the *Press*. They were good friends who remained convinced of Ness's integrity and who sensed that since his separation and divorce, Ness had been a lonely man who needed to unwind from the stress of his job. The bright lights, the music, the drinking, and the women seemed to help. Still, there were a few who cautioned the director to slow down or even halt his nightly excursions. Ness, however, didn't appear to mind the gossip.

By spring, the Torso investigation had reached another standstill. Other cases were given priority, and only Merylo remained engaged full-time in the search for the Butcher. Many of the Homicide detectives, having exhausted every lead imaginable, could not conceive how their indefatigable colleague kept coming up with avenues to investigate. Merylo was perhaps not as resourceful as he was determined. When his singular dedication to the case was once described as an obsession, Merylo had reportedly responded, "I'm just a cop doing my job." But privately, he was pleased at being recognized as the foremost authority on the Torso murders.

Merylo seemed to be willing to go to any length in his relentless quest. He once spent six weeks investigating a suspect on "a good tip." Another time, he found a fraternity pin beneath the East Fifty-fifth Street bridge in Kingsbury Run; Merylo laboriously traced the pin to its owner, who, it turned out, had been at the bridge for a valid reason. In a case where there were almost no clues or solid leads, Merylo played his hunches and long shots. In April of 1939, he arrested a man he came across in a Scovill Avenue beer parlor simply because "he didn't look right." The man, it was revealed, was a Santa Monica, California, attorney who had recently forsaken his practice, his wife, and his child to become a hobo. But he was not the Torso Murderer.

Like any good cop, Peter Merylo spent the majority of his time tracing leads, suspects, and witnesses on the streets. At his desk or at home, he sifted through police and medical reports, reexamined statements, studied criminal files of possible suspects, and read books on serial killings, criminal psychology, and sexual perversion. In contrast to Coroner Gerber and others, Merylo was convinced that the Butcher was a sexual psychopath, possibly a necrophile with "a mania for headless bodies."

Merylo still retained an open mind and did not allow personal theories to interfere with his investigation. When a Third Precinct informant told him that a religious cult was responsible for the murders, Merylo explored the possibility with his customary diligence. He uncovered a wide range of unorthodox sects—blacks practicing Haitian voodoo, covens of self-proclaimed witches and warlocks, and even a Hispanic group observing some obscure, ancient Aztec religion. Each group's doctrine or rituals suggested a potential for violence.

Merylo eventually concentrated on the voodoo practitioners. He was unable to connect the single black victim, the woman tentatively identified as Rose Wallace, to any of the known sects. He did learn, however, that Edward Andrassy had attended a black church not far from Kingsbury Run several months before his death. It was an upstanding, orthodox denomination, and though Merylo never found a satisfactory explanation for why Andrassy had attended church there, there was nothing to suggest that the congregation dabbled in the occult. Merylo investigated Andrassy's black acquaintances, including a former inmate at the workhouse who had reportedly been a close friend. He also tracked down a number of Flo Polillo's black companions, but none emerged as suspects. In the end, Merylo had to scrap the religious theory as another intriguing possibility that lacked supporting evidence.

Early that summer, Merylo discovered he was not alone in his search for the Torso Murderer. His informants in the Roaring Third reported that a private detective and some county deputies were conducting their own investigation. The street talk Merylo tapped into claimed that the other investigators were closing in on a suspect.

To that point, there had been little involvement by county authorities in the Torso case. The repeated appeals by Ness and other municipal officials for a cooperative effort, or at least some assistance, had in fact elicited some rude responses. County Sheriff Martin L. O'Donnell, the successor to Honest John Sulzman, made it clear on several occasions that since each of the victims had been found inside the city, he considered it a Cleveland problem. O'Donnell explained that his department had neither the men nor the money to join in the hunt for the Mad Butcher.

The furor following the lakeside discoveries had forced O'Donnell to soften his stand. Chief Deputy Sheriff John J. Gillespie and Deputy Sheriff Paul McDevitt, two of O'Donnell's favorite officers, were put on the case, but both were laden with too many other duties to mount an effective investigation. Eventually, a private detective, Lawrence J. "Pat" Lyons, had been hired by the sheriff's department to work on the Torso murders for the county.

Lyons was well known to Cleveland lawmen, and he was generally respected for his investigative talents. He had worked closely with police on some of the city's most famous cases. Once, his evidence had cleared a convicted killer; another time, he had provided the proof needed to arrest a temporarily detained murder suspect who would have otherwise been released. Lyons looked like he had stepped from the pages of a Raymond Chandler novel, a muscular, gritty man in his mid-forties with jet black hair and a thick mustache who was always chewing on a fat, cheap cigar.

Each week, Lyons reported his progress to Chief Deputy Gillespie. During his first few months, Lyons had encountered the same dead ends and frustrations as the metropolitan officers, his steps always returning to the overcrowded streets of the Third Precinct. Eventually, Lyons took a room in the area, spending both his nights and days picking up information throughout the region.

It had been almost nine months before Lyons's tenacity paid off. The detective informed Gillespie that he had found a tavern on the corner of East Twentieth and Central where each of the identified victims—Andrassy, Flo Polillo, and Rose Wallace—had been frequent patrons. The clue seemed monumental, since it was the first time any investigator had been able to connect the three to a common hangout. Was this where the Torso Murderer picked up his victims?

Over the next few weeks, Lyons had become a fixture at the tavern, scrutinizing the employees and the regulars and inquiring about any strange behavior. The clientele was a sad, destitute lot— a blind pencil salesman, a legless man on relief, a number of aging prostitutes barely able to scrape together enough change for a couple of drinks. Some patrons spoke of a character named Frank, another regular who reportedly possessed a volatile temper and who often boasted of his prowess with knives. Lyons's suspicions had been further aroused when he checked around the neighborhood and heard more about Frank's unsavory reputation.

Further investigation had revealed the man to be Frank Dolezal, a short, burly, Bohemian immigrant of fifty-two with a squat, powerful build, iron gray hair, and a bull neck. A bricklayer by trade, Dolezal experienced long stretches of unemployment between jobs. Lyons discovered that Dolezal had worked in a slaughterhouse for three months some sixteen years earlier. Dolezal had also been seen with Flo Polillo in the weeks preceding her death. Though Dolezal had no criminal record, the more Lyons learned about him the more he was convinced that he had found a prime candidate for the Torso murders. A fruit dealer near the tavern informed Lyons that Dolezal carried knives and often threatened to use them on people who angered him. A neighbor reported that Dolezal had once hurled a knife at a woman.

Dolezal's antisocial conduct was hardly convincing evidence in itself. Such activities were not uncommon in the Roaring Third. Lyons needed solid proof. He discovered that Dolezal had occupied a first-floor, four-room apartment at 1908 Central Avenue, a mere half a block from the alley where the first pieces of Flo Polillo were dumped. Searching the premises with Gillespie and Deputy McDevitt, Lyons found some dark stains in the cracks of the bathroom floor. He took a sample to his brother, G. V. Lyons, a chemist, who declared that the scrapings were human blood.

O'Donnell and his deputies began to think that Lyons had stumbled upon something. Still, more evidence was needed to warrant an arrest. The suspect and his current address—a second-floor apartment at 2491 East Twenty-second—were placed under surveillance. Lyons, Gillespie, and McDevitt returned to Dolezal's old residence and questioned his former neighbors. Lyons later reported to newsmen, "We managed to uncover some startling facts. We found that Mrs. Polillo had lived with Dolezal for some time. We also learned that the bricklayer had on occasion visited Mrs. Wallace. One informant told us of having seen Dolezal and Mrs. Polillo together on the evening of January 24, 1936."

Not only had Flo Polillo and Rose Wallace been seen with Dolezal, but neighbors also reported having observed a tattooed sailor and a man resembling Edward Andrassy visiting Dolezal's apartment. An informant told the investigators that Dolezal engaged in homosexual activities. One source claimed that Dolezal was in the habit of hanging around Public Square and inviting vagrants back to his apartment. The deputies watching the suspect confirmed that fact, reporting that they had followed Dolezal to Public Square one evening and observed him "accosting strangers." The county officers had realized that a major part of their information was little more than gossip, but taken collectively, it amounted to an impressive mass of evidence against Frank Dolezal. With each day, the investigators had grown more certain they were on the right track.

Then, on Wednesday morning, July 5, 1939, Deputy McDevitt burst into O'Donnell's office. "We got trouble, Sheriff," he reportedly announced in an urgent tone. "Merylo's been sniffing around. . . . He's been checking up on me, trying to find out what I've been working on. He even called at my home the other night when I wasn't there. I think the city boys know we're on to something."

The sheriff called in Lyons, Gillespie, and others working on the case. After a lengthy discussion, it was decided that the suspect should be arrested before the municipal officers could intervene and steal the show. At six o'clock that evening, Gillespie and a pair of deputies quietly placed Frank Dolezal under arrest.

A diligent search of Dolezal's current apartment produced four butcher knives, two of which appeared to be bloodstained. There was also a notebook containing a list of twenty-five names, some with addresses as far away as Ontario, California. Lyons suggested that it might be a list of Torso victims, though it did not include the names of Edward Andrassy, Flo Polillo, and Rose Wallace.

While the investigators' suspicions were further increased, they still had nothing that could be regarded as conclusive evidence. Sheriff O'Donnell realized that if they were to make the arrest stick, they needed a confession. Behind the gray walls of the Cuyahoga County Jail, O'Donnell and County Detective Harry Brown took turns interrogating Dolezal in the hope of obtaining an admission of guilt.

Initially, the Dolezal arrest generated little interest. Suspects in the Torso case had been picked up left and right over the past three years, always with the same disappointing results. Late on

Friday afternoon, July 7, the sheriff's department announced "a major breakthrough in the Torso case." City newsmen, many of them eager to get to their weekend plans, didn't seem enthusiastic as they arrived at the county jail and filed into the outer offices. Then Sheriff O'Donnell entered and dropped the bombshell. "Boys," he proudly declared, "we have a signed confession to one of the Torso murders."

Flashbulbs popped as the sheriff told the story. The suspect, Frank Dolezal, had been subjected to rigorous questioning since his arrest. O'Donnell himself had supervised the interrogation that morning when certain significant details had begun to emerge. Dolezal had admitted an acquaintance with all of the identified victims. Andrassy had been an occasional drinking buddy, while Polillo and Wallace had each visited his apartment many times. Dolezal had also acknowledged a quarrel with Polillo just two nights before her dismembered parts were found in the alley behind the Hart Manufacturing plant, which was only half a block from the apartment Dolezal occupied at the time.

Since that admission placed Dolezal with a Torso victim at about the time of her death near the place where her remains turned up, O'Donnell had pressed for more details. Dolezal had reportedly explained, "We were in my room drinking Friday night. She had two drinks. I had two drinks. She was all dressed up and wanted to go out. She wanted some money. She grabbed for ten dollars I had in my pocket. I argued with her because she had tried to take some money from me before. But I didn't kill her. I didn't kill anybody."

At that point, O'Donnell had decided to call a noon recess. After lunch, the interrogation had been resumed by Detective Brown, who kept pounding the stocky bricklayer with questions about the fight that Friday. About two o'clock, Dolezal had broken down, confessing to Brown, "She came at me with a butcher knife."

"And you hit her?" Brown had asked.

"Yes, I hit her with my fist. She fell into the bathroom and hit her head against the bathtub. I thought she was dead. I put her in the bathtub. Then I took a knife . . . and cut off her head. Then I cut off her legs. Then her arms."

According to his confession, Dolezal had killed and dismembered Flo Polillo between two o'clock and three o'clock in the morning. Dolezal claimed he had next carried some of the body parts and the victim's coat and shoes to the alley, where he placed them against the rear of the Hart building. Close to four o'clock, he had tossed the head, lower legs, and left arm into a basket and carried them to the lakefront near East Forty-ninth Street. He had then crawled on the ice until he reached the breakwater, where he cast the pieces into the open lake beyond. He had burned the rest of Polillo's clothing.

After furnishing the details of the confession, O'Donnell and his men led the reporters into another room to view the prisoner. Dolezal sat motionless in his wrinkled, perspiration-soaked shirt, his face stubbled with a two-day beard, his hands dangling limply in front of him, his eyes glassy and wide as he glared at the newsmen snapping his picture.

The next day, Clevelanders studied the photos of Dolezal with his crazed stare and read the story of the confession. There seemed little doubt that the psychopath who had terrorized the city was finally behind bars.

An editorial in the July 9 *Plain Dealer* stated, "As the matter stands . . . it appears Sheriff O'Donnell and his staff have performed a major task in crime detection. The Cleveland police, at work on the torso case steadily for many months, seem to have had victory snatched from under their noses.

"It is too early to say," the editorial continued. "It is hoped O'Donnell has the right man in custody. When the person responsible for the torso butcherings is finally caught breathing will be a little easier in the community."

Merylo was livid.

The arrest of Dolezal by county officers who had worked part-time on the case for less than a year was a major embarrassment for the entire city police force and for its ace manhunter in particular. Things looked even worse when it was revealed that Merylo had questioned Dolezal a year earlier while checking acquaintances of Rose Wallace's. Merylo had not considered Dolezal a suspect then, and neither did he now. He bitterly denounced the sheriff's methods, the so-called evidence, the confession, everything. Dolezal,

Merylo insisted, had either been forced or fooled into making his statement.

At first, as the news of Dolezal's apparent guilt swept through the city, Merylo stood alone in his criticism of the county officers. Eliot Ness said that the confession was "the most interesting development since the murders began." In his usual diplomatic style, Ness told newsmen, "The sheriff is to be commended for his investigation. The leads he has uncovered will, of course, be followed up to see what possible connection the Polillo case may have with any other. My department and I stand ready to make available to the sheriff any information or facilities that he might feel would be of assistance." Chief Matowitz, Inspector Sweeny, Sergeant Hogan, and the other Torso hunters among the police each echoed somewhat grudgingly the safety director's congratulations and his pledge to aid O'Donnell and his men.

Ralph Kelly, the *Plain Dealer*'s political editor, observed that the Dolezal arrest was more than a case of county lawmen showing up their city counterparts; it was also a positive event for the opponents of Mayor Burton. Kelly wrote, "Democrats were particularly jubilant that the O'Donnell triumph, if it remains a triumph through the intervening weeks, was scored in a field which has been in recent years reserved for Safety Director Eliot Ness, whose activities have remained one of Burton's greatest political strengths."

In an interview with Kelly, O'Donnell stated, "I didn't have any politics in mind at all. I thought if anyone could solve these terrible murders it should be done for the sake of the community." Still, it could not be denied that the Democratic sheriff had greatly enhanced his position in his party while providing a major embarrassment for a Republican administration that relied heavily on the colorful exploits of Ness.

Over the weekend, evidence against Dolezal continued to mount. A twenty-two-year-old woman came forward alleging that only a week earlier, the bricklayer had attempted to murder her. "I was in Dolezal's room," she reportedly told the sheriff, "when he came at me with a knife. I jumped out of a second-story window to get away from him. The heel of one of my shoes was broken when I landed." The woman displayed the shoe as proof of her story. Most found the tale incredible, especially the woman's claim that a leap from a second-story window had resulted in only a busted heel. But O'Donnell stated that the story only increased his suspicions "that Dolezal was connected with other torso murders."

Dolezal, however, refused to speak about the other killings. "He flies off the handle when those other murders are mentioned," O'Donnell told reporters. "We're going to continue our questioning. There are still many things we want him to tell us."

And it was precisely at that point that the case against Frank Dolezal began to unravel at an irreversible pace. To the chagrin of the county officers, it was revealed that Dolezal originally claimed that his quarrel with Flo Polillo had occurred on Saturday night, not Friday night. Upon examining the remains of Flo Polillo early Sunday afternoon, Coroner Pearse had determined that she had been dead at least twenty-four hours. It was only after the sheriff's men informed him of that fact that Dolezal had changed his story.

More weaknesses in Dolezal's confession came to light. He had told his captors that after dismembering the body, he had deposited some of the remains, along with the coat and the shoes, in the alley near his home; he had then tossed the head, lower legs, and left arm into the lake. But none of the victim's clothing had been discovered in the alley. Neither had the upper half of the torso, which was later found with the lower legs and the left arm in a backyard off Orange Avenue. Dolezal had said nothing about discarding any of the body parts there.

In light of what appeared to be serious discrepancies, O'Donnell continued to insist that they had "the right man" and that they only needed Dolezal to straighten out some minor details. The result was another lengthy interrogation and yet another confession, this one conforming more closely to the known facts. Dolezal this time stated that he had disposed of only the head—the lone missing part of the victim—in Lake Erie.

Merylo criticized the new confession as vehemently as he had the first, and now others joined him. Dolezal's language appeared curiously erratic as it was recorded. He rambled aimlessly in places, while elsewhere he was notably precise, suggesting that he had been coached in his statements. As Merylo and others pointed out, the confession amounted to little more than a rehash of the established facts. The only original part was Dolezal's preposterous claim that he had carried the head almost three miles in subzero weather from his apartment to the lakefront and then crawled across the ice to toss it into the open water.

Confronted with the absurdity of his story, Dolezal changed the details again. He had not disposed of the head in Lake Erie, he told Deputy Michael English, but had rather "poured a gallon of coal oil over it and buried it. I can take you to the spot." That afternoon, Dolezal led Sheriff O'Donnell, Detective Brown, and an assortment of deputies to a rubbish-strewn lot on East Thirty-seventh Street only a hundred yards north of the Kingsbury Run pool, where the pieces of "No. 6" had been discovered. The county officers dug for over an hour at the spot designated by Dolezal but found nothing. A few hours later, Dolezal took his captors to a construction site on East Twenty-sixth Street near the lakefront, claiming that he had buried the head "twenty feet down." Again the area was excavated, and again nothing was found. Merylo and others publicly chuckled as the sheriff and his men were led around the city in search of the missing head.

On July 10, O'Donnell escorted his suspect to the East Cleveland police station, where Dolezal was subjected to a lie detector test. The polygraph indicated that Dolezal answered truthfully when he said he had murdered Flo Polillo. On the other hand, his testimony concerning disposal of the head was regarded as inconclusive. Apparently, Dolezal registered positive to each of the versions to which he had confessed. He was not asked about any of the other Torso murders. "At this point," O'Donnell commented, "we are only interested in the Polillo case."

For the first time, Coroner Gerber spoke out about the Dolezal investigation. Though a Democrat and a county officeholder, Gerber joined Merylo and the other municipal officers in criticizing O'Donnell's handling of the case. Gerber stated that it was ridiculous to disregard the other Torso victims, since the one inescapable fact about the murder series was that all twelve killings were the work of the same man. "If Dolezal is not the Torso slayer," Gerber said, "then he had no hand in the killing of Mrs. Polillo."

In the midst of all this, on the evening of July 10, Dolezal attempted to hang himself in his jail cell. The noose broke, and according to the sheriff's account, Dolezal fell against a bench, injuring his side. The act of a guilty conscience? Some thought so. But there were also rumors circulating that the prisoner was being mistreated. On July 11, the American Civil Liberties Union lodged a complaint with the sheriff's office—Dolezal, after six days behind bars, had not yet been charged. O'Donnell immediately arraigned the suspect before a justice of the peace on a charge of first-degree murder in the death of Flo Polillo.

It wasn't until the following day, July 12, that an attorney, Fred P. Soukup, was secured as Dolezal's defense council. After visiting Dolezal in jail, Soukup informed the press that his client had fully retracted the confession. Dolezal insisted that he had been blindfolded, tied to a chair, thrown to the concrete floor, and beaten until he told the officers what they demanded to hear. O'Donnell and his men denied the allegations, but their credibility had suffered greatly by that point. It diminished even further when Dr. Enrique E. Ecker, a pathologist at Western Reserve University, tested the so-called bloodstains found in Dolezal's former apartment and announced that they were not blood. The case that had been crumbling at the edges suddenly began to crack down the middle. The *Plain Dealer* observed, "The glamour of Sheriff O'Donnell's achievement in capturing the 'torso killer' and getting his written confession fades as more light is turned on it."

On July 17, a preliminary hearing was convened before Justice of the Peace Myron J. Penty. Dolezal was escorted by O'Donnell and Gillespie. He took his place beside Soukup at the defense table, staring at the floor and occasionally burying his face in his hands. Coroner Gerber and Sergeant Hogan sat together in the gallery as interested spectators. After a long and confusing debate, the murder charge was reduced to manslaughter, since it was Dolezal's admission of murder in drunken self-defense that remained the county's main piece of evidence.

Five weeks passed. Dolezal remained in the county jail, a despondent figure kept separate from the other prisoners and watched constantly after a second bungled attempt at suicide. On the outside, the sheriff's men continued their investigation, still insisting that Dolezal was the Mad Butcher. Chief Deputy Sheriff Gillespie informed the press that new evidence against Dolezal in the Polillo case was gradually being amassed. The sheriff's department, Gillespie hinted, was also close to linking Dolezal to another Torso murder, presumably that of Rose Wallace.

The county's ongoing investigation received almost no publicity. The interest of both the press and the public had greatly waned since the charge against Dolezal was reduced to manslaughter. Besides, Clevelanders, along with the rest of the world, were focusing their attention on the tumultuous events in Europe. The Nazi juggernaut stood poised to invade Poland, and the entire globe seemed ready to go to war.

August 24 began as a routine Thursday at the Cuyahoga County Jail. Deputy Sheriffs Hugh Crawford and Adolph Schuster were assigned to prisoner supervision, which included, among many other duties, keeping a watchful eye on Frank Dolezal. According to the two deputies, the usually lethargic bricklayer seemed "in good spirits" that day. Following lunch, the prisoners were allowed visitors, a monotonous routine for Crawford and Schuster that required them to take turns ushering visitors in and out of the meeting rooms and prisoners in and out of their cells. Dolezal was usually visited by his lawyer, his younger brother, Charles, or his priest from Our Lady of Lourdes Church, but he had no callers that day. At quarter of two, Schuster was escorting some visitors out; Crawford suddenly realized that another prisoner's visiting time was over, and he left the cell block to bring the prisoner back. According to the official report, Crawford was gone approximately three minutes.

When he returned, he found Dolezal's stocky body dangling against the bars of his cell. Dolezal was limp, his knees bent, his tongue protruding, his eyes open but glassy; his noose had been fashioned from strips of cleaning rags tied together and fastened to a low-hanging hook on the ceiling. Crawford's shouts brought Sheriff O'Donnell and Assistant Chief Jailer Archie Burns racing to the scene. Crawford fumbled with the keys and finally got the cell door open. Burns cut the noose with O'Donnell's knife. O'Donnell and Crawford laid Dolezal on the floor. One of the safety director's emergency teams arrived within minutes and desperately attempted to revive the prisoner, but their efforts failed. Frank Dolezal was dead.

Later that afternoon, Soukup arrived at the jail to criticize the sheriff and his officers in full view of newsmen. The lawyer said that his client had "complained other prisoners taunted him and deputy sheriffs called him 'names.' I had a hunch something like this would happen before Dolezal ever came to trial. What kind of jail are you running, anyway? I thought you were keeping a twenty-four-hour watch on him!"

"We were," responded Chief Deputy Sheriff Charles M. Tylicki. "We tried to watch him all the time."

"Oh, I suppose you gave him all the protection you could," Soukup said.

Since it was plain that Dolezal's death was a suicide and that no criminality was involved, Coroner Gerber announced that there was no need for an autopsy. An immediate protest was raised by Soukup and others, including Dolezal's brother and sister. It was insisted that there be not only an autopsy but an inquest as well. Soukup claimed that there were certain discrepancies that needed to be examined. Chief among them was how the five-foot-eight Dolezal had managed to hang himself from a hook only five feet, seven inches from the ground. William E. Edwards of the Cleveland Crime Commission agreed that the Dolezal case should not be closed without further inquiry. As he put it, "In view of all the street corner rumors and other reports of brutal treatment of Dolezal, I think it only fair to the sheriff and the public to make as thorough an investigation as possible to ascertain the truth or falsity of these reports."

The next day, Friday, Gerber performed the autopsy assisted by his pathologist, Dr. Strauss, and by Dr. Harry Goldblatt, a professor of pathology at Western Reserve University's medical school. Their findings, formally announced at an inquest presided over by Gerber on the morning of Saturday, August 26, raised more questions than they answered. Frank Dolezal had died from asphyxiation. What was startling was the coroner's conclusion that Dolezal must have dangled in his cell anywhere from twelve to fifteen minutes. Gerber's estimate sharply contradicted Deputy Crawford's claim that no more than three minutes had elapsed while the prisoner was unattended.

Though grave doubts were cast upon the story supplied by the county lawmen, there was no way to prove how long Dolezal had been left alone. The critical point Gerber wished to emphasize was that even had the suspect hung for ten minutes, he could have been saved had Crawford immediately cut him down instead of calling others to the scene first. According to the county officers, Dolezal had still been breathing when he was cut down, but he had died before the emergency squad could supply him with oxygen. Had the lawmen attempted to administer mouth-to-mouth resuscitation or chest massage? "No," O'Donnell replied. "We thought the rescue team would arrive in time." The series of obvious blunders by the county officers was declared "unfortunate" and even "inexcusable" by Gerber.

But the coroner had an even bigger bombshell to drop at the inquest. The autopsy had also revealed that Dolezal had suffered six fractured ribs one to two months before his death. That discovery appeared to be a powerful corroboration of Dolezal's claim that he had been physically abused by county officers intent on obtaining his confession, a charge that O'Donnell and his staff had angrily denied for more than a month.

Soukup supplied a detailed account of the alleged abuses his late client had reported to him. Since he was blindfolded, Dolezal had been unable to see his assailants, but he had been certain he recognized the voice of one of them, Chief Jailer Michael F. Kilbone. Kilbone was not present, but most of the newsmen knew him; Kilbone was one of the county officers most delighted in the Dolezal case, having boasted that he was the man who stood guard over the Torso Murderer.

Dolezal was "constantly in fear of what they might do to him," Soukup continued. Responding to the speculation that Dolezal might have been injured before he was taken into custody, Soukup pointed out that Dolezal had been working as a bricklayer almost to the very moment he was arrested. "It is absurd," he insisted, "to imagine Dolezal could have done the work he did if he had received the fractures to his ribs before he went to jail."

Patrolman Frank Vorall, the husband of Dolezal's youngest sister, testified that on the several occasions he had visited his brother-in-law in jail, Dolezal had spoken of the beatings he endured at the hands of county officers. Vorall was followed by a doctor who had examined the prisoner on July 11, the day after the first attempted suicide. The doctor reported that Dolezal's chest had been taped and that there were noteworthy bruises on his left arm and right eye. Dolezal had complained that his left side ached terribly, and the doctor had prescribed some pain relievers.

County Detective Harry Brown gave an account of the questioning that had led to Dolezal's initial confession. With an indignant voice, Brown claimed that the bricklayer had been "treated like any other prisoner. If anyone had an opportunity to beat him it was me. I certainly never touched him." While Brown was adamant that there had been no physical abuse of the suspect, it was revealed for the first time in the course of his testimony that considerable pressure had been placed on Dolezal to confess. From the time Dolezal was arrested at six o'clock on the evening of July 5, he had not been allowed to sleep until nine o'clock on the evening of July 7.

Finally, Sheriff O'Donnell was examined. "Dolezal was never subjected to any violence," he stated. "I have always instructed my deputies never to strike a prisoner except in self-defense. He confessed to murder July 7, so why should there have been any violence?" O'Donnell insisted that Dolezal's injuries had resulted from his first attempt at suicide. "Dolezal said he hurt himself when the noose slipped and he fell to the floor, striking a bench. He promised me, after the second attempt, never to try suicide again. We did all we could to keep him from committing suicide."

As the questioning continued, it became evident that many present had serious doubts about the sheriff's claims. William Edwards, one of the most vocal in the room, interjected regularly with accusations. After one of Edwards's outbursts, Deputy Tylicki, in a voice loud enough to be heard by all, called him a "publicity seeker." Edwards shot up from his seat and responded with the challenge, "If this is going to be a fight of personalities, I'm going to take my coat off and make a real fight of it." A shouting match ultimately erupted between the county lawmen and their accusers before Gerber, rapping his gavel, managed to restore order.

With mounting anger, O'Donnell finished his testimony by declaring, "We treated the man too well. We have nothing to hide. Any and all investigations in the past on alleged beatings in the jail have led to no findings whatever by the investigating body. Dolezal must have been afraid to face the grand jury. I'm sure we had the right man. We did all we could in the case. We got a confession from him and we were close to tying him up with another of the Torso murders. We did everything we could to prevent him from committing suicide. He was in good spirits. We never bothered him at all."

In the end, the inquest resolved almost nothing. The sheriff and his men could be accused of a certain degree of negligence, but specific misconduct that might have either motivated or prevented Dolezal's suicide could not be proven. Their conduct was not deemed criminal.

Editorialists for both the *Press* and the *Plain Dealer* let loose with a barrage of criticism aimed at the sheriff's department. The *Press* was the harsher, charging that the county officers had completely bungled the case in their zeal to "scoop the city police." It was doubtful, the editorial declared, that Dolezal could have been convicted of manslaughter in the Polillo case, let alone connected to other Torso victims. In conclusion, the *Press* observed, "It may sometimes appear that holding a man without communication and hammering his ribs is a shortcut to the truth, but actually this kind of procedure usually leads not to the truth but to confusion, as in this instance."

The Dolezal affair had begun by offering Clevelanders hope of a solution to the Torso murders, but it ended by offering only additional mysteries—Crawford's three-minute absence, Dolezal's battered ribs, the motive behind the suicide. The single issue about which there seemed almost no doubt was Dolezal's alleged guilt. Few in Cleveland believed that the Mad Butcher had died by his own hand in a county jail cell. The twelve Torso murders remained officially unsolved. Merylo, at his own request, remained assigned full-time to the case.

But if Dolezal was not the Torso Murderer, then who was? And where was he? A full year had passed since the last victims were discovered, and many sensed that a chapter in the Torso case had come to an end with the death of Frank Dolezal. After a while, the mere fact that no more bodies turned up in Cleveland prompted some to suggest that Dolezal really had been the killer, a belief that gained a little momentum as time passed. But most people knew better. As Coroner Gerber later declared, "The arrest of Dolezal didn't stop the murders; they had already stopped."

That fall, Eliot Ness began to reminisce about his gangbusting days in Chicago. The people who knew him best took notice of Ness's sudden openness in discussing exploits of the Untouchables he had formerly downplayed.

The suicide of Frank Dolezal may have helped to revive his memories. Eight years earlier, Ness had aided in the arrest of Tony Napoli, a suspected Capone triggerman Ness hoped to groom as an informant but who instead took his own life in a Cook County Jail cell, another instance of a promising opportunity squandered at the end of a hand-fashioned noose.

More likely, it was the recent news reports about Capone himself that had inspired Ness's nostalgia. After serving seven years of his eleven-year sentence in three federal institutions including Alcatraz, Capone was about to win his freedom. Since January, he had been an inmate at Terminal Island near Los Angeles, a comparatively comfortable and humane prison. Capone had become a different man in the latter days of his incarceration. His body besieged and his mind deteriorated by the advanced stages of syphilis, the almighty mobster had been reduced to a harmless hulk.

Much of Capone's time was spent languishing in Terminal Island's hospital ward or wandering its corridors unhampered by the guards. During periods of lucidity, Capone expressed regret for his crimes. Once, at a prison revival service, he came forward to accept Jesus Christ as his Savior. When his release came, Capone was immediately hospitalized until he was judged well enough to retire to his Palm Island, Florida, estate in the care of his family. Rumors that Capone might return to Chicago and reassert his rule over the mobs were put to rest by his former business manager, Jake Guzik, who told reporters, "Al is nuttier than a fruitcake."

Though stories of Ness's old nemesis were playing in the media, critics took the view that Ness was looking to the past because he had grown disinterested in his role as safety director. They noted that for several months the usually active Ness had been a fixture at his city hall office. There was a grain of truth behind the accusations, but not much more. After nearly four years in his post, Ness was simply slowing down. In fact, since his divorce a year earlier, he had undergone a noticeable transition, becoming less of a workaholic and devoting more time to personal interests.

His chief interest at that time was Evaline McAndrew. Their relationship had blossomed, and only a handful of close friends were privy to the fact that they were engaged. The truth was finally revealed when Ness obtained some long overdue vacation time from his job; the couple traveled to Greenup, Kentucky, where they were married on October 14.

Back in Cleveland, the news of Ness's wedding was barely noticed. Part of the reason was that the latest development in the Torso investigation had the city buzzing. Just the previous day, October 13, a pair of railroad workers repairing rails outside New Castle had stumbled upon the nude, headless, and badly decomposed body of a young man resting on some paper in the weeds near the tracks. The victim had a short, slender build with small hands and feet and had probably been in his early to middle twenties. He had been dead about two weeks.

The murder seemed a carbon copy of the Cleveland slayings with two curious exceptions. The neck wound was jagged, indicating that the killer had used a saw or similar instrument to remove the head; a Cleveland pathologist who examined the remains confirmed that the weapon had definitely been one with serrated teeth. There was also the unusual fact that the victim's palms had been scorched. It could not be determined whether the burning had occurred before or after death. If before, lawmen theorized, the killer must have tortured his victim, something completely foreign to the Kingsbury Run Butcher, as far as existing evidence showed. If after, it most likely represented an attempt to prevent fingerprinting. Partial prints were obtained, but they failed to identify the young man.

As soon as the report reached Cleveland, Merylo set out for New Castle accompanied by David Cowles, the department's forensic expert, who had recently risen to the rank of deputy inspector. While Cowles worked with the medical examiners, Merylo joined the search in the Murder Swamp for the missing head and clothing. After dark, Merylo spoke with railroad employees at the New Castle train yards. He found a lineman who claimed to have noticed a small fire shortly after ten o'clock on the evening of September 29 near the tracks where the headless corpse was soon to be found. Believing the fire to be the work of "a tramp or just some kids," the lineman had not regarded it as suspicious.

On the morning of October 19, the missing head was found in a coal hopper at West Pittsburgh, some thirty miles southeast of New Castle. A check of the car's movements revealed that it had been in the New Castle yards for several weeks before its departure on October 9. The victim had soft, handsome features with reddish brown hair neatly combed and greased into a pompadour; it was not the face of a hobo. Merylo thought that the victim looked "effeminate," reinforcing his belief that the killings were sexually motivated.

In a report presented to Ness upon the director's return from his honeymoon, Cowles stated that there were definite similarities between the latest New Castle slaying and the Cleveland murders, but he stopped short of suggesting that there were any solid facts linking the crimes. Merylo, writing in his personal notes, claimed that the murders in New Castle and Cleveland were "beyond a doubt" the work of the same maniac. Merylo returned to Cleveland convinced that the Torso Murderer was still alive, still at large, and still killing.

NINE

On May 3, 1940, a team of train inspectors at the Pittsburgh & Lake Erie Railroad yards in McKees Rocks, Pennsylvania, a small suburb on the northwest corner of Pittsburgh, began a routine check of a string of nineteen old boxcars recently arrived from Ohio and scheduled for destruction. Sliding back the door of one of the cars, the inspectors were greeted by a horrible stench. In a corner beneath a swarm of flies was a large burlap sack. It contained the rotting remains of a human being hacked into seven pieces. The head was missing.

Police were still arriving on the scene when another grisly discovery was made. Just three cars away was a second body, this one sprawled on the floor of a boxcar, stripped naked, and decapitated. Again, the head was nowhere to be found. Carved into the second victim's chest with crude, capital, five-inch letters was the word *NAZI*, the *I* ending just below the neck and the *Z* reversed. It was apparent from the great quantity of blood staining the floorboards and spattered upon the nearest wall that the victim had been killed where he was found. Next to the body was the bloody imprint of a rubber-soled boot or overshoe, size twelve. On a plank a few feet away was a circular mark in blood. Lawmen theorized that it might have been left by a peg leg or the heel of a woman's shoe. Also discovered was the crushed butt of a hand-rolled cigarette some would later insist was marijuana. Several bloodstained pages of the December 11, 1939, *Youngstown Vindicator* were found nearby.

The remaining boxcars were hastily searched. Near the end of the line, another victim was discovered, this one a woman. Like the first victim, she had been dissected at the neck, waist, hips, and shoulders, the pieces stuffed into a burlap bag. Again, only the head was missing. As with the last New Castle victim, parts of her body appeared to have been charred.

Early the next day, Cleveland lawmen arrived in McKees Rocks to assist in the investigation. The group included Assistant Safety Director Robert Chamberlin, Deputy Inspector David Cowles, and Detectives Peter Merylo and Lloyd Trunk. The gory details of the triple homicide were all too familiar. "I think it is safe to say," Merylo told reporters, "that the Mad Butcher's victims now total twenty-three."

Pittsburgh Deputy Coroner Anthony Sappo announced that all the cutting had been performed with precise strokes of a long, heavy butcher knife. The killer, Sappo said, had "a definite knowledge of surgery." The bodies were four to five months old; the victims had been killed within a couple of weeks of each other around mid-December. The advanced decomposition of the remains prevented the determination of anything but general characteristics. Each victim had been between thirty and forty years of age, dark haired, and of slightly below-average height. The woman and the dismembered man had been on the stocky side. A clump of dark brown hair, apparently ripped from the scalp of one of the missing heads, was found beside one of the bodies. Significantly, a single, short strand of blond hair was also discovered—three years earlier, Cowles had found a blond hair with the pieces of the dark-haired "No. 9." Merylo and a few others were convinced that the blond strand and the bloody footprint belonged to the killer.

The decomposed state of the remains rendered conventional fingerprinting useless. Nevertheless, an astute forensic expert in Pittsburgh managed to obtain partial prints of all three victims by photographing their fingertips and enhancing the images. A few days later, on May 10, FBI officials in Washington reported that they had identified the man with *NAZI* scrawled upon his chest as James David Nicholson, a thirty-year-old vagrant from Chicago who had been convicted and imprisoned twice for burglary. Nicholson's photograph revealed a narrow, boyishly handsome face with sleepy eyes that some found hauntingly reminiscent of Andrassy and the tattooed man.

For Merylo and the rest of the Cleveland officers, the identification seemed like a monumental development after so many nameless bodies. The investigators carefully examined the details of Nicholson's past in the hope that his movements, habits, or acquaintances would provide some clue to the identity of the killer. Nicholson had first been arrested for burglary in Pontiac, Illinois, in November of 1929 at the age of twenty. Sentenced to ten years, he had served less than half that time. He was next arrested in May of 1936 in Wisconsin on the same charge, and he was sentenced to the state prison at Waupan for one to three years. Once again a model inmate, he had been paroled after only a single year. From that point, Nicholson apparently drifted aimlessly, living as a vagrant. He had next surfaced in Greenville, South Carolina, where he was arrested for trespassing on railroad property in July of 1938. Nicholson was arrested twice more in Greenville for vagrancy, the second time on November 4, 1939. He was released ten days later with the understanding that he would leave town. Nicholson had kept his word. No one could be found who had seen the young man before his beheaded body turned up in the boxcar at McKees Rocks.

Once again, a promising lead had ended in disappointment. Nicholson's final month alive remained a blank. Officers could only speculate that he had ridden the freights and lived among the hobos up to the time he encountered his murderer. Merylo talked to as many acquaintances of the victim as he could find. A few informed him that Nicholson had been a homosexual.

"The Train of Death," as newspapers were calling it, had arrived in McKees Rocks on April 22. It had passed through New Castle on its journey but had stopped only once, at Struthers, Ohio, some fifteen miles west of New Castle. Prior to that, the string of nineteen obsolete boxcars had stood undisturbed for fifteen months in the train yards at Youngstown, Ohio. It was apparent that the murders had been committed there. A railroad worker at the Youngstown yards distinctly remembered finding articles of clothing beneath the boxcars in question the day after Christmas.

Youngstown had caught Merylo's attention a year earlier. On June 30, 1939, the skeletal remains of a woman had been discovered in a Youngstown dump. Only eighteen of the victim's bones were recovered, but it was established that she had been carefully dismembered. A pile of women's clothing was found two hundred feet away, but it hadn't helped in identifying the victim. The publicity over the Youngstown murder and Merylo's plans for checking for a connection to the Torso case had abruptly come to a halt with the arrest of Frank Dolezal on July 5.

With the permission of their superiors, Merylo and a partner traveled to Youngstown, an industrial city roughly half the size of Cleveland with major steel mills, foundries, and train yards. Disguised as vagrants, the pair rode the freights through Youngstown, Cleveland, New Castle, and Pittsburgh, mingling with the tramps and occasionally dwelling in the hobo camps. They listened intently to stories of sadistic railroad employees and various strange characters. They also attempted to locate a peg-legged tramp the hobos talked about, though Merylo seriously doubted that a man with such a handicap could be the Torso Murderer. After three weeks, Merylo and his fellow detective returned to Cleveland no closer to a solution to the case then when they had started.

In the meantime, the McKees Rocks investigation had ended in disappointment. The three heads were never found, and the two unidentified victims remained so. The triple murder joined the Cleveland and the New Castle killings in the files of the unsolved.

As it turned out, the McKees Rocks investigation was the last major assignment for Robert Chamberlin as assistant safety director. The increasing prospect of war prompted the Ohio National Guard to call in its reserve officers in the summer of 1940. Chamberlin would not return to Cleveland until after the war, and then as a decorated brigadier general. After bidding his close friend goodbye, Director Ness selected Thomas Clothey, one of his special undercover investigators, as his new assistant.

That fall, another powerful Ness ally departed Cleveland. Harold Burton had easily won reelection as mayor on November 7, 1939, but only a few months into his third term, he began to consider offering himself as a Republican candidate for the United States Senate. Retaining a strong image of independence from party constraints, Burton easily knocked off his Cincinnati-based opponent in the spring primary. He then went on to defeat Democrat John E. McSweeney in the November election. Before leaving Cleveland, Burton appointed his law director, Edward Blythin, to perform the duties of mayor for the second half of his term.

While serving in the Senate, Burton became good friends with Missouri Democrat Harry S. Truman. When Truman became president in 1945, he appointed the Ohio Republican to a vacancy on the Supreme Court. Burton remained an associate justice on the nation's highest court until 1958, when Parkinson's disease forced his retirement. He died in Washington a few years later.

The final two years that Eliot Ness served as safety director were relatively quiet and, for some, disappointing. Ness was by no means idle, but it was obvious that he no longer possessed the zest and urgency with which he had formerly approached his work. The departure of Chamberlin and Burton certainly was a major factor. It was also apparent that since marrying Evaline, Ness was spending less time on the job; the couple had become part of Cleveland society, hobnobbing with the wealthy, attending numerous social engagements, and entertaining frequently and lavishly at their new Lakewood boat house.

There were some like Alvin "Bud" Silverman at the *Plain Dealer* who complained that the safety director's extravagant lifestyle made him vulnerable to his critics and removed from the city's working-class population. But despite such criticism, Ness's charisma with the majority of local newsmen, the police force, and the general public continued intact once the furor over the Torso killings subsided.

As a result of the twenty-three indictments Ness and Prosecutor Cullitan had secured against the Mayfield Road Mob in the spring of 1939, a number of local gangland figures were beginning to come to trial. Some had plea-bargained or been caught for other crimes and were already behind bars. A few had gone underground or left the city and were being sought by lawmen. But the majority of the indicted mobsters remained calm and convinced that their lawyers would get them off.

In the months leading up to the trials, there were attempts by the mob to learn the names of the seventy witnesses Ness had recruited to testify. Ness discovered through his undercover men that a thousand dollars was being offered for names. Several identities were eventually leaked, and the wife of one witness was terrorized in her home by four gunmen. Ness responded by enlisting the aid of federal agents in increasing the protection of witnesses and their families. He then turned the tables by unleashing his own reign of terror on Cleveland's underworld, a series of raids and arrests that made it known that any harassment of witnesses would be answered tenfold. From that point on, the mobsters used the system to fight the charges.

Big Angelo Lonardo, son of the slain Big Joe Lonardo, was the first major mob figure to appear in court. A decade earlier, Big Angelo Lonardo had been acquitted of the murder of one of the Porello brothers when the principal witness abruptly left the country. But this time, and thanks largely to Ness, the witnesses implicated Lonardo as the moving force behind the city's policy rackets. The result was a two-year sentence in the Ohio State Penitentiary.

Little Angelo Scirrca, Big Angelo Lonardo's cousin, was under the same indictment. After Lonardo's conviction, Scirrca cleaned out his bank accounts and fled. Federal agents caught him in Acapulco. He was extradicted to Cleveland, where he stood trial and was sentenced to prison for five years. To add insult to injury, Scirrca was immediately deported to his native Italy upon his release.

The convictions gained wide publicity and further enhanced the stature of Ness and Cullitan. The removal of chieftains like Lonardo and Scirrca played a key role in the disintegration of the Mayfield Road Mob. Not long afterwards, Moe Dalitz and his associates moved their operations out of Cleveland, never to return. While it is tempting to suggest that Ness's uncompromising crackdown on gambling prompted the crafty Dalitz to look elsewhere, the criminal possibilities in Havana and Las Vegas were what actually drew him away. By that time, the Cleveland syndicate of which Dalitz had been the chief architect was firmly established under Al and Charlie Polizzi and the Milano brothers, mobsters who would remain beyond the reach of Ness and other Cleveland lawmen.

Ness also reopened his investigation of union racketeering in Cleveland, a project that continued to infuriate local labor leaders. The main thrust of Ness's probe was the activities of Albert Ruddy, president of the Carpenters' District Council and a powerful figure among Cleveland unions.

Ness's chief source of information about Ruddy was Harry Barrington, the man he had helped send to prison in 1937 in one of his first labor convictions. Ness made several visits to the prison farm in Mt. Vernon, Ohio, where Barrington was serving a sentence of three to fifteen years. In return for a reduction in sentence, Barrington promised to tell all he knew about corruption in the unions. (He had already supplied vital information used by Ness in building the case against Campbell and McGee.) As a bargaining agent, Barrington had once been a close associate of Ruddy's and had played a key role in attempts to elicit shakedown money from local businessmen. He had been privy to a good deal of inside information. In his talks with Ness, Barrington described Ruddy's involvement in six separate acts of extortion. In addition, Barrington claimed that Ruddy had been the man behind a 1933 bombing of a downtown laundry that refused to pay shakedown money, and he also implicated Ruddy in the murder of Albert Whitelock, a rival union boss who had been killed in his home by a twelve-gauge shotgun blast fired by an unknown assassin on May 13, 1936.

Barrington was released into the safety director's custody and stashed in a secret Cleveland hideaway. Ness then plunged into an extensive inquiry, gathering evidence to support his informant's claims. Ness found no way to corroborate Barrington's statements about the bombing and the Whitelock murder, but there were plenty of witnesses to the extortion charges, more than enough to indict Ruddy and his top henchman, Vincent Dylinski, on June 19, 1940.

Controversy surrounded the trial in late September. The old accusations portraying Ness as antiunion were resurrected, and the defense made much of the fact that the chief prosecution witness, Barrington, was a convicted blackmailer and extortionist. As usual, the newspapers stuck by Ness and praised his efforts to purge the racketeers from organized labor. When it was over, Ruddy was found guilty and received a four-year sentence.

The Ruddy investigation proved to be Ness's final campaign against crime. He remained active in his role as safety director, continuing to rejuvenate municipal departments and fight for various reforms. Toward the end of his tenure as safety director, Ness concentrated on modernizing the city's fire department, introducing a more rigorous training program for firemen and procuring new equipment like high-pressure pumpers. As the threat of war increased, Ness was the leading figure in preparing Cleveland's civil defense program. But it seemed that he had no more time for special undercover projects.

Late in 1940, Ness agreed to write a series of articles for *American City* magazine detailing his methods for combating metropolitan crime and reducing traffic accidents. Around the same time, he accepted a post as a consultant with the Federal Social Protection Program, a national public awareness campaign designed to combat venereal diseases. As part of his new duties, Ness made frequent visits to New York and Washington.

Ironically, the harshest reactions to Ness's latest venture came from the people closest to him. Most were genuinely puzzled as to why a man with Eliot's virtues—a brilliant mind, an engaging personality, a reputation for integrity—would commit his time and talents to a cause as unconventional and unrewarding as curbing the spread of social diseases. With the best of intentions, friends and supporters cautioned Ness about his involvement in the federal program, claiming that time spent away from his duties as safety director supplied his critics with ammunition to undermine him in the eyes of the public.

There was also a sizable movement among local Republicans to get Ness to run for mayor in the 1941 election. With the departure of Burton, the Republicans were searching desperately for a candidate. Many predicted that Ness's reputation in Cleveland would make him an easy winner. Ness, however, had always found politics distasteful, and it came as no surprise when he refused the offers. A number of Cleveland businessmen, many of them good friends, attempted to convince him to abandon public service altogether and enter the business world his college training had prepared him for. Some offered him positions in their companies, one promising to triple his safety director's annual salary of seventy-five hundred dollars. Others vowed to provide Ness with financial backing in a business of his own choice. Ness expressed his appreciation for the offers but ignored the advice.

The allegations that Ness had grown complacent and arrogant in his post became a sizzling topic in November of 1941, when Democrat Frank J. Lausche was elected mayor. Lausche's chief supporter was Ray Miller, the county chairman of the Democratic party, a former Cleveland mayor himself, and one of Ness's most vocal critics. There seemed little doubt that Ness's days as safety director were numbered.

But when Lausche took office and swept the Republicans out of city hall, he left Eliot Ness. Part of the reason was that Frank Cullitan, Lausche's friend and fellow Democrat, made a strong appeal to keep Ness on as safety director. Lausche had been the judge who issued Cullitan the warrant to raid the Harvard Club, and ever since Ness's colorful intervention in that affair, Lausche had been a private admirer of the safety director's crusade for law and order. Lausche was also a careful politician who realized that despite some recent failings, Ness remained a powerful figure in Cleveland with an adoring public and numerous allies among the ranks of the police, the city council, and the newspapers. Both the *Press* and the *Plain Dealer* had voiced their support for Ness, citing his remarkable record and demanding that the office of public safety director not be regarded as a political post.

On the other hand, Ness had his share of enemies in high places. Lausche's decision to retain Ness as safety director placed him in a precarious position with Ray Miller. Miller, it was revealed, had accepted huge donations from union officials with the understanding that if Lausche were elected Ness would be removed. Miller had even promised that he would go directly to J. Edgar Hoover to get "a real G-Man" to replace Ness. Despite the pressure from his fellow Democrats, Lausche stuck by his decision, and he and Miller remained bitter enemies for the next twenty years as a result.

But even with Lausche's support, Ness did not last long under the new administration. On a rainy March evening four months after the election, the safety director and his wife dined, drank, and danced with another couple at the Vogue Room in the Hollenden Hotel on Superior Avenue, one of Eliot's favorite night spots. The four were celebrating the publication of an article Ness had written for the *Annals of the American Academy of Political and Social Services* on the national menace of venereal diseases. Well after midnight, the group retired to the other couple's hotel room for another lengthy session of drinking and chatting.

It was almost four-thirty when Eliot and Evaline finally departed. A frigid north wind had transformed an earlier drizzle into an icy glare. Driving along West Shoreway, their car went into a skid and smashed into an oncoming vehicle driven by twenty-one-year-old Robert Sims of East Cleveland.

Patrolman Joseph Koneval, the first officer on the scene, found Sims's car empty at the side of the highway. The driver, Koneval learned, had been taken to the hospital by a passing motorist. Sims was suffering from bruises and a wrenched neck when Koneval arrived at the hospital to speak to him. The young man gave his version of the accident and stated that the other driver had rushed over, inquired briefly about Sims's injuries, and driven away. Patrolman Koneval also discovered that the unknown driver had phoned the hospital to check on Sims's condition. Asked point-blank for his name, the man had refused to identify himself.

The mystery was swiftly solved. License plate EN-1 was as good as a name in Cleveland. The news of Ness's involvement in a hit-and-run accident rocked the city. Adding fuel to the fire were reports that Ness had been drinking in public prior to the accident. His enemies showed no mercy. The director of public safety leaving the scene of an accident? The former Prohibition agent and scourge of the Capone mob intoxicated behind the wheel?

Looking more serious than usual, Ness appeared before newsmen a few days later to give his account of the incident. He freely admitted consuming "several drinks during dinner," but he insisted he had not been drunk. "It was very slippery and the thing just happened like that," Ness told the reporters, snapping his fingers to emphasize the point.

His immediate concern had been for Evaline, as she was dazed and had the wind knocked out of her. Ness claimed that after speaking with Sims, he had driven away with the understanding that Sims would follow him to the hospital. When the young man failed to show after a short distance, Ness had returned to the scene of the accident to find Sims gone. By that time, Evaline had recovered, and she asked to be taken home instead of to the hospital. Ness had phoned the hospital from his house "to make sure the injured man was all right." He had promised to have his insurance company take care of the matter, but he had seen no reason to identify himself over the phone. "It was a very unfortunate thing all the way through," Ness stated, "but there was no attempt at evasion in any particular."

The explanation was reasonable enough to satisfy official inquiries into the accident. No charges were brought against Ness. The damage to his exalted image, however, was irreversible. Clevelanders recalled the scandal surrounding the failure of Ness's predecessor, Martin J. Lavelle, to report the accidental drowning of a young girl, and many perceived a distinct parallel in the Ness incident. The safety director's admiring public was disillusioned upon realizing that its hero was capable of bad judgment. The white knight had toppled from his perch.

It was an ideal situation for Ness's foes, an odd coalition of Democratic bosses, labor leaders, crooked cops, and assorted figures with gangland ties. Together, they put tremendous pressure on the mayor to discharge Ness. Lausche refused to fire the director outright, but he finally agreed to urge him to move on. Ness got the message. On April 30, less than two months after the accident, he submitted his resignation.

Ness's departure was a quiet, respectable affair that was barely noticed by the city that had hailed him as its champion of law and order. At the *Plain Dealer*, Phillip Porter was one of the few to look back over the past six years.

> One way in which the Ness administration has differed sharply from the others has been that he

rooted out and minimized departmental politics and when it popped up, he got tough with it. He was always several jumps ahead of the chair warmers and the connivers, and even to this day they couldn't figure him out, but spent a good deal of their time criticizing him. . . .

When Ness enters full-time federal service, an era will have ended here. We may never again achieve the heights of law enforcement and competence which have been built up during his six-year administration. It is so outstanding among American city experiences as to be a little amazing when you get away from town and begin to analyze and compare it.

When he took office, the town was ridden with crooked police and crooked labor bosses. A dozen such were sent to prison, and scores of others scared into resignation or inactivity. There were gambling hells in every block and lush casinos in the suburbs. The little joints mostly folded and finally the big joints quit when a couple of Ness' honest cops were put in the sheriff's office. The town reached such a condition of comparative purity that about all the continual critics had to complain about was occasional bingo, strip-teasers, and some policy games.

To their eternal credit, Mayors Burton and Blythin supported Ness to the limit, and Ness was allowed to have a personal staff of loyal operatives who could be depended on. To Lausche's credit, he saw the same civic value in having a guy like Ness, and he reappointed him amid the anguished screaming of unimaginative party hacks. It was natural, for Lausche as judge had co-operated and even taken the lead in rooting out the suburban gambling joints.

We'll probably never have perfection in any municipal police administration. But we have gradually achieved something as near it as any big city is ever likely to, and we ought to be grateful to Ness for it.

Over at the *Press*, Ness's close friend Clayton Fritchey, soon to leave Cleveland himself to become an editor at a New Orleans newspaper, observed the director's departure with a brief, eloquent tribute. Thanks to Ness, Fritchey wrote, "Policemen no longer have to tip their hats when they pass a gangster on the streets. . . . Labor racketeers no longer parade down Euclid Avenue in limousines bearing placards deriding the public and law enforcement in general. . . . Motorists have been taught and tamed into killing only about half as many people as they used to."

An era had indeed ended, but Clevelanders were almost too busy to notice. The world was at war. Cleveland industry was booming, helping to supply the nation's military needs. People followed the reports of the war and watched young men march off to battle. The metropolitan problems of unemployment, rampant crime, and police corruption had diminished to insignificance. Cleveland was on the threshold of a new age of prosperity. But the man who more than any other had transformed Cleveland into the "safest city in the U.S.A." no longer had a place in it.

TEN

Two months later, on the morning of June 27, 1942, three boys playing in Kingsbury Run stumbled upon the dismembered pieces of a young black woman scattered along a slope near East Sixty-ninth Street. A chill swept through the city at the thought that the psychopath who terrorized Cleveland for nearly three years had suddenly returned.

The fear was quickly dispelled. At the morgue, Coroner Gerber determined that the disarticulation had been a hack job "too crude" to even remotely resemble the work of the Torso Murderer. The killer had used a hatchet or an ax and left abundant clues. Within two hours, the victim was identified as Marie Wilson, age twenty, a known prostitute. The crime was solved in a few days. William Johnson, Marie's boyfriend, confessed to killing her during an argument in his apartment. Johnson had chopped up her corpse, packed the pieces into two suitcases, and deposited the pieces in the Run.

At the time of that brief sensation, Peter Merylo, the only Cleveland cop still working on the Torso case, was just returning from Pittsburgh, where the beheaded body of a man had been discovered near some train tracks on June 21. Though there was no solid evidence to link the Pittsburgh murder to the Cleveland killings, Merylo insisted that the pattern was the same and that they were the work of the same man. He also believed that a Pittsburgh body discovered in 1941 and a year-old skeleton found in the New Castle swamp about the same time were the work of the Mad Butcher. But the killer, if indeed it was the same man behind all the crimes, remained as elusive as ever, leaving no clues, only dismembered bodies.

Merylo's fellow detectives were convinced that he was chasing a phantom. Four years had passed since the Butcher last struck in Cleveland, and most viewed the case as ancient history. It was time, they urged Merylo, to give it up and move on to something else.

Merylo, nevertheless, remained officially assigned to the case at his own request, unwavering in his belief that the killer was still at large and still operating. Merylo's superiors in the Detective Bureau allowed him to continue, not so much in the hope of a resolution to the case as out of respect for his amazing perseverance. In his six-year hunt for the Torso Murderer, Merylo had made more than a thousand arrests, with all but a mere twenty-six suspects convicted. Over a hundred had been convicted of sex offenses; one had been convicted of murder; and the rest were a motley assortment of abortionists, illegal aliens, drug peddlers, burglars, and fences. In addition to his remarkable arrest record, Merylo had uncovered and helped destroy a white slavery operation in the city.

Even so, the fact remained that there had been no progress in the case for several years. The enormous demand for men in the armed forces had begun to deplete police personnel. Merylo's talents were needed elsewhere. On October 1, 1942, he was taken off the case and reassigned. The Torso file, encompassing some thirty-five hundred pages of material, was tucked away with the records of other unsolved cases, where it has remained dormant ever since.

Merylo had the bug worse than anyone realized. He continued to work on the case during off-duty hours. Regular assignments no longer held his interest. Shortly after the war, he retired from the force and went into business as a private detective, still devoting spare time to his search for the Butcher. "I believe this man would not stop the killing as long as he is at large, and alive," Merylo once wrote. "I will never give up my work on these Torso Murders."

Over the next few years, Merylo kept in touch with old friends and former partners, occasionally enlisting their aid in checking obscure leads or hunches. He also studied accounts of unsolved murders across the nation. Several times, he contacted police in other cities when a crime seemed to resemble the Mad Butcher's pattern.

On October 13, 1945, the headless, mutilated remains of a woman were discovered in a swamp twelve miles northwest of Pontiac, Michigan. The victim had been dead less than twenty-four hours. Merylo closely examined early reports of the murder. The pattern seemed to fit, but as it turned out, the victim did not. She was soon identified as Lydia Thompson, the forty-seven-year-old wife of a wealthy Detroit car dealer. Mrs. Thompson had last been seen alive two days earlier outside her home in suburban Orchard Lake, Michigan. Exactly how she came to be butchered in a desolate swamp many miles away remains a mystery to this day, despite an enormous investigation. But the theory that she had somehow encountered the Cleveland Butcher seems extremely unlikely. Lydia Thompson's body had been hacked up, not neatly dismembered, and the probable murder weapon, a meat cleaver, was found in the swamp a month later. Police considered her husband, Louis, the most likely suspect, especially after learning that he had spent more time in recent months with his mistress than with his wife. Lydia, it was revealed, had been indignantly aware of the relationship. Louis Thompson and his mistress were indicted for the murder over a year later, but they were eventually released for lack of evidence.

Early in the morning on January 15, 1947, police in Los Angeles were summoned to a vacant lot on South Norton Avenue. Even the most hardened veterans arriving on the scene were sickened by the sight that awaited them. A young woman, naked, horribly mutilated, and cut in half at the waist, was sprawled amid the weeds and rubbish. The halves of her body rested only a few feet apart, the lower one near the sidewalk. There were deep, vicious cuts on her face, arms, breasts, and thighs. The corners of the victim's mouth had been sliced back to the ears, leaving her with a gaping, grotesque grin. She had been dead only about seven hours. The killer had drained the blood from the remains, then carefully washed and scrubbed them clean; the medical examiners reported finding bristles embedded in the victim's flesh.

Merylo, among others, immediately perceived some startling similarities to the work of the Torso Murderer. The bisecting of the torso was a trademark of the Butcher, one he had performed on at least six of his Cleveland victims. (The decomposition of the eighth and twelfth victims had prevented pathologists from determining whether they had been so carved.) The Los Angeles coroner reported that the cutting had been skillfully executed by a person with surgical knowledge. There were abrasions on the victim's wrists and ankles, suggesting that she had been bound and held prisoner much as Andrassy and one of the Youngstown victims had apparently been. The fact that the Los Angeles victim's body had been carefully cleaned and drained of blood was another remarkable similarity. Though the Torso Murderer was not noted for the kind of ghastly mutilation performed on the Los Angeles woman, some pointed out that he had eviscerated "No. 9" and slashed the thigh of "No. 10."

But there the similarities ended. There had been no decapitation in the Los Angeles case, the one particular that linked all the victims in the Torso cycle—the Butcher's signature, if you will. The Los Angeles woman had also been tortured, and quite horribly, for hours or even days before she expired. There were bruises and cigarette burns all over the body, and the coroner was certain that the victim had been hung upside down for a time. Torture had never been associated with the Torso Murderer. In all instances, the Butcher had apparently dispatched his victims swiftly and cut them up after death.

The Los Angeles killer had carved the initials BD into the victim's right inner thigh. Detectives soon surmised that the letters stood for Black Dahlia, the victim's nickname. She was identified as Elizabeth Ann Short, age twenty-two. It was the beginning of one of the most sensational and enigmatic murder cases in the history of California, a state that has had its full share of bizarre crimes. The name Black Dahlia itself helped to ignite intense public interest in the case.

The odyssey of Elizabeth Short was a tragic and progressively sordid story. At age seventeen, she had left her home in Massachusetts and headed west in an attempt to break into motion pictures in Hollywood. But her break never came, and she had drifted among the hustlers and flesh peddlers of Santa Barbara, Long Beach, San Diego, and Los Angeles during the next five years. Her romance with a young pilot ended tragically when he was killed in the war; her lover's death marked a turning point in Elizabeth Short's brief life. For a time, she operated as an expensive call girl with a flashy lifestyle. Some of her clients were Hollywood producers who promised her movie roles, but before long she degenerated into a common street prostitute hooked on alcohol and drugs, posing for nude photos to earn extra cash and occasionally living with a lesbian lover.

Two qualities had set Elizabeth Short apart from other streetwalkers. She had been an astonishingly beautiful young woman, with lustrous black hair, blue eyes, and a milky complexion. And she had exhibited a penchant for black clothing. Her blouses, her dresses, her hosiery, her shoes, and her undergarments, as the detectives who searched her apartment found, were exclusively black. It was easy to see how Elizabeth Short had come by her nickname. She apparently relished it; there had been a tattoo of the exotic black dahlia on her left thigh that her killer viciously gouged out.

The public's fascination proved to be insatiable. Almost every newspaper in the nation devoted pages to the sad tale of Elizabeth Short, the small-town girl with the big-city dreams whose virtue was stolen and who came to a horrible end at the hands of a sadistic maniac. The story grew more intriguing as the investigation progressed. At the height of the publicity, the killer, like Jack the Ripper, contacted the press and the police, first by phone and then by mail, boasting that he would never be caught. He was right. Though at one point nearly 250 officers were working on the case, and though the investigation continued for over two decades, the Black Dahlia murder remains unsolved.

In retrospect, there seems little doubt that the investigators were greatly hindered by the incredible press coverage. The Los Angeles police were swamped with worthless information and crank calls. No fewer than thirty-five people falsely confessed to the murder. Each was disqualified for failing to describe the mutilations accurately; the police had wisely withheld certain gruesome details from the press. Much worse, there were six more Dahlia-style murders in Los Angeles before the year ended. The ominous letters BD were scrawled on one victim's breast. Though only one of the killings involved dismemberment—that of Mrs. Evelyn Winters on March 11, 1947—some of the investigators believed that at least a few, and possibly all six, had been perpetrated by the same individual. Others disagreed. Detective Harry "Red" Hansen, who remained assigned to the Black Dahlia case until he retired in 1971, was convinced that all six were copycat slayings inspired by but unrelated to the murder of Elizabeth Short.

When Merylo suggested that the Black Dahlia murder and some of the similar Los Angeles homicides that followed might have been the work of the Torso Murderer, his theory was not taken seriously by the California authorities or by anyone else. Merylo himself considered it only a possibility, though an interesting one. It should be remembered that the letter written to Police Chief Matowitz by someone claiming to be the Mad Butcher was mailed from Los Angeles. Almost everyone still doubted the letter's authenticity, but Merylo continued to keep an open mind, as was his custom. The writer had stated that he had disposed of a victim's head "in a gully on Century Blvd. between Western and Crenshaw." No remains had been found there, but interestingly enough, the site was not far from the vacant lot where the Black Dahlia's dismembered body was discarded. Was it possible that the letter writer, though very likely not the Torso Murderer, had eight years later slaughtered Elizabeth Short? Like many other questions in the case, it was one that could be raised, considered, and debated, but never answered.

What ultimately proved to be the final chapter in the Torso mystery began on July 22, 1950, with the discovery of a man's decomposed leg in a field near the Pennsylvania Railroad tracks along Cleveland's lakefront. The limb had been gnawed by an animal, presumably a dog that had dragged it into the open. Two hundred feet away, behind a factory on East Twenty-second Street, police found the torso, both arms, and the other leg of the victim beneath some steel girders. Discovered with the remains were pages from a year-old newspaper and pages 457 and 458 of the Cleveland phone directory, which contained listings for the letter *K*. A search of the area produced some ragged clothing that might have belonged to the victim, including a pair of pants with a "lucky coin" in the pocket. The head was found four days later under some wooden beams only twenty feet from where the other parts had been dumped.

According to Coroner Gerber, the remains were six or seven weeks old. The victim had been six feet tall, with gaunt features, unusually long brown hair turning gray at the sides, and blue eyes; he had been badly in need of a shave when he was murdered. The victim's buckteeth had caused his upper lip to protrude noticeably. Four of his teeth were missing, while three others had poorly made fillings. Partial fingerprints and the condition of the teeth led investigators to an identification weeks later; the victim was Robert Robertson, age forty-four, an ex-convict, a drifter, and a suspected homosexual. Detectives who spoke to Robertson's acquaintances and attempted to trace his movements failed to find anything that shed light on his murder.

The resemblance to the Torso killings was remarkable, if not downright chilling. Gerber announced that the murderer had used "the Kingsbury technique" in disarticulating the corpse, skillfully beheading the victim in the midcervical region and amputating the limbs at the hip and shoulder joints. But while admitting that the remains gave him a sense of déjà vu, Gerber could not bring himself to state that the Butcher was back. "After all," he said, "it's been twelve years." Captain David Kerr, the successor to the retired Sergeant Hogan as head of Homicide, considered the resemblance "a curious feature" but nothing more.

Local interest in the case had undergone a modest revival with the publication of an article entitled "Butcher's Dozen" by John Bartlow Martin in *Harper's Magazine* the previous November. Captain Kerr and Coroner Gerber conceded that an unbalanced individual might have been inspired to pattern Robertson's murder after the Torso crimes. Merylo and some reporters at the *Plain Dealer* went one step further in suggesting that the actual killer had read of himself and decided to return to his favorite hunting ground and resume his bloody activities.

The city was still pondering the possibilities when two workmen employed at the factory behind which the remains had been found came forward with a bizarre story. Six weeks earlier, about the time Gerber believed the dismembered parts were discarded, the workmen had observed an unusual character loitering in the area. They claimed that the unknown man had stretched out and sunbathed for several hours on the pile of steel girders directly above the place where the body was soon to be discovered. The man had performed his ritual daily for more than a month, unbuttoning his shirt or removing it altogether. Then, about a week before the remains were found, he failed to appear and was never seen by the workmen again.

Though they had only viewed the man from a distance, the workmen were able to describe him as huge and heavyset, about fifty years of age, with thinning gray hair; the man had "dressed like a tramp." Police were unable to locate the stranger or to find anyone else who had encountered him. Officially, the sunbathing story was treated as an odd coincidence. The theory that the killer had revisited the scene of his crime day after day was irresistible to some and ridiculous to others.

If the mysterious sunbather was the Mad Butcher, it was his farewell appearance in Cleveland. The Robertson murder was not, as some prematurely predicted, the start of a new wave of Torso slayings, and there was nothing conclusive to link it to the original twelve. The case generated only moderate public interest. It was obvious that the passing of more than a decade had faded the memory of the phantomlike killer and his reign of terror.

There were people who talked about the Torso Murderer for years to come—railroad laborers on the graveyard shift in Kingsbury Run, veteran cops on nightly prowls of the Roaring Third, aged hobos telling stories as they passed a bottle back and forth. But any hope of capturing the Butcher had long since vanished. The man who must rank among the bloodiest of mass murderers had somehow managed to remain unidentified in one of the most massive manhunts in history.

Or had he? Eliot Ness waited almost fifteen years after his departure from Cleveland before sharing his personal version, and his alleged solution, of the Torso murders.

The official announcement of Ness's resignation as safety director of Cleveland stated that he was leaving to devote more time to his advisory post with the Federal Social Protection Program. Within a few months, Ness was appointed national director of the program, a position he held for the next three years. Accompanying the job was a huge house in the nation's capital and an introduction into Washington society. Ness relished his new status and socia' life. Evaline, on the other hand, found playing socialite and hostess boring. The couple began to grow apart.

Ness was apparently too consumed with his duties to notice. A primary goal of his job was the stamping out of prostitution around military bases, a task that kept him traveling and that sometimes brought him into conflict with organized crime. More often, the prostitutes themselves provided the opposition; once, prostitutes picketed a Ness speaking engagement in Peoria, Illinois. For the most part, however, his efforts were successful. The work kept alive Ness's image as a valiant public servant and eventually won him the navy's Meritorious Service Citation. But he lost Evaline in the process. In 1944, she walked out, moving to New York to pursue a highly successful career as an artist and fashion designer.

Toward the end of the war, Ness resigned from his government post and directed his full attention to the business world. For some two years, he had been representing the interests of Mrs. Ralph K. Rex, a wealthy Cleveland widow, and her daughter, Janet, in Diebold of Canton, Ohio, the nation's third largest safe and vault manufacturer. The Rex family owned a dominant 38 percent of the company, which had been bogged down by mismanagement in its efforts to fulfill wartime government contracts for armor plating.

Ness was elected chairman of the board at Diebold on June 15, 1944, and he swiftly made his presence felt with the same aggressive demeanor he had displayed as safety director in Cleveland. Ness eliminated administrative waste and instituted a program to promote young, unnoticed talent through the ranks of the company to the corporate offices. Once the crop of fresh executives with modern ideas and methods was in place, Ness oversaw the expansion of Diebold's manufacturing and marketing into such areas as plastics machinery and microfilming equipment. His greatest coup as chairman was in bringing about a merger with Diebold's major competitor, the York Safe & Lock Company of York, Pennsylvania, in January of 1946. As a result, York's safe and vault business, along with its branch offices and its sales force, came under Ness's direct control.

The merger closely followed Ness's divorce from Evaline on the grounds of gross neglect and extreme cruelty. By that time, he had already entered into a romance with Elizabeth Andersen Seaver, a divorced sculptress and a graduate of the Cleveland Art Institute. Betty was a petite, pretty brunette with dark eyes and a radiant smile. She and Ness were married on January 31, 1946. About a year later, the couple adopted a son, Robert Warren Ness. It was Eliot's first experience with fatherhood.

Around the time of his third marriage, Ness formed a partnership with Daniel T. Moore and James M. Landis, two Cleveland friends who had been attempting to draw him into the business world for years. Moore, the brother-in-law of columnist Drew Pearson, was a prominent Democrat who had served as securities commissioner in Ohio; he had made a number of important contacts while serving in Egypt during the war, and he had decided to start an import-export firm under the name Middle East Company upon his return home. Landis was a former dean of Harvard Law School. Ness became vice-president and treasurer of the company.

By the early months of 1946, Eliot Ness, at age forty-two, seemed established as a successful business executive, living in New York with an office in Rockefeller Center and earning a respectable twenty-four thousand dollars a year. Articles in *Newsweek* and *Fortune* magazines depicted him as a bright, ambitious, young businessman with keen administrative abilities that would take him far. Ness characteristically downplayed the flattering image accorded him. "Maybe I'll fall flat on my face," he told one writer, "but I'm sure having fun."

Before long, however, the fun, the glamour, and the challenge of overseeing business operations and directing policy began to fade.

Restless as always, Ness sought a more rewarding career. In one interview, he said, "I am so situated financially that I do not have to worry about a livelihood. I have some ideas about public service—and I want to try them."

Those who knew Ness could hardly believe that he was talking about seeking an elective office. Throughout his career in law enforcement, Ness had exhibited disdain for politics and politicians, with a few notable exceptions. Cleveland Republicans had attempted to persuade him to run for mayor in 1941 and again in 1945, assuring him that he could win in a walkaway. Ness had politely declined both offers.

The Democrats appeared to have a firm hold on the mayoralty in Cleveland. After serving two triumphant terms, Frank Lausche had moved on to become governor of Ohio in 1945. His successor was Thomas A. Burke, a staunch Democrat who had nevertheless been a prominent figure at city hall and a good friend of Ness's during the Burton years. Burke had also proved to be an extremely popular mayor. Now, with the 1947 mayoral contest approaching, Burke was seeking reelection, and the Republicans were desperate for a candidate to oppose him.

A group led by Senator George H. Bender and Councilman Alexander M. DeMaioribus contacted Ness in the fall of 1946 and tried to persuade him to run against Burke on the Republican ticket. Ralph Kelly, an old friend at the *Plain Dealer*, met with Ness and expressed great enthusiasm over the proposed candidacy. Kelly suggested that Ness's entry into politics was long overdue and that Cleveland was the natural place to start.

A few months later, Ness made it official. His return to Cleveland as the Republican candidate for mayor generated a wide range of reactions. The city's merchants and industrialists, having benefited greatly from Ness's zealous crusade against racketeers, rallied behind him and contributed generously to his campaign. Many of Ness's former associates at city hall and in the police department turned out to pledge their support. Even Mayor Burke was there to welcome back his old friend, wish him luck, and voice his hope for a clean contest. The newspapers, while maintaining a cool neutrality, printed stories about Ness's feats as safety director and pointed out his qualifications to run the city. On the other hand, the powerful forces of organized labor made it clear that they still regarded Ness as a threat, and they zealously pledged their support to Burke. Even more disturbing to the Ness campaign was the apparent apathy of the public. A mere five years had passed since Ness's departure, yet much of the city showed little interest in his bid for office, almost as if they had forgotten who he was and what he had done for Cleveland.

Ness set out to remind them. With a campaign fund estimated at nearly $150,000, he saturated the city with leaflets and billboards urging people to "Vote Yes for Eliot Ness." Full-page advertisements extolled his virtues. On street corners, campaign workers handed out *The Ness News*, a four-page tabloid informing Clevelanders of the ways that Ness would better their city. Ness toured the Flats, shaking hands and distributing his literature at factory gates.

After the nonpartisan primary in early October, it became painfully evident to Ness and his supporters that their vigorous campaign had been largely ineffective. Ness trailed Burke by a wide margin. He was just not the politician that others told him he could be or should be. It was especially evident in his public appearances; Ness was nervous and stiff before crowds, delivering his speeches in a flat, awkward manner. Worse yet, he failed to address significant issues, relying instead on his faded fame as a crime fighter to sell his candidacy. Those who recalled the flamboyant young lawman who had won the hearts of the citizens of Cleveland had difficulty realizing that this Ness was the same man. Even his appearance had changed dramatically. Ness's face was growing lined. His shoulders were slouched, and his paunch was noticeable.

The Ness camp understood that its only hope of victory was in capturing the support of Cleveland's undecided, non-Irish Democrats, who numbered about a quarter of the city's voters. Ness's advisors recommended that he get tough and discredit his opponent, a tactic he had avoided up to that point. But with his campaign on the line, Ness began to describe Burke as disinterested, uninspired, complacent, weary, and confused. The soft-spoken Burke responded by simply stating, "The best politics is good government. My record speaks for itself."

No one could argue the point. Burke's performance as mayor had been impeccable, and his reputation was too great to impugn. His wisdom in not stooping to name-calling only heightened his integrity in the public's eyes while revealing Ness's desperation.

On November 4, the people of Cleveland made their choice. Ness received a dismal 85,990 votes, barely half of the 168,412 Burke registered in a landslide victory, one of the most lopsided in the city's history. The humiliating defeat completely crushed any political aspirations Ness held.

John Patrick Martin, a member of Mayor Burke's cabinet, offered a perceptive evaluation of Ness's bittersweet career in Cleveland, stating, "We all like Eliot, and we all admired him as an honest, thoroughly competent expert in the field of law enforcement. There was never anybody like him in Cleveland. He really captured the imagination of the public in his early years, and he was given a hero worship unlike that given any city official within my recollection.

"But Eliot missed the boat," Martin said. "He should have run for mayor in 1941, against Frank Lausche, who was then a comparative unknown with a name hard to pronounce. He would have beat Lausche then because at that time Ness was the most famous man in the city and the most admired."

Ness never recovered financially and even emotionally from his political defeat. The singular zeal and confidence that had energized him in the past evaporated. Many of Ness's old associates shunned him now that he was no longer in the limelight. An acquaintance who encountered Ness around that time later said, "He was still a fairly young man, but he simply ran out of gas. He didn't know which way to turn."

The time that Ness invested in his unsuccessful campaign for mayor greatly weakened his executive status in the business world. Diebold changed hands, and Ness was ousted by the new ownership. About the same time, the Middle East Company began to suffer heavy financial losses. There were quarrels among the partners, along with scandalous charges of mismanagement. Ness departed soon afterwards, though it is not known whether by choice or order.

Almost a decade of obscurity and near poverty followed. Few details are available. About a year after the election, Ness returned briefly to Cleveland, inquiring with an old friend about a job paying sixty dollars a week. Ness explained that he was experiencing hard times and needed a favor. When the friend regretfully said that he could not be of help, Ness left Cleveland again, this time never to return.

Almost desperately, he searched for new ways of making a living. Bad luck seemed to follow him everywhere. He drifted through an array of business ventures that began promisingly, then soured. Most of the unsuccessful projects plunged him further into debt. Ness was, as some later said, "a lamb among wolves," naively taken advantage of and even used as a front by unscrupulous individuals.

In 1953, still looking to turn his misfortune around, Ness became associated with the Guaranty Paper Corporation, a Pennsylvania subsidiary of the Cleveland-based North Ridge Industrial Corporation. His introduction to the company apparently came through his friendship with Joseph Phelps, a tall, talkative former baseball player and one of the company's founders. Guaranty's most promising project at the time was a new, patented process for watermarking checks to prevent forgery. The crime-prevention angle must have appealed to Ness, and it seemed like an opportunity to get in on the ground floor of something big. Ness poured time, energy, and whatever money he managed to raise into the company, soon becoming Guaranty's president and a full partner with Phelps.

The watermarking process never caught on, despite an enthusiastic promotion. Guaranty tottered on the edge of bankruptcy, and only some intelligent marketing moves in more conventional areas kept it from going completely under. As Guaranty's president, Ness eked out a meager salary of $150 a week, enough to provide for his family but not much more.

In the fall of 1955, Ness and Phelps made a business trip to New York to promote their company's paper products. Phelps took the time to look up a former classmate, Oscar Fraley, a lanky journalist with a humorous face who was working in the city as a sportswriter for United Press International. Fraley accepted his old friend's invitation to join them at Phelps's hotel room at the Waldorf-Astoria. After Phelps introduced Ness as his business partner, the three men spent the evening chatting and sipping scotch. Ness listened as Phelps and Fraley reminisced about their high school days and their adolescent antics.

Close to midnight, Phelps told Fraley, "You'll have to get Eliot to tell you about his experience as a prohibition agent in Chicago. He's the guy who dried up Al Capone. Maybe you never heard of him, but it's real gangbuster stuff; killings, raids and the works. It was plenty dangerous."

Phelps was right; Fraley had never heard of Eliot Ness. For the first time that evening, the journalist looked closely at his friend's partner. Fraley found it difficult to imagine that the dapper, soft-spoken man with the pleasant smile and the affable manner had been a pistol-packing G-man who took on the Capone mob. Fraley noted that when Phelps made his statement, Ness seemed to blush slightly. "I guess it was dangerous," Ness replied with a modest shrug.

Prodded by Phelps and Fraley, Ness began to recount his days as leader of the Untouchables. For the next five hours, Fraley sat totally enthralled by vivid images of stakeouts and wiretaps, of death threats and dumdum bullets, and of Ness and his young raiders smashing down the doors of Capone breweries with their truck. Before the three men realized, it was six o'clock and sunlight was filtering into the room. Ness, who had kicked off his shoes and stretched out on the floor with his back propped against the couch as he told of his exploits, stood up and said, "Let's knock this off and get some breakfast."

As they prepared to leave, Fraley suggested, "Someday you should write a book on your experiences. You might make some money with it."

Ness looked up from the shoelace he was tying and answered, "I could use it."

A few months later, Ness and Phelps returned to New York on another sales venture. Fraley took the pair to dinner and again spoke to Eliot about telling his story in print. Ness had been considering the proposition, but he confessed that he didn't know where to start. He asked Fraley if he would help. Fraley said that he would be glad to if Ness could supply him with some material.

Several weeks after the second meeting in New York, Fraley received a package containing twelve large, dusty scrapbooks crammed with newspaper clippings, magazine articles, citations, case reports, private papers, letters, personal notations, photos, and actual handwritten wiretap reports detailing the story of Ness's fifteen years in law enforcement. At first, Fraley was overwhelmed by the mass of material. Gradually, working mostly in his spare time, he put the pieces together in accordance with Ness's verbal version.

In August of 1956, Eliot, Betty, and ten-year-old Bobby moved to Coudersport, Pennsylvania, a small, sleepy town of fewer than two thousand inhabitants nestled along the bank of the Allegheny River in the mountainous northern region of the state. Ness and Phelps opened a Guaranty branch office in a storefront on South Main Street, only a few blocks from the modest, two-story house Ness found for his family. Though he had lived in big cities all his life, Ness seemed to fall in love with the tranquility of the tiny community, the crisp, pine-scented air, and the magnificent, rolling landscape covered by thick forests. "You know," Ness once told Phelps in words that proved to be prophetic, "I wouldn't mind spending the rest of my life here."

Almost everyone in Coudersport came to know Eliot Ness. Most considered him a warm, likable, friendly man who had a sincere interest in his neighbors and the community. Ness and his family faithfully attended a local Presbyterian church. A boyhood friend of Bobby's who stayed overnight at the Ness house on occasion later described it as a "very homey" environment. Ness himself, Bobby's friend recalled, was "a nice gentleman," but "he always seemed to have a drink in his hand." A few Coudersport residents thought Ness peculiar. Often, at the end of the day, Ness dropped in at a local bar and, after a few beers, began to talk at length about his days as a crime fighter. Many regarded the colorful stories as boastful talk. Fred Anderson, the principal of the elementary school in Coudersport, remembered of Ness, "He'd tell us these things, and we didn't believe him. . . . He was a down-to-earth, quiet sort of guy. We just never realized who he was until 'The Untouchables' came on television several years later. . . . We thought, if he's so important why is he driving such a beat-up old car?"

The people of Coudersport also had trouble understanding why Ness had such a strong distaste for guns, if he was really who he claimed to be. Coudersport was in the heart of deer country, and each autumn the little town was overrun with hunters. Instead of participating in the town's enthusiasm, Ness made it clear that he wanted no part of it. When young Bobby asked if they could go hunting together, his father replied that he had no desire to pick up a gun again or even to allow one inside their home.

In December, Ness was given a full medical examination by a local physician, Dr. George C. Mosch, for insurance purposes. He was found to be in good health except for a slight heart murmur that the doctor explained was not serious at present but was worth keeping an eye on.

Soon afterwards, Ness received a call from Oscar Fraley in New York. Fraley was proud to announce that he had worked up an outline and sample chapters from Ness's material, presented them to a publisher, and immediately been offered a contract. Ness could hardly believe it. Fraley said that the next step was for him to get together with Ness to pound out the pages in as much detail as Eliot could recall.

A week later, Fraley and Ness took time off from their respective jobs and sequestered themselves in a Coudersport hotel room. Their sessions sometimes proved long and difficult for Ness, who struggled to remember and recreate specific events after almost a quarter of a century. Fraley came to realize that Ness's days as a lawman were so filled with action that they had begun to run together in Eliot's mind. Occasionally, Ness threw up his arms in disgust and said, "The hell with it, let's go for a walk. I've got to get out of this room for a while or I'll go off my rocker."

The fresh night air helped. As Ness strolled with Fraley along the silent, snowy streets of Coudersport, details fell into place. Though the book was structured around the Untouchables' crusade against Capone, Ness also talked about the periods he had spent tracking down moonshiners around Cincinnati, serving as Cleveland's safety director, and stamping out prostitution around military bases. Fraley listened intently to everything. Confident that their project would be a success, he was already considering Ness's Cleveland years as a sequel.

There were things that Ness did not talk about, of course—his two divorces, the hit-and-run accident, his humbling defeat in the mayoral election. Fraley did not learn of those things until many years later. Ness did, however, speak briefly of the Torso murders and the massive, maddening three-year search for the psychopathic slayer. For the first time, and for whatever it was worth, he also gave his personal solution to the murder cycle.

According to Ness, not long after the bodies of "No. 11" and "No. 12" were discovered at the lakeside dump in the summer of 1938, two of his special investigators had come to him voicing strong suspicions about a young man from "a well-to-do and rather influential family." Ness referred to the suspect as Gaylord Sundheim, an obvious pseudonym; he was still reluctant to reveal the suspect's or the family's true identity. Sundheim had once been a premed student with a promising future, but he had abruptly abandoned his studies, severed his connection to his family, and moved into a house near Central Market in the Roaring Third, where he lived alone and kept late hours. One of the contacts of Ness's undercover men alleged that homosexuality had prompted Sundheim's self-imposed exile.

After further investigation, Sundheim had emerged as a viable suspect. In relating the story to Fraley, Ness was vague about the evidence that had been found. As desperate for suspects as the Cleveland police had been, the evidence might have amounted to little more than rumors about the young man. At any rate, Ness eventually ordered Sundheim brought in for questioning. The "interview," as Ness termed it, was conducted in a hotel room. Sundheim proved to be "a giant of a man" with a powerful build and a discomforting stare. He had treated the questioning as a joke, toyfully refusing to either admit or deny involvement in the murders. Ness convinced Sundheim to submit to a polygraph test; Sundheim's answers to questions about the Torso killings indicated that he was not being truthful. When the questions were repeated and the lie detector registered the same results, Ness had been certain that they had their man. He decided to confront Sundheim with his suspicions. "I think you killed those people," Ness had said suddenly.

"Think?" Sundheim reportedly replied. "Prove it."

Ness couldn't prove it, leaving him no choice but to release the young man. He ordered a full-scale investigation of Sundheim including round-the-clock surveillance. But before Ness's men could even get started, Sundheim had made a totally unexpected move, signing papers to commit himself to a state asylum, placing himself comfortably beyond the reach of the law.

Ness claimed that he had received a steady stream of jeering, obscene letters over the next two years, many of them signed "Your Paranoidal Nemesis." Ness was sure that the writer was Sundheim. Near the end of his tenure as safety director, the letters had suddenly stopped. Ness checked and was informed that the man he believed to be the Torso Murderer had died in the state asylum.

Was that the solution to the Torso murders? Ness's story seems extremely unlikely, and it is totally unverifiable. The very fact that Ness failed to furnish Fraley with any specific names, dates, and locations makes it all the more suspect. Why did Ness refer to the "murderer" by a pseudonym? Where in the Third Precinct had Sundheim lived? At what hotel had the questioning been conducted? Where had Ness obtained a polygraph to test Sundheim?— the one and only polygraph in northeastern Ohio at the time was owned by the East Cleveland police. To which state institution had Sundheim committed himself? Ness's so-called solution presents too many unanswered questions and too many generalities for it to be considered seriously.

Was it merely a story concocted by Ness to show the world that he had, after all, solved the case? Perhaps. It seems incredible that Ness would have said nothing about Sundheim at the time, especially since Merylo, Chamberlin, and others kept the case open and continued to check leads over the next several years. And what of the later murders at New Castle, Youngstown, and Pittsburgh that appeared to many to be the work of the same maniac? According to Ness, Sundheim was in the asylum long before those crimes were committed.

To be fair, however, it must be pointed out that Ness's account is as impossible to disprove as it is to verify. It might be suggested that the reason Ness did not speak about Sundheim earlier was that he simply had no proof other than the inadmissible results of a lie detector test. The fact that the alleged suspect came from a wealthy, prominent family may also have been a factor in Ness's silence. Once Sundheim had committed himself, what advantage was there in making the story public?

Not long after the discovery of the lakeside bodies, about the time Ness claimed he had learned of Sundheim, the safety director had abruptly disassociated himself from the Torso case and, except for a few isolated comments, refused to talk about the murders. Had Ness become so baffled by the murder cycle that he simply gave up, or had he known something that the others didn't? During Ness's campaign for mayor in 1947, a reporter asked him about the old Torso slayings. "That case," Ness snapped back, "has been solved." Everyone at the time took it for granted that he was talking about Frank Dolezal. Had he actually been referring to Sundheim?

We will never know for sure. Even if there was a Gaylord Sundheim, Ness himself admitted that there was no conclusive proof of his guilt. Ness's "solution" must remain another enigma in the Torso case.

Several days after his fifty-fourth birthday, on April 19, 1957, Ness approved the galley proofs of his book. *The Untouchables* was scheduled to appear in bookstores that fall. His acquaintances later said that Eliot was happier and more excited than he had been in years. Ness hoped that the book would both ease his financial plight and help him recover some of his faded fame. No one at the time, Ness included, had any idea of the amazing success *The Untouchables* would enjoy. Tragically, Ness would never know.

On the evening of May 16, Ness and his business partner were preparing to leave their office when Phelps complained of a headache. "Personally," Ness remarked as he slipped on his coat, "I've never felt better in my life."

A few minutes later, after the brief walk from the office, Ness arrived home and went to the kitchen for a glass of water. In the next room, Betty noticed that the faucet was running an unusually long time and called out to her husband. There was no answer. She found Eliot crumpled on the floor in front of the sink. Dr. Mosch, the same physician who had detected Ness's heart murmur only a few months earlier, was summoned, but it was too late. Ness had died of a massive heart attack.

"His death at 54," reported the *Press*, "is untimely and unexpected, and will come as a shock both to the countless Clevelanders who knew him personally, and to those to whom he was, as safety director, a symbol of courage and decency."

Only in Cleveland was Ness eulogized on the front page and in editorials. He died just five months before achieving his greatest national fame, and his passing earned no more than a brief note in most papers. Ironically, in Chicago, Ness's hometown and the site of what would soon be his most acclaimed exploits, newspapers made no mention of his death.

An accounting of Ness's finances revealed that he was almost $10,000 in debt. He left behind no real estate and no savings. His assets were less than $1,000. Ness had a mere $273 in his checking account, and the 13,150 shares of stock he owned in Guaranty amounted to only a little more than $300 in cash value. His "beat-up" 1952 Ford convertible was worth $300. Also listed with Ness's meager estate was a $200 advance from his publisher, Julian Messner. When *The Untouchables* appeared in bookstores that November at $3.95, it became an instant bestseller. In an epilogue, Fraley proclaimed the book to be Ness's epitaph.

The Untouchables proved to be only the beginning of Eliot Ness's rise to the status of folk hero. In April of 1959, "Desilu Playhouse" presented a two-part dramatization of the book that evolved into a weekly hour-long series. Through four seasons and 114 bullet-riddled episodes, television audiences were transported back to Prohibition-era Chicago for fast-moving stories of the exploits of Eliot Ness. As portrayed by Robert Stack, Ness said little, shot fast, and usually proved his mettle as a lawman by fanning the scenery with staccato bursts from his submachine gun.

Of course, in creating an action-packed feature each week, the show's writers were forced to plunge into fantasy, but the shows had a stark, gritty, realistic look and documentary-style narration by Walter Winchell that convinced most viewers that they were watching factual stories. "The Untouchables" drew consistently high ratings for the American Broadcasting Company, but it was controversial almost from its inception. For its era, the show was excessively violent, and some local network affiliates either refused to carry "The Untouchables" or pushed it to a later, more obscure time slot. There were protests that the show promoted a negative stereotype of Italians; members of Al Capone's family—his widow, son, and sister—even attempted to sue Desilu Productions and the show's sponsor, Westinghouse Electric, for defaming the Capone name and using it for profit. Had it not been for those objections and many more, "The Untouchables" would certainly have enjoyed a longer run.

But no matter. The series introduced Eliot Ness to the American television audience and established him as a genuine legend.

ELEVEN

For years after the Torso murders had ended in Cleveland, Peter Merylo kept hunting the shadowy killer. To a lesser degree, Coroner Sam Gerber continued to write about the Butcher, realizing as he did so that the only real utility of his theories was in satisfying his own fascination with the case, and not in aiding the police. In one of his last reports, Gerber attempted a sociological and psychological profile of the murderer:

WHAT TYPE OF PERSON
IS THE TORSO MURDERER?

All facts elicited from the anatomical examination of the so-called "Torso Murder Victims" and of the examination of the localities in which the bodies have been discovered and of the known surroundings and social history of the two victims that were identified leads to the belief that these victims come from the lowest strata of society originally or may have sprung from an upper strata of society and because of incidents in their lives sank to association with the lowest strata.

Therefore, the murderer must be a person that associates with this strata of life. In all probability, he was at one time or another associated with people in the upper strata of life but through unfortunate incidents either sank to association with persons in the lowest strata of life or has himself become a member. He may have been a doctor or medical student sometime in the past, butcher, osteopath, chiropractor, orderly, nurse or hunter in order to be able to accomplish the dissection with such perfect finesse.

The murderer undoubtedly gained the confidence and probably the friendship of these victims before killing them. The type of person most likely to commit murder falls into three groups: (1) the truly insane group, under which the paranoid may be classed, will commit murder as the result of his delusions of persecution. . . . The schizophrene kills entirely without motive and without passion. (2) The constitutional psychopath is the borderline type of insanity where individuals are not able to comprehend the difference between right and wrong and the desire to kill is accompanied by an abnormal sexual urge, such as some form of perversion. (3) The feeble-minded individuals . . . usually commit murder to obtain some object, trinket, money or something else that they may desire at the time of the killing.

From the anatomical examination of the twelve so-called "Torso Murder Victims" the murderer may possibly be a schizophrene, considering the cold-blooded method of killing and then the dissection of the body and the apparent simple disposition of the remains. In some of the earlier cases there were some genital mutilations of the individual and it is conceivable that the murderer may

belong to the borderline group of insanity, the constitutional psychopath.

Gerber's conclusions were based on two sources—the remains of
the twelve sure victims and the psychological patterns recognized
among murderers at the time. If his report appears indistinct or
archaic, it is only because he had little to go on.

The Butcher had performed a remarkable feat. Over the course of
three or more years, he had managed to murder and disarticulate at
least twelve human beings without leaving a single clue to his
identity. Not one fingerprint was left behind; not one witness to his
activities was ever found; and with the possible exception of a size-
twelve footprint and a couple of strands of blond hair, not one hint of
what the killer looked like was ever discovered. Even the generally
accepted notion that his carving and disposal of the victims indicated
a large, powerful man with a knowledge of anatomy was no more
than an assumption, though a good one. The one and only conclusive fact that Gerber and his pathologists were able to determine was
that the killer was "definitely right-handed," a clue that narrowed
the list of suspects to about three-fourths of the earth's population.

In his attempt to categorize the Torso Murderer, Gerber was
hindered by a weak basis for comparison, since mass murderers,
and especially sexual psychopaths, were a relatively rare phenomenon prior to World War II. Aside from Jack the Ripper and his four-
month reign of terror in London in 1888, there had been Joseph
Vacher, "the French Ripper," who committed eleven murders between 1894 and 1897; Bela Kiss, the necrophilic slayer of over two
dozen women in Hungary during World War I; Earl Nelson, "the
Gorilla Murderer," who raped and strangled twenty-two women in
the northwest United States and southwest Canada before he was
captured and hanged in Winnipeg in 1927; and sexual sadists like
Haarman and Kurten in Germany in the 1920s. With the exception
of Jack the Ripper and Earl Nelson, these maniacal killers were
little known in America, and what few details had been published
delicately avoided the sexual overtones inherent in the cases. Of
course, there had been other serial killers—George Joseph Smith
and the team of Burke and Hare in Great Britain, H. H. Holmes
and the mysterious Belle Guinness in America, and Henri Landru

in France. But while each of these murderers accumulated many victims over a considerable period of time, they had all operated more as murderers for profit than as sexual slayers. We can expand on Gerber's evaluation of the Butcher only because there has been an alarming rise in pathological mass murderers in the last fifty years, most notably in America.

One of the foremost questions about the Torso Murderer concerns his reasons for killing, an issue the Cleveland police grappled with from the onset of the case. Merylo was convinced that the killings were sexually motivated. Gerber disagreed at first, but he grew inclined to accept the sexual component of the case as the years went by. Even Eliot Ness, who remarked early in the case that there appeared to be "no clear motive" for the murders, eventually came to regard the killer as "a pervert."

None of the existing accounts of the Torso murders emphasizes the sex factor. Most, like John Bartlow Martin's "Butcher's Dozen," openly discredit the idea. While rightly recognizing the Torso Murderer as "America's preeminent mass murderer" in his 1949 article, Martin insisted that if the killer had been no more than a sexual degenerate, the police would have caught him. Martin preferred to classify the Butcher's work as murder for its own sake or, as it is more popularly if somewhat inaccurately known, "motiveless" murder. A multitude of early writers attempted to argue the same point in the case of Jack the Ripper. It was ridiculous, they claimed, to suggest that a sexual psychopath could have appeared in Victorian London; they considered the Ripper's crimes as acts inspired by mere blood lust or hatred of women. In commenting on the case, George Bernard Shaw wryly speculated that Jack the Ripper might have been a social reformer intent on casting a spotlight on the squalor of London's East End.

Looking back after a century, one fact about Jack the Ripper emerges clearly—his murder and mutilation of five London prostitutes were acts springing from a psychotic sexual impulse that associated erotic ideas with acts of violence. Upon closer examination, there can be little doubt that the motivating factor behind the Torso murders was much the same.

The major objections to the sex theory are the same ones voiced by Gerber in 1937. The fact that the Torso Murderer killed both men and women was said to rule out a sexual motivation. Another factor given considerable weight was that the decapitation and dismemberment performed by the Butcher did not fit any known "pattern of perversion."

Both of these arguments are weak. There are numerous examples of sex killers who preyed upon both males and females before the Torso Murderer ever appeared. "The French Ripper," Vacher, was one. Peter Kurten, "the Düsseldorf Vampire," was another. Child murderers, in particular, seem to choose their victims without regard to gender. Such killers tend to strike when the opportunity presents itself rather than when they are attracted to a particular individual. It is often difficult to apply the term *bisexual* to them, though in the case of the Butcher bisexuality remains a distinct possibility. In answer to the objection that the Torso Murderer's mutilation of his victims did not typify sex killings, there is abundant evidence to the contrary. Examples go all the way back to the fifteenth century and Gilles de Rais, a French aristocrat who indulged his sadistic sexual fantasies by murdering and mutilating dozens of young boys and girls. The youths were usually tortured, then strangled, and finally decapitated and disemboweled. De Rais performed his atrocities for many years in the privacy of his castle before he was detected. In one of the more commendable acts of the Inquisition, he was executed in 1440.

Most agree that de Rais was a historical oddity, his crimes more akin to the acts of a perverted, egocentric despot than those of a homicidal psychopath. What is often considered the first documented sex killing was committed in England in 1867 by Frederick Baker, a young man who molested and murdered an eight-year-old girl; Baker decapitated and dismembered the body in his sexual frenzy. A similar case occurred in Paris in 1880, when a four-year-old girl was abducted and killed by a retarded young man of twenty. The remains, again, were disarticulated. Jack the Ripper appeared eight years later. The Ripper is best known for his systematic slashing and gruesome evisceration, but a point seldom emphasized is that he came very close to beheading all of his victims, slicing their throats right down to the spinal column and in two instances leaving the heads attached by only a few shreds of flesh.

The twentieth-century sex murderer who sheds the most light on the psychological makeup of the Cleveland Butcher might be Edmund Kemper, who attained a brief infamy in California in the early 1970s as "the Co-ed Killer." The victim of a broken home, Kemper exhibited a disturbed personality from an early age, mutilating his sister's dolls and dismembering the family cat. At age fourteen, he shot and stabbed his paternal grandparents to death and was placed in a mental institution. He was released as cured five years later and placed in the care of his mother, whose persistent mockery, coupled with Kemper's unusually strong sex drive, led him to develop a pathological view of women. A formidable figure at six foot nine and 280 pounds—the sort of dimensions popularly attributed to the Torso Murderer—Kemper was so sensitive about his appearance that he found it difficult to even talk to women. Between May of 1972 and February of 1973, Kemper picked up six young, pretty hitchhikers in the San Francisco area, drove them to a secluded spot, killed them, brought them home in the trunk of his car, engaged in necrophilic acts in his room, and drove to the mountains to discard the remains. He sometimes dismembered the bodies with a large hunting knife he called "the General," and he later spoke of his great sexual excitement in decapitating his victims and enjoying intercourse with the headless remains. Kemper ultimately beat his mother to death with a hammer, strangled a friend of hers, and turned himself in. He was judged legally sane and sentenced to life imprisonment.

The psychological profile that emerges from studying Kemper and killers of his kind goes beyond mere sexual deviance. A great many writers on the subject have agreed that sex murderers are by and large lonely, brooding, repressed, and unfulfilled men who feel alienated from society and who grow out of touch with reality. Unsatisfied with their relationships, they seek fulfillment within their imaginations, often withdrawing into self-indulgent fantasies to the point of obsession. While a significant number of antisocial individuals may daydream of performing criminal acts, only a rare few cross the line into violence.

It has also been pointed out that most sex murderers are the products of large cities. Whether Paris, London, New York, Boston, Chicago, San Francisco, Los Angeles, or Cleveland, every major town seems to have had its sexual serial killer. It is ironic that the greatest population centers are also the best breeding grounds for loneliness and withdrawal. Unable to establish any fruitful contact with the multitude around them, unable to satisfy their basic needs of sexual gratification and self-assertion, unable to be a meaningful part of the society they inhabit, sex killers become society's enemy, striking back at a world they consider unjust and cruel.

Other common denominators among sexual psychopaths are their youth (most begin to kill before they are twenty-five), their above-average intelligence, and their lifestyles of inactivity. This last point, often overlooked, is a critical one. At the most basic level, many obsessive individuals simply have too much time on their hands. Often, they are unemployed or work jobs that allow little contact with others. They are unchallenged. The lack of social interaction or a productive means of expending energy may only heighten their sense of alienation and unreality. It should not be forgotten that certain kinds of crimes are relatively low among the working middle class and notably higher at the ends of the economic spectrum, among the unemployed lower class and the bored rich.

It is impossible to fit the Torso Murderer neatly into any recognized profile of the sexual psychopath, but certain hypothetical notions about him can probably be discarded—the theories that he was an insane doctor performing mad experiments, a religious fanatic slaying the unrighteous, or a man committing murder for its own sake. For over a hundred years, similar theories have been advanced about Jack the Ripper, the most popular among them claiming that the Ripper was a person of prominence (like Queen Victoria's grandson) for whom the authorities covered up. Such theories are intriguing but highly unlikely. Colin Wilson was probably closer to the truth when he wrote in his *Criminal History of Mankind* that Jack the Ripper was probably "an anonymous unknown" such as "a street sweeper or a market porter." The Cleveland Butcher may have been much the same, a man trapped in an isolated, unfulfilling life with an abundance of time to brood over his fantasies.

The Butcher's identity is an unanswerable question, though certain occupations present themselves as likely candidates. The theory that he was a homicidal tramp who dwelt among the hobo camps has its merits, but it appears unlikely in light of the Cleveland evidence. There seems little doubt that he operated in the privacy of a room or a house, though much later Merylo came to think it possible that the Butcher's "laboratory" was no more than an abandoned boxcar. There seems even less doubt that he used a car to transport the remains. All of this suggests an income of some kind. Perhaps he was one of the seventy thousand in Cleveland on work relief or someone who was self-employed, like a junkman, a possibility that seems to fit the facts of the case. The most intriguing possibility is that he was employed by the railroads. Conductors, engineers, brakemen, firemen, switchmen, and signalmen all had lonely jobs that alternated between periods of strenuous labor and utter idleness. Such an occupation would have provided the murderer with easy access to hobos and to prostitutes, who were known to apply their trade in the train yards. Employment with the railroads would also have provided a familiarity with Kingsbury Run and ample opportunity to operate there. It has even been suggested that the killer was one of the railroad police. If Gerber was correct in his belief that the killer had fallen from the "upper strata," then the Butcher's unwilling association with destitute people may have contributed to his motivation.

How the Butcher murdered his victims is the question most easily answered. Of the twelve Cleveland victims, seven died as a result of decapitation; four were too decomposed for a determination to be made; only one, "No. 7," died before her head was removed. The key mystery is how the killer was able to incapacitate his victims. The absence of drugs or alcohol in the bodies, the lack of evidence of blows to the head in the instances when heads were found, and the absence of cuts, bruises, and scratches and of traces of the Butcher's skin under the fingernails of the victims left the investigators baffled. A few theorized that the Butcher used hypnosis on his victims. Even an enormously powerful man could not have restrained a victim with one hand while so neatly cutting off his or her head with the other. The killer may have struck while the victims slept, slashing their throats and waiting as they hemorrhaged to death before completing the decapitations. At least two of the victims, the tattooed man and "No. 10," exhibited wounds consistent with this theory. But in five other cases, the pathologists observed few or no hesitation marks, indicating that once the murderer began slicing through the neck he hadn't stopped until the job was done.

The best explanation, and one that was never given due consideration at the time, is that the killer strangled his victims into unconsciousness before bringing out his knife. An arm choke requires no special strength or skill, and it can interrupt the flow of blood to the head within three seconds. Albert DeSalvo, "the Boston Strangler," used this technique, working his way to the back of a woman, choking her with his arm, raping her while she was unconscious, and then strangling her to death. In *The Complete Jack the Ripper*, Donald Rumbelow offers a strong argument for his theory that the Ripper struck in similar fashion, strangling his victims from behind before cutting their throats. The Torso Murderer may well have done the same. This theory presents a plausible explanation for why "No. 7," a petite, small-boned woman, died before decapitation; the murderer may have used a little too much force and killed her outright. "No. 7" was beheaded lower on the neck than the other victims, a detail that may represent the killer's effort to disguise his actual mode of murder.

What followed decapitation is anyone's guess. There seems little doubt that the Butcher was a necrophile. Necrophilia is considered a relatively rare phenomenon in the annals of murder, with only a few classic cases like those of Kemper and Edward Gein, the Wisconsin farmer and middle-aged virgin with a pathological fear of women who began by robbing graves and using the corpses for sexual fulfillment and ultimately graduated to murder. Actually, many sex murders contain at least a hint of necrophilia. In contrast to violent rapist-killers who derive sadistic pleasure from the plight of their victims, some sexual psychopaths kill quickly and with a minimum of fuss. Their fascination is with bodies that do not resist, reject, or pose a threat. Men like Gein or Kemper might well have proven impotent with live partners.

There seems no clear answer as to why some cases of sex murder involve decapitation. The key may rest in the fact that the killer is interested in a body, not a person. The head may represent a multitude of characteristics that are disturbing to a paranoid mind—

a mouth that speaks things he does not want to hear, ears that hear things he does not want heard. The face represents an individual's identity, and some psychotic killers need to totally depersonalize their victims before they can gratify their twisted sexual desires. The throat is also a critical feature. Kemper expressed particular delight in severing the necks of his victims, especially that of his mother, "because she bitched at me so much." For a killer with a pathological fear of what people say about him, it is an essential part of the act of murder to strike at the throat. Decapitation is carrying that mania to its extreme.

When self-assertion is a factor in such crimes, a number of other possibilities present themselves. Since mass murderers often feel inferior to and intimidated by others, the act of decapitation might be viewed as the ultimate expression of domination. Historically, there is a tradition of conquerors lopping off the heads of their vanquished foes. Dismemberment is perhaps only a radical correlative. What more dramatic fashion of asserting one's ego and proving a demented superiority than reducing an individual to a pile of disarticulated parts?

Another feature of self-assertive killers is their tendency to flaunt their crimes and horrify society with their atrocities, as was notably the case with Jack the Ripper and the unidentified San Francisco Zodiac killer. There seems no doubt that it was also true of the Butcher. Why else had he taken the time and energy and risked the danger of transferring the remains of his victims to public places when it would have been safer and simpler to burn or bury them? At the beginning of the cycle, the killer may have felt ambiguous about displaying the remains, as reflected in the strange fact that the bodies of the first two victims were left in the open while the heads were buried nearby. By the end, however, the urge to show off his butchery was evident in the Torso Murderer's decision to leave his final pair of Cleveland victims on the busy lakefront in full view of city hall and the office of Safety Director Ness.

Why some body parts, including five of the twelve heads, were never found is another matter for speculation. It is obvious that the Butcher kept some remains longer than others, whether for necrophilic purposes or merely as trophies. He applied a chemical preservative to the Lady of the Lake and to his second confirmed Cleveland victim, the man found beside Andrassy, apparently with the aim of stopping decomposition. Both of the lakeside bodies were in his possession for a considerable time, the woman for several months and the man perhaps as long as six months; as Gerber noted at the time, the remains of the female showed evidence of having been refrigerated or frozen. It is difficult to imagine, however, that the Butcher kept the missing parts indefinitely. Most likely, they were discarded like the rest of the pieces and were simply never found. The thought that the Butcher had a laboratory crammed with body parts waiting to be discovered haunted Cleveland police for years.

A highly controversial feature of the case was the Torso Murderer's reputed surgical skill. Some maintain that Coroner Pearse underemphasized the matter in the first six murders, while others suggest that Coroner Gerber overemphasized it with the final six. The terminology used by both coroners may have been misleading; the fact that the Butcher's dismemberments were skillful and precise and even the fact that he displayed a certain amount of "anatomical knowledge" fell far short of actual evidence of surgical training. Though the theory that the killer had some kind of medical background remains a distinct possibility, and an attractive one, it is by no means conclusive. His precision might be interpreted instead as suggesting that he had performed similar mutilations before his appearance in Cleveland.

The Butcher's methodical workmanship may say a great deal about his character. While it does not prove any surgical skill, it strongly suggests a patient, careful, orderly personality, a man who took a morbid pride in his work. This curious characteristic was also evident in the neatness with which some of the early victims were laid out, the way the head of the tattooed man was carefully bundled in his own pants, and the tidy manner in which the torso of "No. 11" was swathed in the patchwork quilt while her limbs were wrapped in brown paper and fastened with rubber bands. Another example was in the Torso Murderer's diligent efforts at cleaning the remains before discarding them. Lawmen have encountered this bizarre feature numerous times, from the Black Dahlia slaying to the more recent Detroit child murders; many murderers are discovered to be fastidious or even obsessively neat. The Butcher's careful washing and draining of the bodies of his victims and his propensity for placing the remains in the river, the lake, or the Kingsbury Run pool may suggest a ritualistic cleansing. On the other hand, Merylo, with his great respect for the killer's cleverness, favored the pragmatic view that the Butcher washed the bodies to remove any traces of fingerprints, semen, and hair.

Characterizing the Butcher's victims is an uncommonly difficult task, as most of them remained as anonymous as their killer, a feature that gives the case a haunting distinction in the annals of modern crime. Most people enjoy some small comfort in knowing that they will be remembered after death by relatives, friends, and fellow employees, or at least that their passing will be commemorated by a grave marker. But of the twelve Cleveland victims, all but three (or two, if the identification of Rose Wallace is rejected) remained unidentified and apparently unmourned. To have one or two unknown victims in a chain of a dozen murders is not unlikely, but to have nine or ten is nothing short of incredible.

The assumption that the Headhunter deliberately selected people who would not be identified is highly suspect. The fact that he chose Andrassy, Flo Polillo, and the tattooed man is sufficient contradiction. Neither can it be considered a tribute to his butchery that they remained unknown, since he often left a complete body and did not mutilate features or fingerprints. That he preyed upon the destitute, the homeless, or the unemployed seems obvious. Such people are often the targets of violent crime. The prostitutes slain by Jack the Ripper instantly come to mind; all five were streetwalkers, four of them in their forties. A more contemporary example is the Skid Row Slasher, a psychopathic sex killer in Los Angeles in the early 1970s whose victims were drunks and vagabonds, many of them approaching middle age.

But each of the Skid Row Slasher's victims was identified, as were Jack the Ripper's victims almost a century earlier. How did the Torso Murderer enjoy such astonishing success in randomly selecting his prey? The answer may be more a sad commentary on the times than a tribute to the Butcher's cunning or luck. Whether the victims were tramps, street people, prostitutes, migratory workers, or some other unfortunate products of the depression, it is difficult to believe that they lived in such total anonymity that they were impossible to trace and that they were not in some way missed. Two of the women were mothers. Fingerprints were obtained from three victims. A few had distinguishing features— "No. 4" had tattoos, "No. 12" had a broken nose, and "No. 11" had notably poor dental work. But such clues were ultimately of no use in reconstructing the victims' lives before they met up with the Butcher.

How many victims were there? Like so much else in the Torso case, it is impossible to determine. Aside from the twelve Cleveland murders, there were, in order of likelihood, the 1934 Euclid Beach torso; the three Youngstown victims found at McKees Rocks; the three later New Castle killings; the two Pittsburgh murders; the six earlier New Castle bodies; and over a dozen isolated cases, including the 1950 Cleveland killing. The official total remains at twelve, though many Cleveland authorities accepted the Euclid Beach victim and though at least a few accepted the Youngstown bodies and some of the later New Castle victims. Those killings would place the body count at close to twenty. Merylo believed that the Headhunter was much more prolific. He claimed that the killer was responsible for at least thirty-four deaths, though he privately considered the total to be closer to forty.

Most lawmen and writers at the time considered such a figure outlandish, but during the same period the Butcher was operating in America, German mass murderer Bruno Ludke was amassing an appalling number of sex killings—eighty-five between 1927 and 1944, when he was finally captured. Fritz Haarman butchered about fifty young vagrants in Hanover, Germany, after World War I. In our own generation, there have been astonishing cases like those of John Wayne Gacy, who murdered thirty-three young men, and Ted Bundy, who police have positively linked to at least twenty sex murders, though Bundy once confided to a Florida lawman that the actual number of his victims was in the triple digits. Volumes have been filled with accounts of serial killers who accumulated enormous numbers of victims over many years before they were finally caught. Who can say that the Torso Murderer, never caught, did not kill before he came to Cleveland and continue after he departed?

In many such cases, the activities of the killers have been interrupted by terms in prison, usually for obscure crimes unrelated to murder. Ludke and Bundy fit that mold. When released, they resumed their killing almost immediately. This raises an interesting point about the Cleveland Butcher. Many rejected the six New Castle murders from 1923 and 1924 because they were perpetrated so long before the confirmed Torso killings, and a full ten years before the Lady of the Lake washed up at Euclid Beach. It is possible, however, that the Butcher spent the interval behind bars. If so, men who served corresponding terms of incarceration should have emerged as key suspects. Yet Merylo, who considered the early New Castle killings part of the Torso cycle, certainly must have considered the possibility, and his failure to solve the murders can hardly be attributed to lack of perseverance.

In the end, there remains only speculation. The Torso case is a giant jigsaw puzzle with only a few of the pieces available. Andrassy's rope-burned wrists, the patchwork quilt, the cryptic word *NAZI* carved into the chest of one of the McKees Rocks victims, and dozens of other ominous details beg an explanation. Unfortunately, when the Torso Murderer stepped back into the oblivion from which he came, he took his secrets with him.

Even mass murderers can have a positive effect on a city, and the Mad Butcher, in his own way, left a mark on Cleveland.

His horrible crimes and the ferocious public outcry they inspired brought attention to the plight of the city's unfortunates dwelling in the squalor of the Third Precinct. Everyone knew about the impoverished conditions in the Roaring Third, but it was the murder cycle that created the prolonged uproar that finally prodded city officials. Sadly, the effects were minimal. Law enforcement in the region was increased dramatically, but the city managed only a superficial face-lift, replacing one slum with another. Any lasting improvements have yet to be realized. Violence and poverty still reign in the Roaring Third; tramps and vagrants continue to roam through the Flats; and children still play in the congested train yards of Kingsbury Run despite the admonitions of parents and grandparents who, perhaps recalling the Butcher, speak of a bogeyman who inhabits the ravine.

Among the enduring achievements credited, in part, to the Torso Murderer was the construction of a new, modern county morgue on the campus of Western Reserve University. The project was prompted by complaints by Gerber and his staff during the Torso investigation that their facilities were too outdated and ill equipped to effectively handle such a case. The county poured close to a million dollars into the project. The structure now contains a massive refrigerated chamber, an elaborate autopsy room, a crime laboratory furnished with modern, scientific equipment including intricate photographic and X-ray devices, and an enormous auditorium. With such technology at his fingertips during the Butcher's reign of terror, Gerber might well have brought the case closer to a solution.

Perhaps the murders are best remembered in Cleveland for the limelight they threw on Gerber himself. The enthusiasm and professional zeal that the newly appointed coroner displayed during the latter half of the case made him a celebrity in the city and helped to establish him as a Cleveland institution. In a remarkable career that spanned almost five decades, Gerber's election to the office of coroner every two years was automatic. He coauthored *The Physician in Court* and assisted in the writing of two other books. His lectures took him all over the nation and even to England, where he once advised forensic experts from Scotland Yard. Gerber was regarded as a prototype of the big-city coroner, setting many of the standards, both by his example and his teachings, for the scientific detection of crime and the postmortem investigation of evidence.

Ironically, both the high and the low points of Gerber's career involved his key role in the conviction of Dr. Sam Sheppard in the most famous murder case in Cleveland history.

When Sheppard's wife, Marilyn, was discovered bludgeoned to death on July 4, 1954, in her Bay Village bedroom, Gerber was among the first to arrive on the scene. In the days that followed, he was the first to cast suspicion on her husband. At the trial, Gerber was the prosecution's star witness, testifying that in his opinion the undiscovered murder weapon was a surgical instrument. As Sheppard was a surgeon, the coroner's conclusions were devastating.

The *Press*, which had conducted a shameful crusade against the doctor, led the chorus of praise for Gerber's skillful testimony.

After ten years in prison, Sheppard was re-tried in 1966 on the strength of new evidence uncovered by the defense. Gerber was again called as the prosecution's principal witness, and he insisted that the indentations in Marilyn Sheppard's skull indicated that a heavy surgical instrument had been used. This time, Sheppard was represented by F. Lee Bailey, the flamboyant Boston attorney, who proceeded to rip the coroner's testimony to shreds in his cross-examination. Bailey asked what kind of surgical instrument it had been. Gerber said he didn't know. Had Gerber ever used or come across such a surgical instrument? Gerber admitted he hadn't. Had he made any effort to determine the type of surgical tool? In an answer that startled the courtroom and collapsed the case against Sam Sheppard, Gerber awkwardly admitted that he had searched for such an instrument for twelve years and failed to find one. The defendant was found not guilty.

While the national coverage of Sheppard's second trial portrayed Gerber in the worst possible light, his status in Cleveland never suffered, since most Clevelanders still considered Sheppard guilty even after he had been acquitted. Gerber remained in office for another twenty years as his health slowly but steadily deteriorated from arteriosclerosis. A stroke worsened his condition and forced his retirement on December 15, 1986. On May 16, 1987, exactly thirty years after the death of Eliot Ness, Samuel Gerber died at the age of eighty-eight. All Cleveland mourned his passing.

Only a few weeks later, the Paramount film of *The Untouchables* opened in theaters across the nation. It offered a glorified, ultra-violent version of Ness's battle against the bootlegging empire of Al Capone. Incredibly, the film was even less factual then the television series; screenwriter David Mamet was careful to specify that his script was "inspired" by the writings of Ness and Fraley, and not actually based on their book. It is worth mentioning, however, that in the opening reel of the film, Kevin Costner's portrayal of Ness as a prim, idealistic, and inexperienced young crime fighter was closer to reality than was Robert Stack's gritty, cold-as-steel television persona.

The elevation of Eliot Ness to the status of legend was probably as inevitable as it was irresistible. Ness was an oddly individualistic figure closer in spirit to frontier marshalls than to twentieth-century law officers. Perhaps he was born seventy-five years too late. On the other hand, people who knew and respected him felt that he enjoyed the rare good fortune of being the right man at the right time.

In Chicago, as a young agent of the Justice Department leading his small band of Untouchables, Ness boldly defied the most powerful gangland organization of his time and produced far greater results in two years than the combined efforts of local, state, and federal authorities had over the course of a decade. But while Ness's exploits in Chicago brought him his greatest fame, his accomplishments in Cleveland were greater and more enduring. Almost single-handedly, he waged a relentless crusade against crime and corruption, reformed and rejuvenated sagging municipal departments, challenged key underworld figures, and at the same time provided Cleveland with a sorely needed hero.

Such is the stuff of legitimate legend. That Ness greatly encouraged his own mystique, especially with the writing of *The Untouchables* in the twilight of his life, is undeniable. The charge that he suffered from an excess of pride may be valid, but in all probability, Ness would have been embarrassed by the exaggerated proportions his celluloid image has attained.

And yet there were times when the real Ness lived up to the myth, when he seemed almost too good to be true. While *The Untouchables* was in galleys, an editor suggested to Fraley that he cut out the scene in which Ness angrily refuses the two-thousand-dollar bribe offered by Capone mobsters. "It makes him sound too goody-goody," the editor complained. But that, in essence, was the actual Eliot Ness, a man whose incorruptibility was more a part of his nature than a requirement of his job. Fraley insisted that the account remain as it was written. Interestingly, the bribe scene was the only incident in the book included in both the television pilot and the motion picture.

It was a curious twist of fate, and Ness's bad luck, that he launched his career in Cleveland at the same time that the Torso Murderer appeared. Stranger still was the fact that at the moment of some of Ness's greatest accomplishments, new Torso victims seemed to turn up to draw away the attention. Everybody expected Ness to be the one to catch the killer, but it was the unknown murderer who ultimately won the contest, and Ness's failure in the Torso case seemed to set the stage for the downhill side of his life. It is more than appropriate, however, that Eliot Ness has since become one of the most exalted figures of American law enforcement, while the Butcher is barely remembered, an obscure, enigmatic character buried in the annals of crime.

In that respect, at least, good has managed to triumph over evil.

Bibliography

The *Cleveland Press*, the *Cleveland Plain Dealer*, and the *Cleveland News* were the main sources for this book. To a lesser degree, material from the *Chicago Herald-Examiner*, the *Chicago Tribune*, the *Chicago Daily News*, the *New York Times*, the *Pittsburgh Press*, and Pennsylvania's *Potter County Ledger* proved useful.

All of the materials listed below contributed to the shape of this book, some to a great degree, others in only minor details. An assortment of police reports, medical and autopsy records, private papers, unpublished photographs, and personal communications also played an essential role.

Books

Bayer, Oliver Weld, ed. *Cleveland Murders*. New York: Duell, Sloan & Pearce, 1947.

Condon, George E. *Cleveland: The Best Kept Secret*. New York: Doubleday & Co., 1967.

Fraley, Oscar. *Four Against the Mob*. New York: Award Books, 1976.

Fraley, Oscar, and Paul Robsky. *The Last of the Untouchables*. New York: Pocket Books, 1988.

Karpis, Alvin, and Bill Trent. *The Alvin Karpis Story*. New York: Berkley Medallion Books, 1972.

Kobler, John. *Capone*. New York: G. P. Putnam's Sons, 1971.

Martin, John Bartlow. *Butcher's Dozen and Other Murders*. New York: Harper & Brothers, 1950.

McPaul, John J. *Chicago, City of Sin*. Englewood Cliffs, N.J.: Prentice-Hall, 1962.

Messick, Hank, and Burt Goldblatt. *The Mobs and the Mafia*. New York: Thomas Y. Crowell Co., 1972.

Meyers, Richard. *TV Detectives*. San Diego: A. S. Barnes & Co., 1981.

Nash, Jay Robert. *Open Files*. New York: McGraw-Hill Book Co., 1983.

Ness, Eliot, and Oscar Fraley. *The Untouchables*. Englewood Cliffs, N.J.: Julian Messner, 1957.

Porter, Phillip W. *Cleveland: Confused City on a Seesaw*. Columbus: Ohio State University Press, 1976.

Rumbelow, Donald. *The Complete Jack the Ripper*. Boston: New York Graphic Society, 1975.

Sifakis, Carl. *The Mafia Encyclopedia*. New York: Facts on File, 1987.

Toland, John. *The Dillinger Days*. New York: Random House, 1963.

Wilson, Colin. *A Criminal History of Mankind*. New York: G. P. Putnam's Sons, 1984.

Articles

Brennan, Ray. "The Capone I Knew." *True Detective* (June 1947): 25.

"Crime in Cleveland." *Newsweek* 11 (March 21, 1938): 12.

Fraley, Oscar. "The Real Eliot Ness." *Coronet* 50 (July 1961): 25–30.

"G-Man." *American Magazine* 123 (May 1937): 103.

High, Stanley. "Cleveland Versus the Crooks." *Reader's Digest* 34 (February 1939): 48–51.

Martin, John Bartlow. "Butcher's Dozen." *Harper's Magazine* 199 (November 1949): 55–69.

Ness, Eliot. "Radio-Directed Mobile Police." *American City* 56 (November 1939): 35–36.

"Ness the Safe Man." *Newsweek* 27 (January 7, 1946): 56.

"Selling Ness to Cleveland." *Newsweek* 30 (October 13, 1947): 25.

"There Goes Eliot Ness." *Fortune* 34 (January 1946): 196.

Watson, Ernest W. "Evaline Ness, Rising Star in the Illustration Firmament." *American Artist* 2 (January 1956): 28–33.

Index